BUSINESS DATABASE TECHNOLOGY

BUSINESS DATABASE TECHNOLOGY

An Integrative Approach to Data Resource Management with Practical Project Guides, Presentation Slides, Answer Keys to Hands-on Exercises for Students in Business Programs

SHOUHONG WANG
HAI WANG

Universal-Publishers
Boca Raton

Business Database Technology: An Integrative Approach to Data Resource Management with Practical Project Guides, Presentation Slides, Answer Keys to Hands-on Exercises for Students in Business Programs

Universal-Publishers
Boca Raton, Florida
USA • 2014

ISBN-10: 1-61233-288-9
ISBN-13: 978-1-61233-288-8

www.universal-publishers.com

Cover image © Can Stock Photo Inc./ kgtoh

Credit: ORACLE, MySQL are trademarks of Oracle Corporation. IBM DB2 is trademark of IBM. Windows, Microsoft SQL Server, Microsoft Office, Microsoft Access, Microsoft Excel, and Microsoft Visual Studio are trademarks of Microsoft Corporation.

Library of Congress Cataloging-in-Publication Data

Wang, Shouhong.
  Business database technology : an integrative approach to data resource management with practical project guides, presentation slides, answer keys to hands-on exercises for students in business programs / Shouhong Wang and Hai Wang.
     p. cm.
  Includes index.
  ISBN-13: 978-1-61233-288-8 (pbk. : alk. paper)
  ISBN-10: 1-61233-288-9 (pbk. : alk. paper)
  1. Business--Databases. 2. Information technology--Technological innovations. 3. Database management. 4. Database design. 5. Management information systems. I. Wang, Hai, 1973- II. Title.
  HF5548.2.W2992 2013
  005.74--dc23
                                                                    2013039227

Table of Contents

** Electronic teaching material for this textbook includes model syllabus, answers to all assignment questions, sample exams, answers of the exams, lecture PPT, the Microsoft Access database for the textbook SQL examples, Microsoft Access database for Technical Guide A, Microsoft Access database for Technical Guide C, and others.

PREFACE

Data are valuable assets of the organization. Database is a key component of the information systems in business. Database technology is critically important to business. This book is designed for business students who study database technology for data resource management.

The database management systems are powerful tools for constructing and accessing databases. Currently, many user-friendly end-user oriented relational database management systems are available on the commercial software market or are accessible as open source software products. However, people often do not fully realize the importance of understanding accurate concepts of database. In fact, a poorly designed database or misuse of database management systems would do more harm than good for the organization. The objective of this book is to help students understand the precise concepts of database and develop practical skills of database design, implementation, and application. Upon the completion of study of this book, students should be able to build and to manage databases in a professional way. More importantly, students should be able to develop their independent learning ability to learn advanced features of database design, implementation, application, and management.

IT has been the most innovative field in the modern era. Ironically, after it was first introduced to the computational world longer than three decades ago, the relational database model is still the most popular database model in the IT industry. Although research into object-oriented database has been carrying on for many years, the relational database model is still the main stream of databases in business. There is no evidence that the relational database model will phase-out any soon.

There have been hundreds textbooks of database on the market. Given the long history of database, many database textbooks were written decades ago and revised for numerous times. The volumes of these database textbooks are usually huge since they contain many secondary contents which might be useful decades ago but are no longer essential to know, especially for business students. On the other hand, contemporary topics, such as physical database design and database application for business intelligence (e.g., OLAP) are lacking in these textbooks. Furthermore, some textbooks are totally database management systems independent, but others seem to overemphasize specific database management systems (e.g., Oracle or Microsoft Access). This book maintains a good balance between the core concepts and secondary concepts, and includes both basic knowledge of database and hands-on material for Microsoft Access, a widely available end-user oriented relational database management system. In this book, a huge amount of material about database design, implementation, and application is boiled down to a practically workable volume.

The book is self-contained. It includes ten chapters of fundamentals of database technology, sufficient problem solving exercise questions for each chapter, answers to the representative exercise questions, key learning objectives of each chapter, three tutorials for projects of database technology applications or large assignments, and a set of PPT slides handouts of the lectures.

The book is organized as follows. Chapter 1 provides an overview of database systems. It highlights the key difference between data, information, and knowledge, as well as the key concept of data redundancy. Chapter 2 introduces the important data structure techniques that are commonly used in databases. Chapter 3 describes the entity-relationship model which is a key element of the foundation of database design. Chapter 4 discusses the relational database model. It ties the entity-relationship model with the relational database model. Chapter 5 provides details of normalization process which is another key element of the foundation of database design. Chapter 6 explains SQL, a standard database processing language. Chapter 7 discusses the concept and major techniques of physical database design which is critical for large-scale databases. Chapter 8 discusses the major database administration functions. Chapter 9 discusses the key concept of distributed databases in the Internet environment. Chapter 10 discusses the application of relational databases for business intelligence in the data warehouse context. The book also contains a comprehensive set of student study guides. Technical Guide A is a tutorial of database implementation and application through the use of Microsoft Access. Technical Guide B is a tutorial of data normalization process and ER diagram construction based on data samples. Technical Guide C is a tutorial of OLAP using Microsoft Office. Answers to selected exercise questions, review sheets for preparation for exams, and a set of PPT slides handouts are attached at the end of the book.

Nowadays, students and young managers are the digital generation. They expect to learn more about information technologies to meet the challenge of the "Big Data Problem" in business. The vast amount of data creates an increasing degree of needs as well as pressure for managers to understand and to use information for their business. We believe that the basic foundation of database technology and data resources management is definitely needed for business students to become successful business professionals.

In summary, this textbook is written for university students in all majors who study database technology for data resource management in business.

Shouhong Wang, PhD
University of Massachusetts Dartmouth

Hai Wang, PhD
Saint Mary's University

CHAPTER 1. INTRODUCTION

1.1. Database Technology

Database technology includes theory and application methodologies for building information systems that manage, access, and process data. Database technology is critically important for business in many aspects.

• Database technology supports the database development for information systems. The database design is parallel with the business process analysis and design for the information system development.

• Database technology empowers organizations to manage data resources to meet the challenges of the "**Big Data Problem**". Big data are a collection of data sets that are large and complex. The challenges include capture, preservation, storage, search, sharing, transfer, analysis, and visualization. The major objective of big data analysis is to derive information from analyses of separate but related large sets of data to determine global trends. Generally, big data are characterized by three dimensions: volume (amount of data), velocity (speed of data in and out), and variety (range of data types and sources).

• Database technology enables the society and business organizations to develop organizational knowledge and to sustain organizational learning.

1.2. Data Are Resource of the Organization

Data are valuable resource of the organization. Data can be used for the organization in day-to-day operations as well as in developing competitive advantages. There are many types of data in business. For the time being, no commonly accepted taxonomy of data is available, but the following types of data can be readily observed in business organizations.

• Master data (e.g., customers)

• Transaction data (e.g., sales)

• Historical data (e.g., credit history)

• Secondary data (e.g., industrial publication)

• Subjective data (e.g., end-user survey)

Master data characterize the properties of stakeholders of the organization. They are resident in the system permanently, and are usually used for the daily activities. Transaction data record the transactions of business, and are usually temporary. They might be kept in the system for a certain period for specific purposes such as auditing. Historical data are chronicle records of useful facts. Secondary data are facts obtained from outside sources. Subjective data are human opinions.

One of the critical issues of data resource management is **data quality**. Generally, data quality is measured by many attributes of data, including accuracy, objectivity, believability, reputation, access, security, relevancy, value-added, timeliness, completeness, amount of data, interpretability, ease of understanding, concise representation, and consistent representation. The ultimate objective of databases is to provide quality data for the organization in these data quality attributes.

1.3. Data, Information, Knowledge

Although the distinction between **data**, **information**, and **knowledge** can never be unambiguous, we must differentiate the three for this database course. For our purpose, data are raw facts; information is a product of processed data in a given context; and knowledge is human interpretation of the real world. While tacit knowledge is in the human's mind, explicit knowledge can be represented and stored by computers in a form of information. For instance, sales figures are data which record the facts of sales. *"The total of sales"* is information because it is not a raw fact, but is a processed result of sales of all sales teams over a certain period. A proposition such as *"the low total of sales is a result of the slow economy"* is knowledge, because it is not a raw fact, nor an immediate product of processed data, but is a human perception and judgment. Note that data, information, and knowledge are not interchangeable terms in this book. In principle, a database stores data (not information, nor explicit knowledge), and is able to process the stored data to generate information for the user to develop knowledge. Certainly, a computer can always store information and explicit knowledge, but not in the normal form of database. In fact, "information repository" and "knowledge base" are ambiguous terms for less structured digitalized resources.

1.4. Common Mistakes in Data Resource Management

Data is a valuable resource of the organization. However, many people do not know much about the database technology. They use non-database tools, such as Excel spreadsheet or Word document, to store and manipulate business data, or use poorly designed databases for business processes. Eventually, the data are redundant, inconsistent, inaccurate, and corrupted. The corrupted data storage is actually a garbage can. The common mistakes in data resources management are discussed as follows.

(1) No control of redundant data

People often keep redundant data for convenience. Redundant data could make the data set inconsistent. We use an example to explain why redundant data are harmful. Suppose the registrar's office has two separate files that store student data: one is the registered student roster, and the other is student grade roster, as shown in Figure 1.1. You can find in Figure 1.1 that the fact *"the student holding the student number 1432 is Ann Riley"* is stored in both spreadsheets in multiple places. Such a duplication occurrence that repeats the same fact stored in the data system is called **data redundancy**. Redundant data often make data access convenient, but can be harmful. For example, if Ann Riley changes her name, then all her names stored in the system must be changed altogether. However, practically, making changes to all redundant data is difficult if the data set is huge. As a result of data redundancy, the entire data set can eventually be corrupted.

(2) Violation of data integrity

Data integrity means consistency among the stored data. We use the example in Figure 1.1 to explain the concept of data integrity and how data integrity can be violated if there is no systematic means to maintain data integrity. In Figure 1.1, you can find in the grade roster that Chris Smith received a grade in MKT211; however, you can't find Chris Smith in the student roster. In this example, the two rosters are not consistent. Suppose we have a data integrity control procedure to enforce the rules, say, "no student can receive a grade unless she/he has registered", then such a violation of data integrity can never happen.

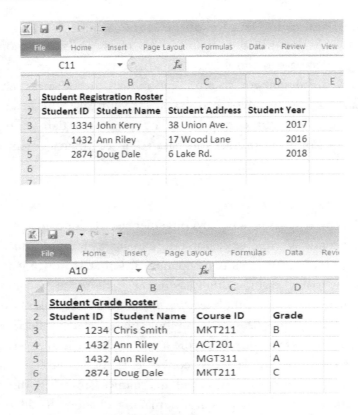

Figure 1.1. An Example of Mistakes in Data Resource Management

(3) Relying on human memory to store and to search needed data

The third common mistake in data resource management is the over-use of human memory for data search. A human can remember what data are stored and where the data are stored, but may forget what data have been stored and where these data are stored at any time. If a piece of data is stored in an un-remembered place, it has actually been lost. As a result of relying on human memory to store and to search needed data, the entire data set eventually becomes disorganized.

To avoid the above common flaws in data resource management, database technology must be applied.

1.5. Control Data Redundancy

One of the major objectives of data resource management is to control data redundancy. Data redundancy not only waste resources for data entry and updating, but also causes data inconsistence and thus corrupts the database. For instance, suppose a customer holding a certain customer number has filed her data in five store branches of a retail company, and the customer changes her address. The system must remember to change all addresses in the five branches. If only one address is changed and others remain unchanged, then her addresses are no longer consistent in the data system of the retail company. We will further discuss other problems caused by data redundancy later in this book.

Data redundancy occurs when the same **fact** is stored in more than one place. Note that this definition of data redundancy should not be read like "the same number (or text) is stored in more than one place." Let us examine the examples in Figure 1.2 to understand more about data redundancy. There are two cases in Figure 1.2, and both show the storages of the customers' data and purchase data. In case (a), the customer's data repeat in several places. The **fact** that *"the customer holding the customer number 123456 is Smith who lives in Westport Rd. with phone number 508999"* is stored twice. Hence, case (a) is a case of data redundancy. In case (b), the **fact** that *"the customer holding the customer number 123456 is Smith"* is stored in the CUSTOMER table only once. Thus, it does not have the data redundancy problem occurred in case (a). Take a look at the PURCHASE table in case (b). The same customer number 123456 is stored in the two places. Does data redundancy occur here? The answer is no, because the same customer number 123456 represents the two different **facts** in the two places; that is, the customer 123456 had two purchases. Take a look at both tables in case (b). The same customer number 123456 is stored in both tables. Does data redundancy occur here? The answer is no. In the CUSTOMER table, this number represents the **fact** that *"the customer holding the customer number 123456 is Smith."* However, in the PURCHASE table, the customer number 123456 represents different **facts** of purchases made by this customer.

CUSTOMER- PURCHASE

CustomerNumber	CustomerName	CustomerAddress	CustomerPhone	Purchase	PurchaseTime
123456	Smith	Westport Rd.	508999	$200	10/20/2014 09:45am
234562	Green	Eastport Ave.	509343	$300	10/23/2014 01:32pm
123456	Smith	Westport Rd.	508999	$150	11/08/2014 05:04pm

(a) Data redundancy occurs

CUSTOMER

CustomerNumber	CustomerName	Customer Address	CustomerPhone
123456	Smith	Westport Rd.	508999
234562	Green	Eastport Ave.	509343

PURCHASE

CustomerNumber	Purchase	PurchaseTime
123456	$200	10/20/2014 09:45am
234562	$300	10/23/2014 01:32pm
123456	$150	11/08/2014 05:04pm

(b) There is no data redundancy if the data are stored in this form

Figure 1.2. Control Data Redundancy

This example shows that a system can avoid data redundancy, as long as the data are stored in an appropriate way. On the other hand, this example also shows the potential difficulty of **data integration** when the data has no redundancy. For instance, more likely, the user of the data prefers the integrated data as shown in case (a) of Figure 1.2 to find all associated facts in just one table. In case (b), the user has to search the two tables and merge them together every time she wants to obtain the integrated data. If the organization has a huge number of tables, it is impossible for human to perform such tedious jobs. This example explains why computerized database systems are needed to achieve no-redundancy as well data integration for data resource management.

1.6. Database and Database System

Organizations use database systems to manage data efficiently and effectively in the following aspects.

(1) Controlled data redundancy - All data files are integrated into a single logical structure of database. In principle, any fact is recorded once.

(2) Data consistency - As a result of data redundancy control, data in database are consistent.

(3) Data sharing - All authorized users in the organization share the data in the database.

(4) Facilitate application development - A database system provides powerful abilities to access the data in the database.

(5) Wide-ranging data management functions - Database management systems provide integrity control, backup and recovery, and security and privacy control functions.

Key terms of database system are explained as follows:

● **Database (DB)** - A database is a collection of data which is accessed by more than one person and/or which is used for more than one purpose.

● **Database management system (DBMS)** - A database management system is a collection of procedures, languages and programs which can be used to facilitate the design, implementation, operation, and maintenance of the database system.

● **Data model** - The data model of a database is the logical structure of the data items and their relationships.

● **Database administration procedures** - The formal policies and procedures for the data resource management in the organization.

● **Database system** - A database system consists of the database, the DBMS, the computer hardware, **database administrator (DBA)**, and the database administration procedures for the database.

The general architecture of a database system is illustrated in Figure 1.3.

Figure 1.3. Database System

1.7. Database Management Systems

To create and manage a database, a **database management system (DBMS)** must be used. A DBMS is a software system which can be used to facilitate the design, implementation, operation, and maintenance of database systems. The key concepts of DBMS and common functions of DBMS are discussed as follows. Note that an individual DBMS has its own algorithms and procedures to support those functions at its own sophistication level.

1.7.1. Support database construction and data access

A DBMS provides the **interface** between the user and the computer to allow the user to create a database, to input data, to update the database, and to access the data.

1.7.2. Control data redundancy

In principle, there should be no data redundancy in a database. However, in a large database, no redundancy will result in poor performance (i.e., slow response). As explained later, a large database might have controlled data redundancy. Such data redundancy might be temporary and has a limited scale. One of the DBMS functions is to ensure that the controlled data redundancy does not compromise the data **accuracy** and **integrity**.

Data integrity means **consistency**; that is, there are no conflicting facts in the database. **Data accuracy** and **verifiability** are exchangeable terms of data integrity.

A redundant data set often causes **data modification anomaly** and violates data integrity. Chapter 5 will further explain data modification anomaly. The DBMS eliminates the data redundancy and avoids the data modification anomaly.

1.7.3. Provide data integration

Data **integration** refers to the ability to tie together pieces of related data upon the request from the user. For instance, the user might like to have all data about *"the courses John Smith has taken, the grades he has received from these courses, and the instructors of those courses"* in a single table instead of searching several tables. Usually, integrated data contain data redundancy, and are not supposed to be stored in the database permanently. One of the DBMS functions is to support data integration by assembling the available data in the database for the user while controlling the data redundancy.

1.7.4. Maintain data independency

Data are processed by computer programs. On the other hand, the format of data and the way in which the data are stored on the media (disks) are highly dependent on the individual database. One of the DBMS functions is to ensure the data **independency** so that any changes in the data storage within the database do not require changes in the application computer programs.

1.7.5. Monitor and improve data retrieval performance

As will be explained later, performance in a large database is crucial for the success of the information system, and must be taken into account for the **physical database design**. The DBMS monitors the data retrieval performance and provides information for the DBA for the database physical design. A good DBMS has the capacity to support database physical design, or even automatically take actions to improve the data retrieval performance. We will further discuss physical database design in Chapter 7.

1.7.6. Control data security

Data security is an important issue of database. The DBMS acts as a security guard for the database. The DBMS applies the **authentication** process to verify that only registered legitimate users are allowed to access the database. It applies the **authorization** process to determine whether the user is allowed to read, to change, or to delete a specific piece of data.

1.7.7. Enforce business rules and maintain data integrity

Many **business rules** related to the data can be built-in the database through defining cardinality, modality, data access security, etc. For instance, *"one professor can have only one office"* is a business rule. If the DBA builds this business rule in the database through the definition of the cardinality, the DBMS will not allow the database to have a fact that is contradictory to this business rule, and maintains the data integrity.

1.7.8. Manage concurrency control

When multiple users access and update the same piece of data concurrently, the data could become incorrect. This is caused by the time delays between the data access and the data updating among the multiple users, which is known as the **concurrency** problem. A sophisticated DBMS has advanced techniques and procedures, called concurrency control protocols, to manage concurrency control to ensure the correct and prompt data access and data updating by multiple users in the data sharing environment.

1.7.9. Perform backup and recovery

Databases are vulnerable and could be damaged by fire, flood, earthquake, and other human-made or natural disasters. A good DBMS is able to perform **backup** from time to time automatically, and to provide instructions for **recovery** when the database is damaged. We will further explain backup and recovery later in this book.

1.7.10. Maintain data dictionary

A database has a **data dictionary**, as further explained later in Chapter 8. A data dictionary contains data about the database. The DBMS maintains the data dictionary for the data resource management.

1.7.11. Facilitate database restructuring

The business environment keeps changing, so does the database. A DBMS can facilitate offloading, redefinition, reloading, conversion, etc. to accommodate the changes.

1.8. Commonly Used DBMS for Relational Database

There are many commonly used DBMS for relational database in business.

(1) ORACLE is Oracle Corporation's product. It first appeared around 1979, and was one of the first relational DMBS in the IT industry. It has been widely used in business since then.

(2) IBM DB2 (or DB2) is IBM's product. It was also a pioneer of relational DBMS in the early 1980s. DB2 is the first commercialized database product that uses SQL (Structured Query Language) which was also developed by IBM.

(3) MySQL was released in 1995. Later, MySQL becomes open-source software under the GNU General Public License (GPL). MySQL is a popular choice of database for Web applications, because it is closely tied to the popularity of PHP, an open-source server-side programming language.

(4) Microsoft SQL Server was Microsoft's entry to the enterprise-level database market, competing against ORACLE and IBM DB2 in about 1989. It is a widely used DBMS in many enterprises.

(5) Microsoft Access was released in 1992 as an end-user oriented DBMS in the Microsoft Office suite. Microsoft Access is easy for end-users to create their own queries, forms and reports, etc., but does not support many sophisticated database management functions. Microsoft Access is well suited for individuals and small workgroup. Generally accepted limits of Microsoft Access are 2 GB data and up-to 5 simultaneous users.

This textbook uses Microsoft Access as the DBMS for the SQL examples and the course project of database development and application. This is because (a) Microsoft Access possesses essential features of relational DBMS; (b) It is easy to use for database beginners; (c) It is available virtually everywhere. However, since it is an end-user oriented DBMS and is usually used for small scale databases, Microsoft Access does not support physical database design. Hence, the concepts of physical database design and distributed database design covered in this textbook are unable to be applied to Microsoft Access.

Chapter 1 Exercises

1.* Give examples of master data, transaction data, historical data, secondary data, and subjective data for a student information system (e.g., the Student Information System on the campus).

2. Use examples to explain the differences between data, information, and knowledge.

3.* Identify examples of data redundancy in Figure 1.2a.

4.* In Figure 1.2b, the number 123456 appears in the CUSTOMER table as well as the PURCHASE table. Are they redundant data? Why? The number 123456 appears twice in the PURCHASE table. Are they redundant data? Why?

5. Discuss data redundancy and the solution. What are the advantages and disadvantages of each of the two cases presented in Figure 1.2a and 1.2b?

6. Discuss the framework of database systems in Figure 1.3.

7. Discuss the major functions of DBMS.

---

* The questions marked with (*) across the textbook are used for class exercise and discussion. Their answers are listed at the end of the textbook.

CHAPTER 2. DATA STRUCTURE TECHNIQUES FOR DATABASE

This chapter provides an overview of basic data structure techniques used in computer data processing. These basic techniques are used by database management systems at the level of data physical placement and search. The purpose of learning these techniques in this course is to understand how the computer can retrieve the needed data speedily through the DBMS.

2.1. Data Secondary Storage - Disk

Because the CPU memory is limited and volatile, computer programs and data must be stored on the secondary storage. There are many forms of secondary storage, including paper, magnetic tape, magnetic disk, flash disk, and optical disk. Magnetic disk is still the most commonly used second storage media in databases. As illustrated in Figure 2.1, the disk read/write device is able to locate an **address** with the track number and sector number of a particular disk to record or to read a piece of data. A collection of all disk surfaces of a disk group with the same track number is called a **cylinder**. All data on the same cylinder can be accessed quickly without moving the read/write heads. Usually, related data are clustered on cylinders for fast access.

Figure 2.1. Disk

Regardless how fast the disk group spins and how quickly the access arm moves, the speed of data storing and data access on disks is very slow in comparison with that in the CPU. If the data set is huge and the organization of the data set is not well designed, it might take a prohibitive time to retrieve the needed data from the disk.

2.2. File, Record, Attribute, and Key

Logically, data are organized into a hierarchy structure in the traditional file systems, as illustrated in Figure 2.2. Database inherits the concept of file systems in many aspects.

Figure 2.2. Record, Attribute, Key, and File

- **File**: a collection of a set of records. Note that, the term file is often overloaded. For example, a computer program is stored on disk as a "file." However, in this book, we use file exclusively for **data file**, but not computer program file.
- **Record**: a description of a single transaction or an entry in a data file. A record is a collection of a set of data items. Normally, record is the unit of data storage on the disk. A file has its **record structure** for all records in the file.
- **Attribute:** a specification that defines a property of each record in the file. A record has its structure of attributes.
- **Key**: a minimal set of attributes that can uniquely identify each record in the file is called a record key, or key for short. The key can be a specific attribute or a group of attributes that has a unique value for each record in the file. Key is the identifier of unique record of the file.
- **Data item**: the occurrence or the value of an attribute.

2.3. Pointer

A **pointer** is the basic technique that can link two remote pieces of data on the disk to allow the computer to trace the sequence. A pointer is attached to the predecessor and contains the address of the successor. Figure 2.3 illustrates the concept of pointer.

Figure 2.3. Pointer

2.4. Basic File Organizations

Because data retrieval from a disk is much slower than data retrieval from the CPU, the way how data are organized on the disk is crucial for speeding data process. There are three basic file organizations, as discussed below.

2.4.1. Sequential file

The simplest organization of disk file is sequential file. In a **sequential file** (see Figure 2.4), records are stored in physically adjacent locations on the storage medium.

Figure 2.4. Sequential File

In order to find a particular record, the computer has to search the file by checking the records one by one, starting at the beginning of the file, until it finds the desired one, or reaches EOF (End of File) in the case where the search fails. Also, insertion and deletion of records are difficult in a sequential file.

Advantages of sequential files:
(1) Saves space.
(2) No record key is required.
(3) Efficient when all of the records are sequentially processed (e.g. payroll processing for each employee record).

Disadvantages of sequential files:
(1) It would take a long time to find a particular record randomly.

(2) It is difficult to update. For example, it is difficult to insert a record.

2.4.2. Random file

A **random file** organization allows immediate and direct access to individual records in a file. The essence of random accessing is the ability to quickly produce an address from a record's key. The fundamental component of data access in the random file organization is the conversion of the record key of a record to the address of the record on the disk though a formula called **hashing function**. In the general form,

Record key value Address of the record on disk

We use a simplified example to explain the concept of hashing functions. In this example, the hashing function is defined to be

Address of Record = Remainder of [Record Key / 111]

Suppose there is a record with its Record Key = 4567. Then,

Address of Record = Remainder [4567 / 111]= 16

That is, this record (its key value = 4567) is stored at the location with the address 16. Next time, if one wants to find a record with the key=4567, then the computer will quickly calculate the address according to the hashing function and immediately find it at this address.

In fact, hashing functions used in real systems are much more complicated than this simplified example. No matter how sophisticated a hashing function is, **synonyms**, or **conflicts**, can occurs if the file is large; that is, several key values will be mapping onto the same address. For example, suppose the above example hashing function is applied, the data system has three records, and their key values are 4567, 1126, 349, respectively. According to the hashing function, all the three records should be placed at the address 16, but this is impossible.

Key   4567 → Address 16

Key   1126 → Address 16

Key   349 → Address 16

Such a problem can happen frequently especially the data file is large. To solve this problem, an overflow area is created on the disk to hold conflicting records. The pointer technique is then used to trace all conflicting records. Figure 2.5 briefly illustrates the solution. For instance, suppose the record with key value 4567 is stored on the disk first, and occupies the address 16. Later, the record with key value 1126 comes in. Because of the conflict, it is placed to the overflow area at any unoccupied address, say 100. The system updates the pointer of the first record with key value 4567 to 100. Next time when searching the record with key value 1126, the computer uses the hashing function and locates address 16 first. Because the located record has an unwanted key value, the computer then follows the pointer to trace the conflict records until the record with key value 1126 is found, or a "null" pointer is reached which means a failure. Obviously, when the data file is huge, the random file organization is not an ideal option.

Advantages of random files:
(1) It can randomly access an individual record very fast, if there are only few synonyms.
(2) It is efficient in updating (e.g., adding and modifying records).

Disadvantages of random files:
(1) Sequential access is impossible.
(2) The record must have a key.
(3) Storage spaces could be wasted.
(4) Synonyms make search slow.

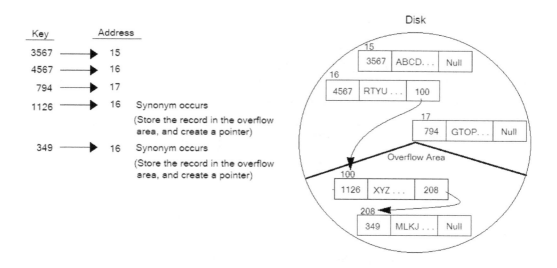

Figure 2.5. Conflict and Its Solution in Random File

2.4.3. Indexed file

An **indexed file** keeps an index table which associates the record keys with the addresses of the records. An index table is comparable to the table of contents in a textbook (see Figure 2.6). When a record is stored, it can be placed anywhere as long as the disk space is available, and then the index table is updated by adding its key and the address. In fact, the index table is a set of pointers.

Usually, an index table is small and can be manipulated in the CPU memory. Hence, the conversion of a record key to the address of the record takes little time. Given a record key, the computer can find the record on the disk almost directly. Also, an index table may be sorted based on a sequence of the record key values if needed. An indexed file is generally good for random access, sequential access, and file updating such as record insertion and deletion. Generally, an index table can also be designed for a non-key attribute.

Figure 2.6. Index Table in an Indexed File

However, if a data file is extremely large, then its index table will be so large that the index table has to be placed on the disk. Then the index table itself becomes a sequential disk file which is poor for random search. This simple indexed file organization is called **linear indexed file** because of this property.

Advantages of indexed files:
(1) It can be used in both sequential and random access. The access speed is fairly good for both, if the indexed file is not extremely huge.
(2) It is efficient in adding a record, sorting and updating the file, if the indexed file is not extremely huge.

Disadvantages of indexed files:
(1) The record must have a key.
(2) If the data file is huge, then the linear index table becomes a sequential disk file, and the speed of data access will be slow.

2.5. B-tree

2.5.1. Overview of B-tree

A **B-tree** is a hierarchical structure with multiple index records. B-tree overcomes the disadvantages of simple linear indexed file organization and improves the performance of search in very large databases. There are many variants of B-tree. Although it has been with us for a quite long time, the concept of B-tree techniques still dominates the modern database systems. In fact, a large database is supported by massive B-trees.

Figure 2.7 shows an example of B-tree. A B-tree consists of index records which organized into a reverse-tree. A B-tree has one and only one index record on the top, which is called root. The index records are organized into levels. A B-tree can have many levels. In the example of Figure 2.7, the B-tree has only two levels. An index record at the bottom level is called leaf. The index records in a B-tree are of the same format. Each index record has a certain number of key-value/pointer pairs, and each pairs hold a key value and a pointer. In this example, the number of key-value/pointer pairs is 4. Suppose the data system has 8 cylinders, and each cylinder has records with a range of key values as illustrated in Figure 2.7. The construction of a B-tree starts from the leaf level. In the example of Figure 2.7, there are three index records at the leaf level. The first leaf index record uses three key-value/pointer pairs to link itself to the first three cylinders in such a way that each key-value/pointer pair keeps the maximum key value of the records on each cylinder and the address of the corresponding cylinder. The other two leaf index records have the similar connections with the rest five cylinders. To build a tree, higher level index records are needed to link themselves to the leaf index records. In this example, because each index record has 4 key-value/pointer pairs and only 3 leaf index records exist at the leaf level, only one index record at the next higher level is needed. The index record on the very top of the reverse-tree becomes the root of the tree. Three key-value/pointer pairs in the root index record are used to link the root to the lower level index records in such a way that each key-value/pointer pair keeps the maximum key value of the lower level index record and the address of the corresponding lower level index record.

In principle, the computer keeps the root of the B-tree in CPU in order to use the B-tree. We use the example in Figure 2.7 to explain how a B-tree can make the data retrieval fast. For example, suppose we want to find the data of the record with key value 6000. The computer starts from the root. Since 3000<6000<6743, the computer uses the second pointer in the root index record to find the second index record at the next level. Since 5123<6000<6743, the computer uses the third pointer in the index record and locates cylinder 6 to find the record. In such a way, the computer uses only two steps to find the needed data record.

Figure 2.7. An Example of B-Tree

2.5.2. Construction of B-tree

The following general rules are applied to the construction of B-tree.

(1) A B-tree consists of index records that are organized into a tree. The tree has its root with one and just one index record on the top, and a number of levels of index records.

(2) Each index record accommodates the same number of pairs (4 in the example of Figure 2.7), and each pair can hold a key-value and a pointer.

(3) Each index record is at least half full (in the example of Figure 2.7, at least 2 pairs in an index record are occupied with key-values and pointers, and the rest pairs can be empty).

(4) In each occupied key-value/pointer pair, the pointer points to an index record at the next level or a disk cylinder if the pair is contained in a leaf index record, and the key-value is the maximum key value in the pointed index record or the maximum key

value on the cylinder.

Other than the above four rules, the construction of a B-tree can be flexible, depending on the situation or arbitrations. For example, the B-tree constructor (the DBMS if not human) determines how many index records are used, how many levels the tree has, whether an index record should have empty key-value/pointer pairs, etc. depending on the case.

Generally speaking, the construction process operates from the bottom of the tree to the top root, and goes through the following steps.

Step 1. List all given disk cylinders in the ascending order of their maximum key values of records.

Step 2. Given a certain number of key-value/pointer pairs of each index record, determine the number of index records at the leaf level for the given cylinders, and create the index records.

Step 3. Following the construction rules, fill each index record, and link the pointers to the cylinders.

Step 4. Determine the number of index records for the next upper level, and create the index record(s).

Step 5. Following the construction rules, fill each index record, and link the pointers to the lower level index records.

Step 6. Repeat Step 4 through Step 5 until the root of the tree has been reached.

In fact, a large database has a large number of large-scale B-trees. The computer constructs and maintains these large-scale B-trees to make the random access efficient.

2.5.3. B-tree maintenance

Data might be added or deleted from the cylinders, and the B-tree has to be updated correspondingly. Follow the example in Figure 2.7. Figure 2.8(a) shows a simple case of B-tree updating when Cylinder 6 is full and a new cylinder (Cylinder 9) must be added to accommodate additional records with key values between 5190 and 6743. In this case, split the records on Cylinder 6 arbitrarily and move a part of the records to Cylinder 9. As there is an empty pair in the index record, the computer simply adds a key-value/pointer pair to the index record.

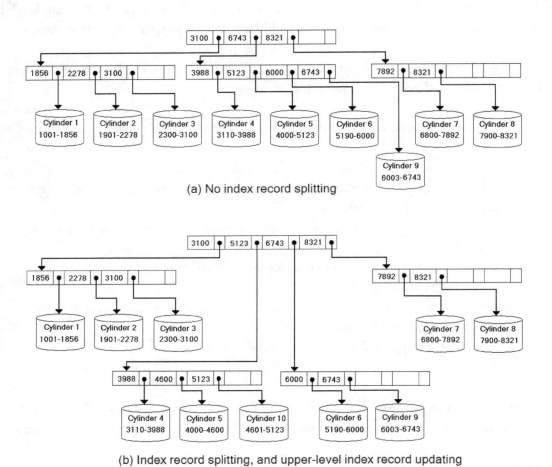

(a) No index record splitting

(b) Index record splitting, and upper-level index record updating

Figure 2.8. B-Tree Updating in Response to Data Insertion

Follow the example in Figure 2.8(a). Figure 2.8(b) shows a little complicated case when Cylinder 5 also happens to be full after Cylinder 9 has been added. To accommodate additional records with key values between 4000 and 5123, a new cylinder (Cylinder 10) must be added. However, as the index record has been full, it must be split into two index records, and each index record must have at least two key-value/pointer pairs (i.e., at least half of pairs are occupied). It is not important whether one index record has two occupied pairs or three occupied pairs in this example, as long as the splitting follows the construction rules. As the lower level of the B-tree has been changed, the upper level of the B-tree (in this case, the root) has to be updated correspondingly, as shown in Figure 2.8(b).

Several points are worth thinking further.

(1) A data deletion may also trigger B-tree updating.

(2) In Figure 2.8(b), the root index record of the B-tree is full. If the data set keeps growing and more and more new cylinders are added, eventually the root index record has to be split into two index records. Then, the B-tree must grow by creating a new root above the two index records.

(3) In our examples, the B-tree is used for indexing key values. Actually, B-trees can also be used for non-keys.

(4) A database management system can construct and maintain a huge number of B-trees so that random data access would be efficient. On the other hand, significant computational resource would be devoted to the B-tree construction and maintenance.

(5) Can the computer avoid splitting the index records of the B-tree by moving key-value/pointer pairs around? For instance, following the case of the B-tree in Figure 2.8(a), it has been said that if Cylinder 5 is full, then the index record is split to add Cylinder 10. Can one use the unoccupied space of the neighbor index record for Cylinders 7 and 8 by moving the key-value/pointer pairs for Cylinder 9? To answer this question, you need to imagine that a B-tree could be huge. If one keeps moving key-value/pointer pairs around, eventually every index record of the B-tree becomes full. At that point, just one data insertion will cause reconstruction of the entire huge B-tree which is the worst case for the B-tree maintenance. Thus, it is a good practice to split the index record when it has no room for an additional cylinder. In such a way, the B-tree maintenance job consumes only tiny computational resource each time.

(6) B-tree is good for random search. In cases where a sequential search occurs, the search process starts from the root and ends with the leaf repeatedly, which is not efficient. To improve the search performance for sequential searches, a variation of B-tree called B+-tree technique has been used. In B+-trees, there are additional pointer-links between the leaf index records at the lowest level.

Chapter 2 Exercises

1. A sequential disk file is as follows:

> Linda...
> Jone...
> John...
> Oldman...
> Youngman...
> Mark...
> EOF (End of File)

In order to find the record of Youngman, how many records the computer has to read from the disk? Explain why sequential file is rarely used in a large database.

2. A hashing function is

Address of record = Remainder of [Record key / 19].

Suppose that a record key is 379. What is the address of this record?

3. An indexed file for the inventory data on disk and its index table are as follows:

Disk file

Disk Address	Record			
	Record Key	Item Name	Quantity	Price
43	130	Pen	300	$4
20	12	Paper	200	$5
05	23	Disk	250	$6
10	43	Watch	100	$7
. . . .	. . . .			

Index Table

Record Key	Disk Address
20	14
130	43
43	10
14	29
. . . .	. . . .

What is the data of the record holding the key value 43? Explain the advantages and disadvantages of linear indexed files.

4. In the indexed file organization presented in Question 3, how can the computer read all of the records from the disk logically sequentially based on the values of the record key in the ascending order?

5. In the indexed file organization presented in Question 3, if one wants to randomly read individual records based on the price of the item, how would you design the index table?

6. The records of a large file are stored on 9 cylinders of disk. The highest key values of the records on each of the 9 cylinders are:

Cylinder 1: 1234
Cylinder 2: 2345
Cylinder 3: 3456
Cylinder 4: 4567
Cylinder 5: 5678
Cylinder 6: 6789
Cylinder 7: 7890
Cylinder 8: 8991
Cylinder 9: 9992

*a) Construct a B-tree for the file, assuming that each index record has 4 key-value/pointer pairs, and the number of index records at the lowest level of the tree is the minimum. Explain how the computer can find the record with the key 5000 using the B-tree.

b) Each index record has 2 key-value/pointer pairs, and the number of index records at the lowest level of the tree is the minimum.

7. Consider the B-tree below. A record has been added to cylinder 6, causing a cylinder split. The empty cylinder is number 20. The highest key value on cylinder 6 is now 5600, and the highest key value on cylinder 20 is now 6000. Update the B-tree.

8.* Consider the B-tree as shown below:

a) A record has just been added to Cylinder 6, causing a cylinder split. The highest key value on Cylinder 6 is now 2111; the highest key value on Cylinder 22, the empty reserve cylinder that received half of Cylinder 6's records, is now 2348. Update the tree index accordingly.

b) A record has just been added to Cylinder 10, causing a cylinder split. The highest key value on Cylinder 10 is now 3770; the highest key value on Cylinder 30, the empty reserve cylinder that received half of Cylinder 10's records, is now 3900. Update the tree index accordingly.

CHAPTER 3. DATA MODELS

3.1. Overview of Data Models

A **data model** is a representation of the complex data structures and their relationships of the target real world, or the system (e.g., Student Information System), for the database design. A data model defines the **semantics**, the meaning of data within the context of application. In the context of business information systems, a data model describes the **business rules** that are applied to the data. In systems analysis and design, data modeling is the data-centered analysis in conjunction with process modeling (the process-centered analysis) for the information system development.

To model the data and their relationships, graphics are used because verbal descriptions are often ambiguous and thus are difficult to be used for database design.

In principle, a data modeling approach (or the type of graphics) does not necessarily tie with a particular type of database system, but actually it does. In the database history, there have been four major types of data models, as listed below.

- **Hierarchical model** for hierarchical databases;
- **Network model** for network databases;
- **Entity-relationship (ER) model** for relational databases; and
- **Object-oriented model** for object-oriented databases.

The hierarchical model and hierarchical databases were used in the 1960s. Some legacy information systems might still run those databases. In the hierarchical model, all data are organized into a tree. Due to the limitation of the hierarchical model, the network model was created in the 1970s. The network model describes the data using network charts. However, the network databases were too complicated, and they had not become popular yet when the relational data model was invented. The entity-relationship (ER) model and relational databases were developed in the late 1970s, and still dominate the database area today. Since the early 1990s, the object-oriented model and object-oriented databases were developed. The **Unified Modeling Language (UML)**, a set of complicated diagramming methods, was created for the object-oriented model. However, for many reasons, object-oriented databases never became widespread. For the time being, it is unlikely that the ER model and relational database will be replaced by something else within a foreseeable time period. Thus, this book focuses on the ER model and relational database.

3.2. ER Model

The ER model is the most widely accepted model of data for database. Ironically, there is no universally accepted standard for **ER diagram** (**ERD**) notations despite of the popularity of the ER model. Historically, there have been many variations of versions of ERD notations. In fact, none of them is perfect. For database professionals, it does not matter which ERD convention is used because they know exactly what a specific notation or symbol means, and what aspect is missing in the convention. It has become a norm that people just use whatever ERD style the organization has already adopted. For teaching beginners, it might be ideal to use just one ERD style to avoid confusion. However, as you will see, any single ERD style cannot convey all important points for database design. Accordingly, our ERD convention includes two ERD styles which are very parallel. In this chapter, we use so-called logical ERD first to explain the concept of data modeling. Later, we will transit from logical ERD to so-called physical ERD. The two styles will convey all essential concepts for database design. More importantly, the conversion of a physical ERD into the relational database will be just one seamless step. Hence, you are recommended to use the physical ERD for your assignments and database project.

Generally, the ER model has two key elements: **entity** and **relationship** between entities, as discussed next.

3.3. Entity, Attribute, and Primary Key

An entity is a class of **objects**. There are three major types of entities in the context of database.

• A **physiomorphic** entity is a class of physically existing objects; e.g., CUSTOMER, STUDENT, and INVENTORY.

- An **event** entity represents a class of events of routine operations; e.g., GAME and CREDIT-APPROVAL.
- A **document** entity is a class of artificial abstractions; e.g., INVOICE.

Each entity has its **attribute**(s) which characterizes the entity. For example, a STUDENT entity would be described by student ID, student name, address, etc. Attribute and field are exchangeable terms. An attribute has its **data type**, such as text (character string), integer, decimal number, etc. An **instance** (or **occurrence**) of attribute is called a **value** of the attribute. For example, "John Smith" is a value of attribute StudentName. An attribute can have many **values**. An object with values in all attributes is an **entity instance**. For example, "01234567, John Smith, 286 Westport, 2012" is an instance of STUDENT.

Each entity has its unique **identifier**, called **primary key** or **key** for short. The key of the entity is a minimal set of attributes that can uniquely identify the unique object in the class. The primary key can be a specific attribute or a group of attributes. For example, the attribute StudentID is the key of STUDENT because it is the identifier to find a specific student object.

Figure 3.1 shows an ERD for entity STUDENT. We use the following convention of diagramming notations for entity.

- Use the rectangular shape for entity;
- Use caps for entity name;
- Use the camel style for attribute names – no space;
- Use the asterisk sign (*) to indicate the primary key of the entity.

Figure 3.1. An Example of Entity and Attributes in the ER Model

One may use any diagramming tool (e.g., a tool at www.gliffy.com) to draw ERD.

3.4. Relationship

A relationship describes the association among the instances of entities. The diamond shape and an active verb phrase are used to represent a relationship in the ERD. Binary, unary, and ternary relationships are the major types of relationships in terms of the number of entities involved, as discussed next.

3.4.1. Binary, unary, ternary relationships

The most common type of relationship describes the association between the instances of two entities, and is called **binary relationship**. For example, *Occupy* is a binary relationship between instances of PROFESSOR and OFFICE, representing *"who occupies which office"* (see Figure 3.2). *Use* is a binary relationship between the instances of COURSE and CLASSROOM, representing *"which course uses what classroom"* (see Figure 3.3). *Teach* is a binary relationship between the instances of PROFESSOR and COURSE, representing *"which professor teaches what course"* (see Figure 3.4).

A **unary relationship** describes the association between the instances of the **same** entity. For instance, *Mentoring* is a unary relationship between the instances of PROFESSOR, representing *"who is the mentor of other professors"* (see Figure 3.5). *Prerequisite* is a unary relationship between the instances of COURSE, representing *"which course is a prerequisite of what other courses"* (see Figure 3.6).

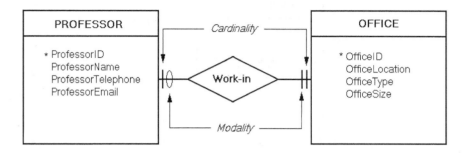

Figure 3.2. Binary One-to-One Relationship

Figure 3.3. Binary One-to-Many Relationship

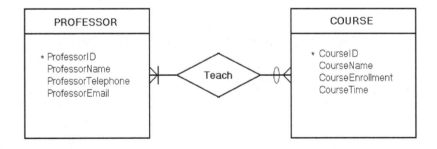

Figure 3.4. Binary Many-to-Many Relationship

Figure 3.5. Unary One-to-Many Relationship

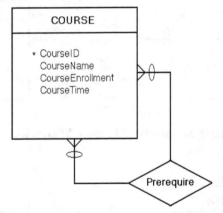

Figure 3.6. Unary Many-to-Many Relationship

A **ternary relationship** describes the association between the instances of three entities. For instance, *Teach* is a ternary relationship between the instances of PROFESSOR, COURSE, and STUDENT, representing *"which professor teaches what course for which student"* (see Figure 3.7).

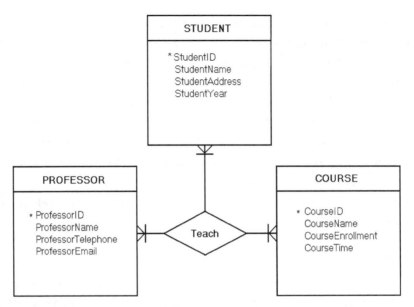

Figure 3.7. Ternary Many-to-Many Relationship

Apparently, one may use two or even three binary relationships to describe the relationships between the instances of PROFESSOR, COURSE, and STUDENT. The difference of semantics between a set of binary relationships and one ternary relationship is significant, and could be complicated if many business rules are considered. Generally, a ternary relationship assumes that the relationship instance (e.g., *Teach* in Figure 3.7) involves the three entities concurrently, while binary relationships relax this assumption and make the entire relationships among the entities flexible. For example, one may describe the relationships between the instances of PROFESSOR, COURSE, and STUDENT using two binary relationships: "*which professor **teaches** what course*" and "*which student **takes** what course*". In principle, a student can take a course without any professor (e.g., a transfer course) in this case. Further, when three binary relationships are used to describe the relationships between the instances of three entities, additional new semantics would be introduced. For instance, suppose that one uses the following three binary relationships to describe the relationships between the instances of PROFESSOR, COURSE, and STUDENT: *"which professor **teaches** what course"*, *"which student **takes** what course"*, and *"which professor **educates** which student"*. The third binary relationship *"which professor **educates** which student"* introduces additional semantics that a professor can educate (e.g., advise) a student without involving a course. The use of three binary relationships to replace a ternary relationship introduces a relationship loop. It is important to note that a relationship loop could contain a redundant binary relationship which in turn causes data redundancy, as discussed later in this chapter, and must be inspected thoroughly to eliminate any redundant relationships.

Practically, higher order relationships (i.e., more than 3-ways relationships) can be used in ER modeling, but are less common.

3.4.2. Cardinality

The **cardinality** is attached to a relationship to indicate the maximum number of instances of entities involved in the relationship. There are three types of relationships between the instances of entities in the ER model in terms of cardinality: **one-to-one** (1:1), **one-to-many** (1:M), and **many-to-many** (M:M). The "crow's foot" notations, as shown in Figures 3.2-3.7, represent the cardinalities.

Figure 3.2 is an example of 1:1 relationship between the instances of PROFESSOR and OFFICE, which means *"one professor can occupy at most one office, and one office can be occupied at most one professor."*

Figure 3.3 is an example of 1:M relationship between the instances of CLASSROOM and COURSE, which means *"one classroom can be used for many courses, and one course can use at most one classroom."*

Figure 3.4 shows an example of M:M relationship between the instances of PROFESSOR and COURSE which means *"one professor can teach many courses, and one course can be taught by many professors."*

Figure 3.5 shows an example of 1:M unary relationship between the instances of PROFESSOR which means *"one professor can be a mentor of many professors, and one professor can have at most one mentor."*

Figure 3.6 shows an example of M:M unary relationship between the instances of COURSE which means *"one course can have many prerequisites, and one course can be a prerequisite of many courses.*"

Figure 3.7 shows an example of M:M ternary relationship between the instances of PROFESSOR, STUDENT, and COURSE which means *"one professor can teach many courses for many students, one student can take many courses taught by many professors, and one course can be taught by many professors for many students."* Note that this ternary ER model implies a business rule that team teaching is allowed in this system.

3.4.3. Modality

The **modality** is the minimum number of instances of entity that can be involved in the relationship. Modality is also called **optionality** or **minimum cardinality**. In the ER model, modality can be either 0 or 1. For example, the modality shown in Figure 3.2 means *"one professor can work in at least one office, and one office can have no professor (i.e., can be empty)."* Similar to cardinality, modality can be used for the database management system to enforce the pertinent business rules. For instance, in our example, the database will not make a mistake that a professor has no office to work-in.

Several important points about the ER model are worth noting.

(1) The relationships between the instances of entities along with the cardinalities and modalities are not God-given, but are modeled by the database designer using the ER diagram as a tool to design the database. The relationships depend on the **business rules** of the business environment, or the **assumptions** made for the particular database. For instance, in our example in Figure 3.3, we assume one course can have only one classroom. If this assumption is not true for another database, the 1:M cardinality must be changed correspondingly.

(2) The cardinalities and modalities will be used by the database management system to enforce the pertinent business rules. For instance, in our example, the database will not make a mistake that a professor has two or more offices.

(3) In relational database, there is no way to present M:M relationships directly in the database. Any M:M relationship must be converted into 1:M relationships through the use of **associative entity**, as discussed in detail later in this chapter.

3.5. Instrument for Implementing 1:1 and 1:M Relationships – Foreign Key

In principle, the ER model is applicable for any types of databases. Practically, however, the ER model is intended for relational database. We will discuss relational database in details in Chapter 4. In this section, we discuss the way any relational database implements 1:1 and 1:M relationships, and describe how the ER model represents the implementation of 1:1 or 1:M relationships for the relational database.

To implement a 1:1 or 1:M relationship, a linkage between the entities is needed. The instrument used for the linkage is **foreign key**. A foreign key is the primary key of one entity and "travels" to another entity to implement the linkage. For example, the ER model in Figure 3.2 can be detailed by adding the foreign key *OfficeID* from OFFICE to the PROFESSOR entity, as shown in Figure 3.8. This foreign key represents *"a particular professor works-in this office."* In this book, we use the *Italic* font for foreign keys.

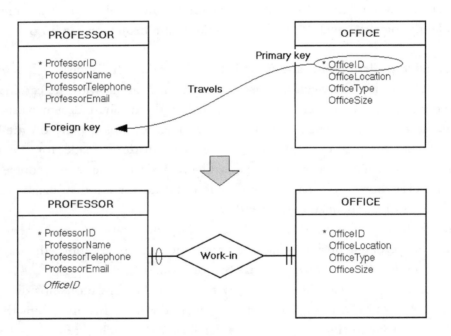

Figure 3.8. Foreign Key (*OfficeID*) Implements the Binary 1:1 Relationship in Figure 3.2

Similarly, the ER model in Figure 3.3 can be detailed by adding the foreign key *ClassroomID* from CLASSROOM (on the 1-side) to the COURSE entity (on the M-side), as shown in Figure 3.9, to represent *"a particular course uses this classroom."* Note that the primary key in one table and its corresponding foreign key in another table must have the same **domain of values**; that is, they have the same data type (e.g., both the primary key ClassroomID in CLASSROOM and the foreign key *ClassroomID* in COURSE are designed to be a text string with 7 characters).

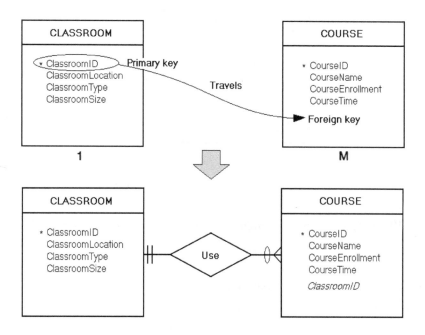

Figure 3.9. Foreign Key (*ClassroomID*) Implements the Binary 1:M Relationship in Figure 3.3

Figure 3.10 is the implementation of the unary 1:M relationship in Figure 3.5. Note that, within an entity, no two attributes can share the same attribute name. Hence, a different attribute name, say, *MentorID*, is created for the foreign key.

It is an important fact that the 1:1 and 1:M relationships which are explicitly annotated in the ERD do not have their independent body inside the relational database other than foreign keys. In other words, 1:1 and 1:M relationships are represented by the relational database implicitly through foreign keys. Because of this, some styles of ERD even do not include relationship diamond symbols. We use the diamond shape to represent the relationships for good reasons as explained later in Chapter 4.

Figure 3.10. Foreign Key (*MentorID*) Implements the Unary 1:M Relationship in Figure 3.5

While it is worth thinking deeper by yourself why foreign key can implement 1:1 and 1:M relationships, you need to understand the following rules.

(1) For a 1:1 relationship, you can arbitrarily choose the primary key from either entity and place it as the foreign key to the other entity. For instance, for the 1:1 relationships in Figure 3.2, you may place *ProfessorID* as the foreign key into the OFFICE entity. However, if one of the modalities is 0, it is better to place the foreign key in the entity with the 0 modality, as we did in Figure 3.8. In such a way, a value of the foreign key can never be empty.

(2) For a 1:M relationship, you place the primary key of the entity with the 1 cardinality into the entity with the M cardinality as the foreign key.

(3) The primary key in one table and its corresponding foreign key in another table have the same domain of values.

3.6. Instrument for Implementing M:M Relationships – Associative Entity

To implement an M:M relationship, the instrument is a little more complicated. In the relational database, there is no way to represent an M:M relationship unless an addition entity, called **associative entity**, is created. The associative entity converts the binary M:M relationship into two 1:M relationships which can then be represented in the relational database. For example, the M:M relationship in Figure 3.4 is converted into two 1:M relationships by adding an associative entity, called TEACH in this example, as shown in Figure 3.11.

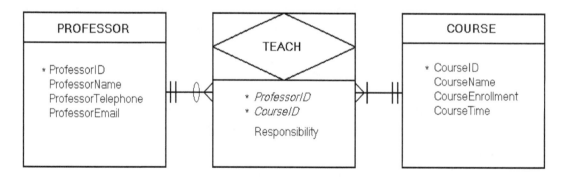

Figure 3.11. Associative Entity Is the Instrument for Implementing the Binary M:M Relationship in Figure 3.4

Important rules you need to understand when applying an associative entity.

(1) Once an associative entity is introduced, the binary M:M relationship becomes two 1:M relationships, and the associative entity is on the M sides between the two original

entities. The original M:M relationship disappears. In the example of Figure 3.11, the original M:M relationship between PROFESSOR and COURSE becomes the combination of the 1:M relationship between PROFESSOR and TEACH and the 1:M relationship between COURSE and TEACH.

(2) To distinct an associative entity from an ordinary entity, a diamond symbol is added on the top.

(3) Follow the same rules of implementing 1:M relationships, place the primary key of the entity on the 1 side into the associative entity as the foreign key. If the original M:M relationship is binary, then the associative entity can have two foreign keys. In Figure 3.11, *ProfessorID* and *CourseID* are the foreign keys from PROFESSOR and COURSE, respectively.

(4) An associative entity usually has its own attribute(s) that is not a part of either of the original entity but describes the characteristics of the associative entity. Those attributes are called **intersection data**. For example, in Figure 3.11, Responsibility is the intersection data attribute to describe the specific characteristics of the relationship between PROFESSOR and COURSE: *"what is the role (e.g., principle-teacher or co-teacher) of the professor who teaches this course?"*

(5) Usually, the combination of the foreign keys in the associative entity is the primary key of the associative entity. In Figure 3.11, the **combination primary key** (or simply **combination key**) of TEACH is [*ProfessorID+CourseID*]. Note that this rule can be altered in some cases as discussed below.

a) One may add an additional intersection data attribute(s) to join the combination key to make the primary key for the associative entity. For instance, in Figure 3.11, suppose the associative entity is used to record the data of TEACH for different semesters. In this case, [*ProfessorID+CourseID*] is no longer the identifier of the records of TEACH. Thus, one needs to add, say, SemesterID to the associative entity as a part of combination primary key to indicate the uniqueness of an instance of the associative entity. Then, [*ProfessorID*+*CourseID*+SemesterID] becomes the combination key of the associative entity.

b) If there are many attributes in the combination primary key of the associative entity, the index of the primary key becomes complicated. One might create a new single attribute as the primary key for the associative entity to substitute the tedious combination key. For instance, in the example of Figure 3.11, it is possible to create a new artificial attribute, say, TeachID, as the primary key of TEACH. Note that *ProfessorID* and *CourseID* are no longer a part of the primary key, but are still the foreign keys in the associative entity.

The above rules can be extended to the unary and ternary relationships. Figure 3.12 is the implementation of the unary M:M relationship in Figure 3.6. Note that, in the unary relationship, the names of the two foreign keys cannot be the same. Thus, *PrerequisiteID* is used for one of the foreign keys. In this example, the associative entity has no intersection data, and just describes "*what course is the prerequisite of what course.*"

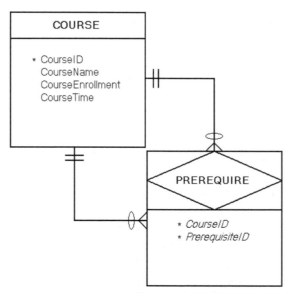

Figure 3.12. Implementation of the Unary M:M Relationship in Figure 3.6

Figure 3.13 is the implementation of the ternary M:M relationship in Figure 3.7. In this example, we add intersection data attribute called Assessment.

As shown in Figure 3.8 through Figure 3.13, in comparison with the logical ERDs in Figure 3.2 through Figure 3.7, the physical ERD include foreign keys, as well as applicable associative entities and intersection data. Note that there is no explicit M:M relationship in the physical ERD, because any M:M relationship will eventually be converted into 1:M relationships for the relational database.

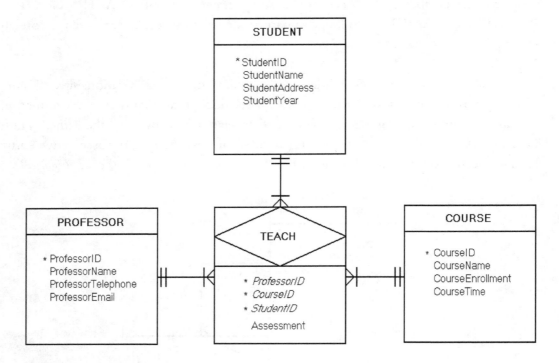

Figure 3.13. Implementation of the Ternary M:M Relationship in Figure 3.7

3.7. Summary of ER Diagram Convention
Figure 3.14 provides a summary of the ERD convention that conveys all necessary and detailed information for database design and implementation.

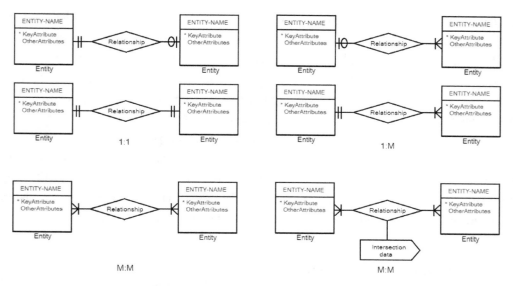

(a) Logical ER Diagram Notations (Tool for Intermediate ERD)

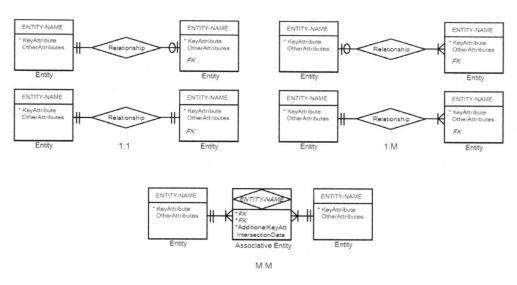

(b) Physical ER Diagram Notations (Tool for Final ERD)

Figure 3.14. Summary of ER Diagram Convention

As pointed out earlier in this textbook, there is no standard set of ERD notations. For example, a five-sided box is commonly used for including intersection data for an M:M relationship in logical ERD. Clearly, Figure 3.14 shows the advantages of physical ERD in that (a) foreign keys are included; (b) associative entities are presented; and (c) any M:M relationships are converted into 1:M relationships. These properties ensure the precise design of databases.

As you will see in Chapter 4, the transition from the physical ERD to the internal model of relational database is just one seamless step. For the database design beginners, the logical ERD can be a transitional tool for constructing ERD, but the physical ERD is strongly recommended to be the final blueprint for the database design in order to avoid any errors during the database construction.

3.8. Construction of ER Diagram

There are two major starting points for the **database designer** to construct an **ER diagram**: transcripts of the target real world, or sample datasheets from the target real world.

3.8.1. Transcript

It is common to use descriptions of the real world for constructing an ERD. A transcript could be a summary of your observations, or records of interviews, or verbal documents of surveys. For instance, we might have the following transcript that describes a school information system.

> *The School wants to create a database to maintain data for the school. Student data should include identification, name, address, and the earliest enrollment year. Professor data should include identification, name phone number, and office. Each professor has her/his own office, and teaches many courses each semester. Several professors might form a team to teach a single course. Each student can take many courses each semester. Course data should include unique course number, title, and enrollment cap. Each course can have its prerequisites. Each course must have a classroom. The school wants to keep track of students' grades.*

Based on the transcript, you might be able to construct an ERD which would look like Figure 3.15.

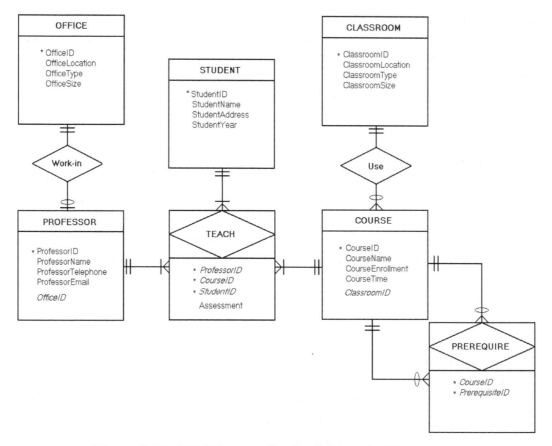

Figure 3.15. ER Diagram Derived from the Transcript

There are several steps you may apply to constructing an ERD based on a transcript.

(1) Identify entities and their attributes through identifying **nouns**.

(2) Identify relationships through identifying **verbs** or verb phrases.

(3) Identify cardinalities and modalities through identifying **business rules**.

(4) Make commonsensical **assumptions** if the transcript does not provide all information you need for modeling the system using ERD.

(5) Construct a logical ERD for the case.

(6) If there is an M:M relationship in your logical ERD, convert the M:M relationship into 1:M relationships by adding an associative entity along with its intersection data attributes.

(7) Add notations for all primary keys and foreign keys, and complete the physical ERD.

3.8.2. Sample datasheets

Another approach to generating an ERD is to collect sample datasheets from the real world, including business reports, forms, Web sites, etc. The sample datasheets collected are usually organized for particular application purposes and contains redundancy or secondary processed facts (e.g., totals). You need to abstract entities and relationships from those datasheets. For instance, Figure 3.16 shows a sample datasheet that you might have not seen before. As an exercise, you can make an ERD for the datasheet in Figure 3.16.

Several rules can be applied to constructing an ERD based on sample datasheets.

(1) Identify the entities that have their attributes in the datasheet table.

(2) Identify the relationships between the entities based on your understanding of the business environment.

(3) Identify cardinalities and modalities based on commonsensical assumptions that can be applied to the business environment.

(4) Construct a logical ERD for the case.

(5) If there is an M:M relationship in your logical ERD, convert the M:M relationship into 1:M relationships by adding an associative entity along with its intersection data attributes.

(6) Add notations for all primary keys and foreign keys, and complete the physical ERD.

Apparently, when sample datasheets are used for constructing ERD, more assumptions would be needed. Also, for a real-world database project, it is more likely to use both transcripts and numerous sample datasheets from a variety of application areas.

Department of Decision & Information Sciences		TEACHING SCHEDULE –		**Spring 2020**				
Instructor's Name:		**Shouhong Wang**			Office Location:		CCB #325	
Office/Conference Hours:		MWF 10:00-10:50 1:00-1:50 3:00-3:50			Telephone Ext.		8579	

		9:00-9:50	10:00	11:00-11:50	1:00	2:00-2:50	3:00
MON	Course Name Course Number (Section) Room Number	MIS 322 (01) Business Systems Analysis & Design T-201	Office Hours	MIS 212 (01) Programming & Problem Solving CCB-Lab	Office Hours	MIS 432 (01) Database Design & Implementation CCB-Lab	Office Hours
TUES		Research, Teaching innovation, Services					
WED	Course Name Course Number (Section) Room Number	MIS 322 (01) Business Systems Analysis & Design T-201	Office Hours	MIS 212 (01) Programming & Problem Solving CCB-Lab	Office Hours	MIS 432 (01) Database Design & Implementation . CCB-Lab	Office Hours
THURS		Research, Teaching innovation, Services					
FRI	Course Name Course Number (Section) Room Number	MIS 322 (01) Business Systems Analysis & Design T-201	Office Hours	MIS 212 (01) Programming & Problem Solving CCB-Lab	Office Hours	MIS 432 (01) Database Design & Implementation CCB-Lab	Office Hours

Figure 3.16. A Sample Datasheet for Construction of ER Diagram

3.8.3. Redundant relationships in ERD

One of the common mistakes in constructing an ERD is the inclusion of **redundant relationships**. We use an example to explain redundant relationships. Figure 3.17 shows an ERD for a customer order database. The ERD does not have redundant relationship.

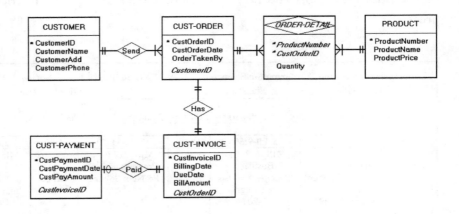

Figure 3.17. ERD of a Customer Order Database

Figure 3.18 shows an ERD with a redundant relationship for this database.

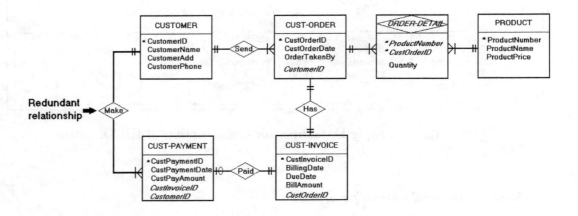

Figure 3.18. ERD with a Relationship Loop and Contains a Redundant Relationship

In Figure 3.18 the relationship between CUSTOMER and CUST-PAYMENT is redundant, because the database shown in Figure 3.17 can always find out which customer made a specific payment by tracing the relationship chain CUST-PAYMENT → CUST-INVOICE → CUST-ORDER → CUSTOMER. More importantly, the redundant relationship between CUSTOMER and CUST-PAYMENT is not only unnecessary but also harmful because it introduces data redundancy through the additional foreign key. Note that the entity CUST-PAYMENT in Figure 3.18 has two foreign keys: *CustomerID* from CUSTOMER and *CustInvoiceID* from CUST-INVOICE. These two attributes are actually interdependent. This interdependency will cause data redundancy which will in turn result in data inconsistency. For instance, due to the redundant relationship "Make" in Figure 3.18, the database allows you to input a customer payment record with a legitimate *CustomerID* value and a legitimate *CustInvoiceID* value, but the involved customer invoice can actually belong to another customer. We will learn data normalization in Chapter 5, and this issue becomes more understandable by then.

Redundant relationships may simplify some database queries and updates, but can cause inconsistency in the database. If redundant relationships exist in an ERD, special treatments will generally be required at the programming level to ensure data consistency.

A redundant relationship in an ERD is caused by a **relationship loop**. However, a relationship loop may not always introduce a redundant relationship. For instance, if one uses three M:M binary relationships to replace an M:M ternary relationship, a relationship loop without a redundant relationship could be generated if the semantics of the three binary relationships are not correlated. In any case, a relationship loop must be inspected carefully to detect any redundant relationship. It is a common practice to remove a redundant relationship by breaking up the relationship loop unless a special means preventing data integrity violations is applied.

3.8.4. Iterations of ERD construction

Thus far, we have learned how to create an ERD for the database based on verbal descriptions of the system or sample datasheets used in the system. One question you might have in your mind is: "*Is there a criterion for judging whether an ER diagram is correct or wrong?*" The answer to this question is "yes." We will return to this question in Chapter 5 on normalization.

The above question tells that, regardless whether the start point of the construction of an ERD is a system description or is sample datasheets, one-shot construction may not result in a good ERD. The construction of ERD and the normalization process should be carried out together. If an initial ERD is generated before the normalization process, this trial ERD might need to be revised after the normalization process to become the approved ERD. In fact, if the start point of the construction of an ERD is sample datasheets, one may perform the normalization process before constructing a trial ERD for the database. This fine point is illustrated in Technical Guide B in this textbook through an example.

An ERD is the design blueprint for the target database. If the ERD is wrong, the target database based on the flawed ERD must be wrong, and could become a collection of garbage.

Chapter 3 Exercises

1. You are planning to open a motel. A rough sketch of the online reservation form is shown below. Create an ERD for the database that can support the online reservation system, making all necessary commonsensical assumptions.

Online Reservation

Reservation Information

Check-In Date: ☐
Check-Out Date: ☐
Number of Guests: 1 ▽
Number of Rooms: 1 ▽   Type of Rooms: ▽

Contact Information

Last Name: ☐
First Name: ☐
Street Number: ☐
City: ☐
Province/State: ☐
Country: Canada ▽
Postal Code ☐
Phone Number: ☐
E-mail Address: ☐

Credit Card Information

Credit Card: ○ Visa ○ MasterCard ○ American Express ○ Discover
Name on Credit Card: ☐
Credit Card Number: ☐ (No spaces or dashes, please)
Expiration Date: ☐ (MM/YYYY)

(**Submit**)   (**Reset**)

2.* Draw an ERD that describes the database of GreenHeating Company to store data of its heating units, the houses in which they locate, and its technicians and the services they perform for the heating units. Each heating unit has a unique unit number, name, manufactory, type, date built, and capacity. House has a unique address, owner, and insurance. A heating unit can be used in one house. A house can have several heating units or it can have no heating unit. A technician has a unique employee number, employee name, title, and year hired. Some technicians supervise others. Each heating unit is cared for by at least one and generally many technicians, and each technician cares for at least one and generally many heating units. Each time when a technician performs a specific service for a heating unit, the service type, date, and time are recorded.

Minicase: *GreenJetNB (Chapter 3)*

GreenJetNB is a regional airline with headquarters in New Bedford. It has several aircrafts and various commute itineraries between hubs and small cities. GreenJetNB wants to have data on the current aircrafts and pilots who works on each of its aircrafts. For scheduling and marketing purposes, it keeps track data of past and future flights and data of the passengers who traveled with GreenJetNB and have booked on the future flights. A flight is identified by a unique flight number. It is described by a departure city, a destination city, a departure time, an arrival time, and a schedule code (i.e., D for daily, M for Monday, MW for Monday and Wednesday, etc.). A flight involves just one aircraft, but an aircraft can serve on many flights. Each aircraft can have more than one pilot and each pilot can drive more than one aircraft. Each aircraft has its attributes include GreenJetNB aircraft number, manufacturing serial number, type, and capacity. GreenJetNB keeps the maintenance records for each aircraft to trace the maintenance work, the time, and the responsible persons. The maintenance work is outsourced to several independent maintenance companies. Each pilot has a unique identification number, name, home address, email, and qualification. Some of the pilots are in supervisory positions for several junior pilots. A passenger is identified by a unique number, name, address, and data of birth. GreenJetNB also wants to keep track of the sale price and the regular price for each airticket as well as the customer satisfaction rating of each trip.

Draw an ERD that models the data for GreenJetNB.

CHAPTER 4. RELATIONAL DATABASE

4.1. Relational Data Model and Tables

Since the 1980s, the **relational data model** has been popularized. At the present time, relational database systems are still the most commonly used database systems. A relational data model is easy to understand and easy to use. Newly developed data bases in business are all relational data bases, with few exceptions.

In the relational data model, an **entity** can be represented by a **table** (or **relation**). For instance, STUDENT is an entity. The instances of STUDENT can be represented by a table, say, tblStudent, in the database, as shown in Figure 4.1.

Several special terms used in the relational data model are shown in Figure 4.1. Each table can have several columns represented by **attributes**. An attribute describes a characteristic of the entity. In this example, the entity STUDENT has four attributes: StudentID, StudentName, StudentAddress, and StudentYear. The table can contain many **rows**, and each row represents a **record** (or a **tuple**). A minimal set of attributes that can uniquely identify each tuple in the relation is called is called **primary key** (or **key**) of the relation. The primary key of the relation can be a specific attribute or a group of attributes. In this example, StudentID is the key. The value of the key of a record is fixed for the database and is not supposed to be changed.

Each attribute has its **data type**. For example, StudentName is **text** (or **character**, or **string**), and StudentYear is **Number**. The definitions and names of data types are highly dependent on the DBMS. Commonly used data types in database are:

- Text (Character, String);
- Number;
- Integer;
- Date;
- Image.

It is recommended to use **text** for the data type of keys to differentiate strings from numbers. For example, "001" is a character string, and its value is placed in a pair of quotation marks. In terms of internal code within the computer, "001" is different from 1.

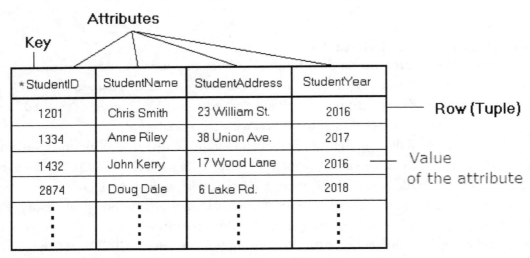

Figure 4.1. Table tblStudent

There are several properties of table (or relation) in the relational data model.

(1) The order of columns of a relation is not important. In other words, it makes no difference whether you put an attribute, say, StudentID, in the first column or in the second column.

(2) The order of row of a table is not important. In other words, it makes no difference whether you put a record in the first row or in the second row.

(3) Each **cell** in the table can have only one single value. The value could be "**null**".

(4) No two records in a table have the same value of the primary key.

4.2. Candidate Key and Alternative Key

A table (or relation) can have more than one minimal set of attributes that can be used to identify the unique record in the table. For instance, if we assume StudentName (including first name, middle name, and last name) is unique in the database, then the

STUDENT relation can have two **candidate keys**: StudentID and StudentName. If the DBA chooses StudentID to be the primary key for the STUDENT relation, then StudentName is called the **alternative key**. If the DBA chooses StudentName to be the primary key for tblStudent, then StudentID becomes the alternative key. The concept of candidate key and alternative key is important for understanding the indexing in databases. Thus far, we have learned four terms about key: primary key, candidate key, alternative key, and foreign key.

4.3. Conversion of ER Model to Relational Data Model

The conversion of an ERD into the relational data model includes two steps: constructing relations, and defining constraints. As you can see in this chapter, it is one seamless step to convert a physical ERD into the relational data model. In fact, the ER model in the physical ERD form (i.e., the form that models 1:1 or 1:M relationships, associative entities, foreign keys, but contains no M:M relationship, as presented in Chapter 3) and the relational data model represent the same concept in the alternative forms. The ER model is the human perception of the target database, and the relational data model is the computer internal model of the target database.

4.3.1. Constructing relations

The general rules of conversion of the ER model to the relational data model are simple if the physical ERD is used.

(1) An entity (including associative entity) in the ER model is a relation in the relational data model.

(2) All attributes (including intersection data items) in an entity in the ER model are the attributes of the corresponding relation in the relational data model.

(3) The primary key of an entity in the ER model is the primary key of the corresponding relation in the relational data model.

(4) The foreign key in an entity in the ER model is an attribute of the corresponding relation in the relational data model.

Figure 4.2 shows the result of conversion of the ER model in Figure 3.9 to the relational model.

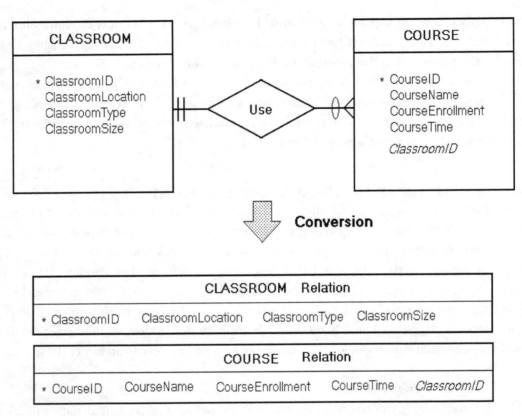

Figure 4.2. ER Model Is Converted to Relational Model

The relational data model in Figure 4.3 is the result of conversion of the ER model in Figure 3.13.

STUDENT Relation			
* StudentID	StudentName	StudentAddress	StudentYear

PROFESSOR Relation			
* ProfessorID	ProfessorName	ProfessorTelephone	ProfessorEmail

COURSE Relation			
* CourseID	CourseName	CourseEnrollment	CourseTime

TEACH Relation			
* *ProfessorID*	* *CourseID*	* *StudentID*	Assessment

Figure 4.3. The Relational Data Model Converted from the ER Model in Figure 3.13

The relations can be created as tables of the database under the DBMS support. There are two ways to create a table using the DBMS: using the standard SQL (Structured Query Language), or using the graphical environment of the DBMS. We will learn SQL in Chapter 6. Technical Guide A in this textbook describes the graphical environment of Microsoft Access to create tables.

A relation filled with data is a **data sheet**. Figure 4.4 is a sample of data sheet of the STUDENT relation.

STUDENT		Relation	
* StudentID	StudentName	StudentAddress	StudentYear
1201	Chris Smith	23 William St.	2016
1334	Anne Riley	38 Union Ave.	2017
1432	John Kerry	17 Wood Lane	2016
2874	Doug Dale	6 Lake Rd.	2018

Figure 4.4. Sample Data Sheet of the STUDENT Relation

4.3.2. Defining constraints

The second step of conversion of the ER model into the relational data model defines the constraints for cardinalities and modalities attached to the relationships between entities. Generally, a **constraint** is a restriction posted on data to enforce rules. To implement the cardinalities and modalities in the ER model, the database designer must define applicable constraints that are attached to the corresponding tables.

The reality is that the methods of implementation of constraints attached to tables vary depending upon the DBMS, although the methods of construction of tables are quite similar in all relational DBMSs. In this textbook, we use a generic form of script, called **pseudo-code**, to define constraints attached to tables.

(1) For a relationship with 1:M cardinality, no constraint is needed as it is the default case.

(2) For a relationship with 1:1 cardinality, define the constraint using the following pseudo-code:

Table {CONSTRAINT *foreign-key* UNIQUE}

For instance, for the 1:1 relationship between PROFESSOR and OFFICE in Figure 3.8, the constraint is defined as follows.

PROFESSOR {CONSTRAINT *OfficeID* UNIQUE}

(3) For a relation with 1 modality, no constraint is needed as it is the default case. Nevertheless, the following pseudo-code can be used to make the default constraint explicit.

Table {CONSTRAINT MANDATORY TO The-Other-Table}

For instance, in the Figure 3.8 example, the following constraint imposes 1 modality to the OFFICE table which means that there must be at least one instance of OFFICE in the relationship between OFFICE and PROFESSOR.

OFFICE {CONSTRAINT MANDATORY TO PROFESSOR}

(4) For a relation with 0 modality, define the constraint using the following pseudo-code.

Table {CONSTRAINT OPTIONAL TO The-Other-Table}

For instance, in the Figure 3.8 example, the following constraint imposes 0 modality to the PROFESSOR table which means that the minimum instance of PROFESSOR could be 0 in the relationship between PROFESSOR and OFFICE.

PROFESSOR {CONSTRAINT OPTIONAL TO OFFICE}

When implementing the constraints expressed in pseudo-code using a particular DBMS, the database designer must examine the support features of the DBMS used for the database construction. Sophisticated commercial DBMS support advanced SQL features that allow the database designer to define those constraints using SQL. Technical Guide A in this textbook shows limited features of implementation of constraints in the Microsoft Access environment.

One interesting point is worth noting that, unlike an entity, a relationship represented by the diamond shape in an ERD has no its corresponding representative in the relational database. That is why some versions of ERD notations even do not have diamond shape for relationships. In our physical ERD notations, we keep the diamond shape for two reasons. First, ERD is a tool for representing the semantic network of the database. To describe the database in a genuine semantic context, we need to represent the relationships explicitly on the diagram for human communication about the meaning of the database. This would be particularly useful for data processing applications development using queries as shown in Chapter 6. Second, as we learned earlier, the nature of associative entities is different from that of ordinary entities, and we need to use the diamond shape to differentiate associative entities from ordinary entities. To make the notations consistent, we must keep the diamond notation clearly in the ERD.

4.4. Data Retrieval from Relational Database

Once the relational data model is established, the DBMS allows the user to create tables, to establish the relationships, and to input data. The tables filled with the data become a relational database. Supported by the DBMS, the user is allowed to retrieve data from the relational database through **SQL (Structured Query Language)**, which will be introduced in Chapter 6, or an alternative tool called **Query By Examples (QBE)** technique, as explained in Technical Guide A of this textbook for using QBE in Microsoft Access.

There is **relational algebra** to formally describe how data can be retrieved from a relational database. Here, we explain how data are retrieved from a relational database.

4.4.1. B-trees for search

At the level of individual table, B-trees play the major role of data retrieval. Once a relational database is built, the DBMS can create B-trees to index the selected attributes for the database to support data search and data direct access of the records. As we learned from Chapter 2, however, excessive B-trees make data retrievals from each of the tables in the relational database efficiently, although they consume computational resource for maintenance.

4.4.2. Simple data retrieval path

At the level of multiple tables, data retrieval is carried out through tracing the chains of

76

key and foreign key that link the connected tables. In simple data retrieval cases, it is possible to define a clear data retrieval path. For instance, in the relational database represented by the tables in Figure 4.3, to *"find the assessment made by professor Fred Brown for student Chris Smith in the Database Design & Implementation course"*, the database goes through the following steps while each step involves just one table, as illustrated in Figure 4.5.

(1) Find the primary key of Professor Fred Brown from the PROFESSOR relation. If the ProfessorName is indexed (e.g., by a B-tree), this operation can be done quickly; otherwise, the computer has to go through the entire table.

(2) Find the primary key of student Chris Smith from the STUDENT relation.

(3) Find the primary key of course Database Design & Implementation from the COURSE relation.

(4) Use the values of the three primary keys as the combination key to find the assessment in the TEACH relation.

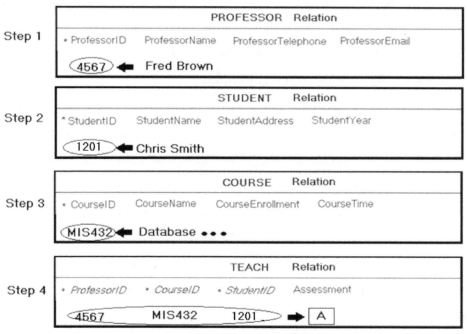

Figure 4.5. Simple Case of Data Retrieval

4.4.3. Join operation

When highly integrated data are retrieved from multiple tables, however, the data retrieval becomes complicated. For instance, in the relational database represented by the tables in Figure 4.2, to *"list course ID, course title, course enrollment, course time for each course along with its classroom's data including classroom ID, classroom type, classroom size"*, the computer must go back-forth between the two tables by tracing the chain of the key and foreign key of the two tables (i.e., COURSE and CLASSROOM) for many times to find the needed data, and meanwhile stores a large amount of intermediate data before it can present the final query result to the user. In such a case, the database actually performs a **join** operation. The join operation matches the values of the key in one relation (ClassroomID in the CLASSROOM relation) and the values of the foreign key in the other relation (*ClassroomID* in the COURSE relation) to merge the two relations into a single table, as illustrated in Figure 4.6. Note that the merged table (COURSE-CLASSROOM) should have the same number of rows as the relation on the M side (COURSE) of the 1:M relationship.

Apparently, the merged table contains redundant data. For example, the fact that *"the classroom T-001 locates in T-Building and is a computer lab"* repeats. However, the merged table provides good data integration so that all related data are presented in a single table which is easy to read. In Chapter 6, we will learn how the DBMS can provide integrated data for the user through queries while having tables without data redundancy.

Clearly, the join operation would take enormous computation resources if the tables involved are huge. Sophisticated DBMS apply advanced algorithms to optimize join operations.

COURSE-CLASSROOM

CourseID	CourseName	CourseEnrollment	CourseTime	ClassroomID	ClassroomLocation	ClassroomType	ClassroomSize
MIS212	Programming	40	MWF 9-10	T-001	T-Building	Comp-Lab	50
MIS432	Database	30	MWF 11-12	T-001	T-Building	Comp-Lab	50
ACT211	Accounting I	40	TR 10-11	L-213	L-Building	Lecture	60
FIN312	Finance	35	MWF 9-10	L-213	L-Buldinbg	Lecture	60
MGT211	Organization	38	TR 10-11	K-123	K-Bulding	Case-Room	40

Figure 4.6. Merge Tables through Join Operation

4.5. Referential Integrity

As the primary key in the table on the 1-side is the foreign key in the table on the M-side in a 1:M relationship, there are potential violations of data integrity. For example, in the relational database represented in Figure 4.2, when the user adds a course to the COURSE table, he might make a mistake that the inputted classroom ID for the course even does not exist. Also, when the user deletes a classroom records but the classroom has already been assigned to several courses, what should the DBMS do? Such issues are known as **referential integrity**.

Any DBMS should be capable to maintain the data integrity and to prevent potential violations of data integrity. When the data are inputted into the database, the DBMS must apply the rule to check the inputted data to maintain the data integrity. For example, the DBMS never allows the user to input a value of ClassroomID (foreign key) in the COURSE table if the value of ClassroomID does not exist in the CLASSROOM table. For data deletion, the referential integrity issue is a little more complicated than data insertion. Generally, there are three **delete rules** as described below.

(1) **Delete Rule: Restrict**

Suppose one wants to delete a classroom record (on the 1-side), and the classroom has been assigned to a course(s) (on the M-side) already. The restrict rule will forbid the delete to take place. A classroom record is allowed to be deleted only when it has not been assigned to any course.

(2) **Delete Rule: Cascade**

If the cascade rule is applied, when a record on the 1-side is deleted, all related records on the M-side will be deleted as well. In the Figure 4.2 example, if one deletes a classroom record, all records of the courses which use the classroom will be deleted automatically.

(3) **Delete Rule: Set-to-Null**

If the set-to-null rule is applied, when a record on the 1-side is deleted, the matching foreign key values on the M-side will be changed to "null". In the Figure 4.2 example, if a classroom record is deleted, the values of *ClassroomID* in all records of the courses that have been assigned to this classroom will be changed to "null" which means "no classroom for these courses".

These delete rules are implemented by the DBMS through constraints. Again, the methods of implementing these constraints vary depending upon the DBMS used. Large DBMSs support advanced SQL features that allow the database designer to implement more constraints. Technical Guide A in this textbook shows some features of delete rule constraints in the Microsoft Access environment.

Chapter 4 Exercises

1.* Consider the ERD in Figure 3.13 and the tables in Figure 4.3. Assume that course names are unique. Mark all primary keys (PK), candidate keys (CK), alternative keys (AK), and foreign keys (FK) on the tables.

2.* A part of the database of a property management company is modeled by the following ERD. Define the non-default constraints for the relationships between the three tables.

3. Convert the following ERD into a relational database model. Explain your assumptions for making candidate keys. Mark all primary keys (PK), candidate keys (CK), alternative keys (AK), and foreign keys (FK) on the tables. Mark the data type (T or N) for each attribute.

4. Consider the following data sheets of the database represented in Question 3.

MANUFACTORY

* ManufactoryName	Representative	PhoneNumber
RedFlower	John	2345
BlueJay	Anne	3456
GreenWorld	Dick	4567
YellowRock	Mary	7890

PRODUCT

* ProductNumber	ProductName	ProductPrice	ManufactoryName
C1234	ThinkPC	2000	GreenWorld
B3456	SmartPhone	3000	BlueJay
A7213	GW-GPS	500	GreenWorld
A8934	YR-GPS	450	YellowRock
C8973	MobilPrinter	480	GreenWorld

SALES

*ProductNumber	*BranchName	*Date	Quantity
C1234	Westport	03/12/2016	123
B3456	Eastport	03/23/2016	234
A7213	Northport	04/02/2016	58
C1234	Southport	03/08/2016	34
A7213	Westport	04/23/2016	134
A8934	Eastport	05/05/2016	88

BRANCH

*BranchName	BranchAddress	BranchManager	RegionName
Eastport	20 Eastport Rd.	Tim	NewBedford
Northport	50 Northport Ave.	Mike	Boston
Southport	60 Southport St.	Susan	FallRiver
Westport	10 Westport Dr.	Cathy	CapeCod

a) Does it cause data redundancy to place ManufactoryName in both MANUFACTORY and PRODUCT tables? Why?

b) Merge the PRODUCT table and SALES table into a single table. Show the products that have sales. Do you see data redundancy in the merged table? Give an example. Does the merged table have any advantage?

5. Consider the relational database represented by the ER diagram in Question 3 and the datasheets in Question 4. Explain how the following data are retrieved from the relational database in step-by-step, and be specific by showing the data.

a) Find the record of product number A8934.

b) Find the record of the product of "ThinkPC".

c) List all of the names of representatives of the manufactory companies that produce "ThinkPC".

d) What is the sales figure of "ThinkPC" at Cathy's branch on 03/12/2016?

e) List all product sales transactions for year 2016, including the product numbers, product names, product prices, sales, branches for the sales, and the manufactories for the products.

f) List the branch names, branch manager names, product numbers, product names, and sales quantity for every sales transaction that occurred during year 2016.

6. Consider the following the database represented in Question 3 and the datasheet in Question 4. What would happen in the following situations?

a) The deletion rule between the MANUFACTORY and PRODUCT relations is restrict and an attempt is made to delete the record for ManufactoryName "GreenWorld" in the MANUFACTORY relation.

b) The deletion rule between the MANUFACTORY and PRODUCT relations is restrict and an attempt is made to delete the record for ManufactoryName "RedFlower" in the MANUFACTORY relation.

c) The deletion rule between the MANUFACTORY and PRODUCT relations is restrict and an attempt is made to delete the record for ManufactoryName "BlueJay" in the MANUFACTORY relation.

d) The deletion rule between the MANUFACTORY and PRODUCT relations is cascade and an attempt is made to delete the record for ManufactoryName "GreenWorld" in the MANUFACTORY relation.

e) The deletion rule between the MANUFACTORY and PRODUCT relations is cascade and an attempt is made to delete the record for ManufactoryName "RedFlower" in the MANUFACTORY relation.

f) The deletion rule between the MANUFACTORY and PRODUCT relations is cascade and an attempt is made to delete the record for ManufactoryName "BlueJay" in the MANUFACTORY relation.

g) The deletion rule between the MANUFACTORY and PRODUCT relations is set-to-null and an attempt is made to delete the record for ManufactoryName "GreenWorld" in the MANUFACTORY relation.

h) The deletion rule between the MANUFACTORY and PRODUCT relations is set-to-null and an attempt is made to delete the record for ManufactoryName "RedFlower" in the MANUFACTORY relation.

i) The deletion rule between the MANUFACTORY and PRODUCT relations is set-to-null and an attempt is made to delete the record for ManufactoryName "BlueJay" in the MANUFACTORY relation.

Minicase: *GreenJetNB (Chapter 4)*

Follow the GreenJetNB minicase in Chapter 3, convert the ERD you generated for GreenJetNB into a relational database. Define (non-default) constraints for each table.

CHAPTER 5. NORMALIZATION AND LOGICAL DATABASE DESIGN

5.1. Normalization

It is possible that the tables created for the relational database have problems of data redundancy, because the ER modeling itself does not ensure no-redundancy. **Normalization** is a process that evaluates the table structures and minimizes data redundancy. Specifically, normalization is an analysis procedure to group attributes into well-structured relations and to obtain "good" relations (tables) for the relational database by eliminating the risk of data redundancy.

5.2. Functional Dependency

An important concept of normalization is **functional dependency** which defines the **determination relationships** between the attributes. The concept of functional dependency is not totally new to you. We have introduced the concept of **primary key** in Chapter 4 that a minimal set of attributes that can uniquely identify each tuple in the relation is called the primary key of the relation. The primary key of the relation can be a specific attribute or a group of attributes. Using the term of functional dependency, we can say "*a record of the table is **functionally dependent** on the primary key of the table*," or "*the primary key of the table is the **determinant** of a record of the table*." In normalization, functional dependency reaches to the attribute level instead of the record level.

A **functional dependency** occurs when the value of one attribute in a table determines the value of another attribute in the table. The statement "*B is functionally dependent on A*" or "*A determines B*", where B is an attribute and A is an attribute or a group of attributes, means that "*if you know the value of A, then you know the value of B.*" The common notation of functional dependency is

A → B

For example, in the database represented in Figure 4.3, if you know the StudentID, then we can determine the StudentName of this student. Formally,

StudentID → StudentName

If you know the value of [StudentID+CourseID+ProfessorID], then we can determine the Assessment for this student, for this course, and made by this professor. Formally,

[StudentID+CourseID+ProfessorID] $\rightarrow$ Assessment

An important point we would like to underline here is the conceptualization. The functional dependencies for a database are assumed by the database designer based on her/his conceptual understanding of the relationships between the attributes in the real world. The functional dependencies for the database are usually objective "common sense", but can also be assumptions which may or may not be totally objective. However, if an assumption of functional dependency is contradictory to what truly happens in the real world, the database might build in errors. As functional dependency is used as the key instrument for the normalization process, different assumptions of functional dependencies for the database may result in different outcomes of database design. Apparently, the conceptualization of the real world is crucial for the database development. Practically, if you design a database, you need to document the assumptions of functional dependencies beyond "common sense" for the database to avoid confusion. These assumptions should be necessary, correct, and as minimal as possible. Incorrect or conflicting assumptions will result in an erroneous database design. The assumed functional dependencies will become the **business rules** incorporated in the database. The validation of the correctness of assumed functional dependencies is discussed in Chapter 5. When you are using a database, you should respect the business rules made for the database, and do not make your own assumptions.

5.3. Normal Forms

A table has its properties in terms of the functional dependencies between its attributes. A **normal form** represents a certain type of functional dependency property of tables. Normal forms are ordered in a series of stages. A table in a higher stage of normal form is better than a table in lower stage of normal form in terms of data redundancy control. The normalization process is to evaluate tables and convert tables in a lower stage of normal form into tables in a higher stage of normal form. We will emphasize on **first normal form (1NF)**, **second normal form (2NF)**, and **third normal form (3NF)**, although will also study higher-level normal forms. For most business databases, tables in 3NF are considered to be acceptable with no serious data redundancy. However, higher-level normal forms would make the database better to control data redundancy.

Note the concepts that (1) if a table in 3NF, it must be also in 2NF; (2) if a table in 2NF, it must be in 1NF as well; (3) the database is in 3NF only if all tables are in 3NF.

5.3.1. Unnormalized form

A table that has a missing value or multiple values in a cell, or has not primary key, is called unnormalized table. Its form is called unnormalized form, or **0NF**. Figure 5.1(a) and Figure 5.1(b) show examples of unnormalized table.

Student ID	Student Name	Course ID	Grade
10001	Chris Smith	ACT211	A
		MIS315	B
		MIS322	
10021	Anne Riley	ACT212	B
		MGT311	
		FIN312	A
10293	John Kerry	MGT212	B
		ACT211	A

Figure 5.1(a). Unnormalized (0NF) Table
(Table with missing values or multiple values)

Student ID	Student Name	Grade
10001	Chris Simth	A
10001	Chris Simth	B
10001	Chris Simth	B
10021	Anne Riley	B
10021	Anne Riley	A
10021	Anne Riley	A
10293	John Kerry	B
10293	John Kerry	A

Figure 5.1(b). Unnormalized (0NF) Table
(Table with no primary key)

5.3.2. Conversion from 0NF to a normal form

The procedure of converting from a 0NF table into a normal form table includes the following steps.

Step 1. Eliminate missing values or repeating values in any cell.

Step 2. Define all functional dependencies among the attributes based on the business environment or common sense. If there is an attribute without involving functional dependency (e.g., Grade in the example in Figure 5.1(b)), you must create a functional dependency for it by adding a new attribute(s) (e.g., in Figure 5.1(b), add CourseID to make [StudentID+CourseID] for Grade in the table).

Step 3: Identify the primary key for the table (e.g., [*StudentID+*CourseID] in Figure 5.2), so that if the value of the primary key is known then the value of any other attribute must be known.

Note that a table with a primary key only but does not have any non-key attribute could be a **trivial table** and should not be included in the database, unless a combination of the components of the primary key records substantial facts. As discussed next, a normal form derived from 0NF could be 1NF, 2NF, or even 3NF.

5.3.3. First Normal Form (1NF)

A table is in **first normal form** (**1NF**) if it meets the following two conditions.

(1) The table has no missing value or multiple values in a cell.

(2) The primary key of the relation is identified based on assumptions of functional dependency among all attributes. These assumptions should be consistent with the **business rules** in the business environment.

Figure 5.2 shows an example of table in 1NF. The assumptions of functional dependency among all attributes are then made, as shown in Figure 5.3.

* StudentID	StudentName	Major	Department	* CourseID	CourseTitle	Grade
10003	John Smith	ACT	Accounting	ACT211	Fin.Accouting	B
10003	John Smith	ACT	Accounting	ENG101	Intro.English I	A
10014	Anne Gold	CHM	Chemistry	CHM101	Intro.Chemistry	C
10014	Anne Gold	CHM	Chemistry	CHM231	Adv.Chemistry	B
12343	Bob Brown	GNS	Biology	BIO101	Intro.Biology	A
12343	Bob Brown	GNS	Biology	CHM101	Intro.Chemistry	B
12343	Bob Brown	GNS	Biology	BIO345	Genetics II	A
13345	Mike Green	ACT	Accounting	ENG101	Intro.English I	B
13345	Mike Green	ACT	Accounting	ENG201	Intro.English II	B
13345	Mike Green	ACT	Accounting	ENG345	Literature	C

Figure 5.2. Table in 1NF

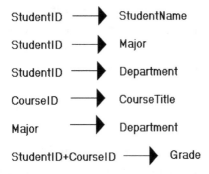

Figure 5.3. Functional Dependencies for the 1NF Table in Figure 5.2

Based on the assumptions of functional dependency, it is conclude that the primary key of this 1NF table is [StudentID+CourseID] (a **combination key**), which is marked with asterisk (*), since [*StudentID+*CourseID] is the determinant of any other attribute in the table. In other words, if you know a value of [*StudentID+*CourseID], you will know all values of other 5 attributes.

5.3.4. Data redundancy and data modification anomaly

The 1NF table in Figure 5.2 has redundant data. For instance, the fact that "student 10014 is Anne Gold" is stored twice. Data redundancy not only wastes resource, but also causes problems called **data modification anomaly**.

(1) **Update anomaly**

In a table with data redundancy, if a repeated fact is changed, all redundant values must be changed in each place they are stored. This is called update anomaly. For example, in Figure 5.2, if the name of the student holding the Student ID 10014 is changed to Anne Smith, all records with Student ID 10014 have to be changed correspondingly.

(2) **Insertion anomaly**

A table with data redundancy could preclude useful facts. For example, the table in Figure 5.2 is unable to record a newly admitted student unless she/he has taken a course because CourseID is a part of the primary key which can't be empty. Accordingly, the table can't record the data of any student who has not registered in a course. This problem is called insertion anomaly. The insertion anomaly in a table with data redundancy actually eliminates useful facts.

(3) **Deletion anomaly**

In a table with data redundancy, a deletion of record from the table can cause unintentional deletion of facts. For instance, in Figure 5.2, if Student John Smith (10003) withdraws his ACT211 course and the first record in the table is deleted from the table, then the fact that *"ACT211 is Fin.Accounting"* will be lost unintentionally. This problem is known as deletion anomaly.

5.3.5. Partial key dependency in 1NF table, and normalize 1NF

As can be seen in Figure 5.2 and Figure 5.3, a great deal of data redundancy is caused by the mixture of student data and course data. The root of this problem is known as **partial key dependency**. A partial key dependency occurs when the value in a non-key attribute of a table is dependent on the value of a part, but not the whole, of the table's combination primary key. In the example in Figure 5.2, the student data depend on StudentID only (but not [StudentID+CourseID]), and the course data depend on CourseID only (but not [StudentID+CourseID]).

To eliminate the partial key dependency in a 1NF table, the 1NF table must be further normalized by splitting it up into two or more tables which do not have partial key dependency. The rule of decomposition is to make such tables that all attributes depend on the entire key. The procedure of normalizing a 1NF table with partial key dependency includes the following steps.

Step 1. Make a list of potential individual key components derived from the (combination) primary key of the original table in 1NF. Each key component will become the primary key of a new table. For example, for the table in 1NF in Figure 5.2, three potential individual primary keys can be derived from [StudentID+CourseID]; they are: StudentID, CourseID, and [StudentID+CourseID].

Step 2. Assign each non-key attribute in the table in 1NF to one of the potential individual keys based on the functional dependency. The further normalized tables are then formed. Using the example of Figure 5.2 and Figure 5.3, you can assign StudentName to StudentID, CourseTitle to CourseID, Grade to [StudentID+CourseID], and so on. The final result of the two steps for the example in Figure 5.2 is shown in Figure 5.4.

Step 3. Revise and preserve the given functional dependencies. A certain functional dependency may be lost as a result of Step 1 through Step 2. One must examine each of the lost functional dependencies. If a lost functional dependency is a trivial derivation of some remained functional dependencies, it means that the lost functional dependency is already preserved and can be simply discarded. Otherwise, one must reconcile the tables obtained from Step

1 through Step 2 to consolidate and preserve the lost functional dependency.

Note that we do not elaborate the last step here, but will revisit this point in the next sub-section. In addition, we provide an exercise question and its answer to explain the concept of revising and preserving functional dependencies.

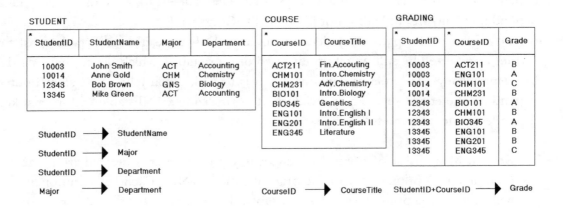

Figure 5.4. Tables Normalized from 1NF Table in Figure 5.2

A special point is worth noting. If a table does not have its non-key attribute, then the database designer must justify assumptions in order to determine whether the table with its primary key only should be included in the database. For example, suppose the table in Figure 5.2 does not have attribute Grade. [*StudentID+*CourseID] could still be meaningful as an independent table without a non-key attribute, indicating "*who had taken what course*". It is clear that the assumption of business rule made here is: "*any value of the combination* [StudentID+CourseID] *is meaningful and unique*". This assumption is true if "*a student can take a particular course with only one record*", but it is not true if "*a student can have many records for a particular course*". If a table has its key only but does not record substantial facts, it is a trivial table and should not be included in the database.

5.3.6. Second Normal Form (2NF) and non-key dependency

Figure 5.4 shows the result of decomposition of the 1NF table in Figure 5.2, and the functional dependencies relevant to each table. The key of the STUDENT table is a single attribute, and thus this table can never have partial key dependency. The COURSE table has the same condition. The GRADING table has a combination key, and Grade fully depends on [StudentID+CourseID]. The normal form of a table that is in 1NF and contains no partial key dependency is called second normal form or 2NF. The three tables in Figure 5.4 do not have partial key dependency, and thus are in 2NF. Clearly, a 2NF table is also in 1NF.

As shown in Figure 5.4, because the partial key dependency has been eliminated, the data redundancy is greatly eliminated as well. Here, we refresh what we have learned from Chapter 1 about data redundancy. In Figure 5.4, StudentID 10003 appears once in the STUDENT table and 2 times in the GRADING table. These values are not data redundancy because they record different facts, and act as the linkage between the two tables.

A 2NF table does not have partial key dependency, but might still contain data redundancy. For instance, the STUDENT table in Figure 5.4 has repeating facts about major and department. This problem is caused by **non-key dependency** (or **transitive dependency**). A non-key dependency occurs when the value in a non-key attribute of a table is dependent on the value of another non-key attribute in the table. In the example in Figure 5.4, the Major attribute is a non-key attribute, but it is the determinant of the Department attribute in the same table.

5.3.7. Normalize 2NF table with non-key dependency and Third Normal Form (3NF)

To solve the non-key dependency problem in a 2NF table, you can do the following steps to eliminating the non-key dependency by normalizing the 2NF table further as follows.

Step 1. Identify any non-key dependency in the table in 2NF. In the example of Figure 5.4, Major → Department is a non-key dependency.

Step 2. Create a new table (e.g., OWNERSHIP in the Figure 5.5 example) for the attributes involved in the non-key dependency (e.g., Major and Department in this example), and assign the primary key for this new table (e.g., Major in this example) based on the given functional dependency.

Step 3. Keep the determinant attribute involved in the non-key dependency (e.g., Major in the Figure 5.5 example) in the original table (STUDENT in this example) as the foreign key from the new table (e.g., OWNERSHIP), and delete other attributes involved in the non-key dependency (Department in this example) from the original table (STUDENT in this example).

Step 4. Revise and preserve the given functional dependencies. A certain functional dependency may be lost as a result of Step 1 through Step 3. One must examine each of the lost functional dependencies. If a lost functional dependency is a trivial derivation of some remained functional dependencies, it means that the lost functional dependency is already preserved and can be simply discarded. For example, the functional dependency StudentID $\rightarrow$ Department in Figure 5.4 is lost; however it is actually preserved in the functional dependencies in Figure 5.5 as StudentID $\rightarrow$ Major and Major $\rightarrow$ Department. However, if a lost functional dependency is necessary to recover, one must reconcile the tables obtained from Step 1 through Step 3 to consolidate and preserve the lost functional dependency.

Figure 5.5 shows the normalization results derived from the 2NF tables in Figure 5.4 as well as the functional dependencies relevant to each table. Clearly, the tables in Figure 5.5 have no non-key dependency. The normal form of a table that is in 2NF and contains no non-key dependency is called third normal form or 3NF. Clearly, a 3NF table is also in 2NF. In other words, a table in 3NF has no partial key dependency and has no non-key dependency.

There is an important point to clarify for the definition of non-key dependency. If an attribute is an alternative key, it is not considered to be a non-key attribute. For instance, in the STUDENT table in Figure 5.5, if StudentName is unique and is considered to be an alternative key of the table, it is not a non-key attribute. In other words, an alternative key is treated as the primary key of the table.

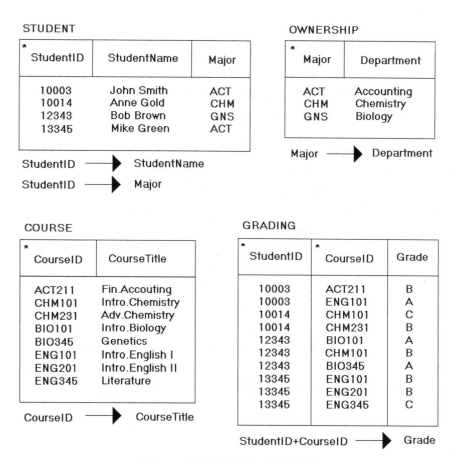

Figure 5.5. Tables in 3NF

5.3.8. Summary of normalization procedure from 0NF to 3NF

Given a table, it is not difficult to determine whether the table is 0NF or is in a normal form because missing values or multiple values in a cell can be easily observed and the key can be easily identified based on commonsensical assumptions. However, the normal form of a given non-0NF table (or normal table) might not be obvious. The following rules can be applied to determine the normal form of a normal table.

1. If the table has partial key dependency, then it is in 1NF.
2. If the table does not have partial key dependency and has non-key dependency, then it is in 2NF.
3. If the table does not have partial key dependency, and does not have non-key dependency, then it is in 3NF.

3NF tables are generally considered to be acceptable for database design. They are also essential for validating the correctness of the functional dependencies identified before the normalization process. If an initial functional dependency identified before the normalization process is correct, it must be preserved in the 3NF tables resulted from the normalization process.

The overall normalization procedure that produces well-structured 3NF tables and their ERD is summarized in the following steps.

Step 1. Arrange the data into basic tables known as "unnormalized" tables (0NF).

Step 2. Normalize each of the tables in 0NF into a table in normal form by eliminating multiple values in a cell, eliminating missing values, and establishing functional dependencies between the attributes and the primary key.

Step 3. If the normal form of the table is 1NF, normalize the table by eliminating partial key dependency. Revise and preserve the identified functional dependencies.

Step 4. Determine the normal form for each of the normalized tables obtained from Step 3. If the normal form of the table is 2NF, normalize the table into 3NF by eliminating non-key dependency. Revise and preserve the identified functional dependencies.

Step 5. Consolidate all tables in 3NF from the analysis, and generate or revise the ERD.

The above steps are depicted in Figure 5.6. Technical Guide B in this textbook provides another example of normalization procedure for database design.

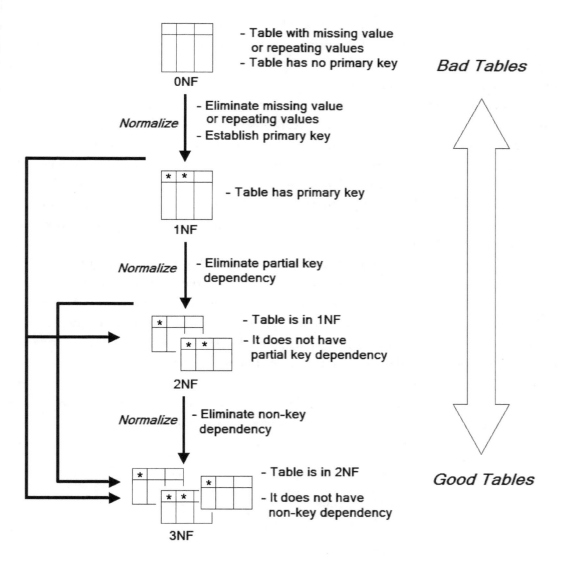

Figure 5.6. Normalization Process

5.3.9. Boyce-Codd Normal Form (BCNF)

Tables in 3NF could still have data redundancy and modification anomalies due to other types of functional dependencies. **BCNF (Boyce-Codd Normal Form)** addresses the problem in a 3NF table where a **non-candidate-key attribute** is the determinant of an attribute of the primary key of the table. Specifically, BCNF solves two special cases not covered by 3NF: (1) a non-key attribute determines an attribute in a combination key; (2) an attribute in the combination key determines another part of the combination key. In the literature, there is no precise common terminology for such functional dependencies. In this textbook, we call such functional dependencies **"reverse dependency"**. A reverse dependency occurs when the value of a part of the combination key is reversely determined by the value of another non-candidate-key attribute. Although the reverse dependency problems are not common, they do cause data redundancy. Accordingly, further normalization is needed for a table in 3NF with reverse dependency. The normal form of a table in 3NF that has no reverse dependency is called BCNF. Here, we present an example that a table in 3NF is not in BCNF. Suppose there is a table called ADVISING, as shown in Figure 5.7. The functional dependencies based on the business rules indicate that [StudentID+Major] is the combination key of the table, Advisor is dependent on [StudentID+Major], and MajorProject is dependent on [StudentID+Major] as well. There is no dependency between Advisor and MajorProject. Thus, the ADVISING table is in 3NF. However, Advisor is not a candidate key of the table, but is the determinant of Major in this business environment. This causes data redundancy. For instance, the fact that Green is a GNS advisor repeats in the table. To solve the problem, decompose and restructure the table into two tables in BCNF, as shown in Figure 5.8.

* StudentID	* Major	Advisor	MajorProject
10014	CHM	Brown	3.5
10014	GNS	Green	3.1
13345	ACT	Smith	3.2
12343	GNS	Green	3.7
13469	ACT	Jones	3.4

StudentID+Major ⟶ Advisor   Advisor ⟶ Major   ("Reverse" dependency)

StudentID+Major ⟶ MajorProject

Figure 5.7. A Table in 3NF but Not in BCNF

STUDENT

* StudentID	* Advisor	MajorProject
10014	Brown	3.5
10014	Green	3.1
13345	Smith	3.2
12343	Green	3.7
13469	Jones	3.4

StudentID+Advisor ──────▶ MajorProject

ADVISOR

* Advisor	Major
Brown	CHM
Green	GNS
Smith	ACT
Jones	ACT

Advisor ──────▶ Major

Figure 5.8. Tables in BCNF without "Reverse" Dependency

5.3.10. Normalize 3NF table with reverse dependency into BCNF

Unlike 3NF, BCNF is not always achievable. Detailed discussions would go beyond the scope of the textbook. Generally, the procedure of normalizing a 3NF table with reverse dependency into BCNF tables includes the following steps.

Step 1. Identify any reverse dependency in the table in 3NF. In the example of Figure 5.7, Advisor → Major is a reverse dependency.

Step 2. Create a new table (e.g., ADVISOR in the Figure 5.8 example) for the attributes involved in the reverse dependency (Advisor and Major in this example), and assign the primary key for this new table (Advisor in this example).

Step 3. Make the determinant attribute involved in the reverse dependency (Advisor in the Figure 5.8 example) to be a part of the combination primary key of the original table (STUDENT in this example), and delete other attributes involved in the reverse dependency (Major in this example) from the original table (STUDENT in this example). Revise all functional dependencies.

Note that the determinant attribute involved in the reverse dependency (Advisor in the Figure 5.8 example) also becomes a foreign key from the new table (e.g. ADVISOR in the Figure 5.8 example) to the original table (STUDENT in this example).

5.3.11. Fourth Normal Form (4NF)

The Fourth Normal Form (**4NF**) is the next level of normalization after BCNF. While previous normal forms all deal with functional dependencies, 4NF addresses a different type of dependency known as **multivalued dependency** (**MVD**). Before presenting the definitions of MVD and 4NF, we examine an example of MVD in Figure 5.9. The STUDENT table shown in Figure 5.9 is in BCNF, but it has data redundancy and modification anomalies when a student has multiple majors (e.g., a student can have both majors in MKT and FIN) or multiple minors (e.g., a student can have both minors in FRA and GER), because the STUDENT table repeats the same facts (e.g., *the student holding the StudentID 10003 has the SPA minor, and the student holding the StudentID 10014 has the MKT major*).

STUDENT

StudentID	Major	Minor
10003	MKT	SPA
10003	FIN	SPA
10014	MKT	FRA
10014	MKT	GER
23540	CHE	BUS
35462	ENG	BUS

StudentID ———▶▶ Major

StudentID ———▶▶ Minor

Figure 5.9. Table in BCNF with Multivalued Dependency

An MVD occurs in a table in BCNF if (a) the table has at least three attributes, say, A, B, and C; (b) for each value of A, there is a set of values for B and a set of values for C, and the set of values for B and C are independent of each other; (b) for any two tuples of the table that have the same value of attribute A, the two tuples resulted by switching the values of attribute B are also in the table. The common notation for

MVD is: A→→B and A→→C. For example, in the first two tuples of the table in Figure 5.9, (a) the two tuples have the same value (10003) of the StudentID attribute can switch the values (MKT and FIN) of the Major attribute; and (b) the table has the Minor attribute that is independent of Major. In the third and fourth tuples of the table, (a) the two tuples have the same value (10004) of the StudentID attribute, and they can switch the values of the Major attribute because of the same value (MKT); and (b) the table has the Minor attribute. Hence, using the notation, the MVD is

StudentID →→ Major

Similarly, in the third and fourth tuples of the table in Figure 5.9, (a) the two tuples have the same value (10004) of the StudentID attribute, and they can switch the values (FRA and GER) of the Minor attribute; and (b) the table has the Major attribute that is independent of Minor. In the first and second tuples of the table, (a) the two tuples have the same value (10003) of the StudentID attribute, and they can switch the values of the Minor attribute because of the same value (SPA); and (b) the table has the Major attribute. Hence, using the notation, the MVD is

StudentID →→ Minor

In summary, an MVD has the following properties.
1. An MVD always requires that certain tuples be present in the table.
2. The table with multivalued dependency has at least three attributes, say, [A,B,C], where A, B, C are the attributes of the table; if A→→B, then A→→C. An MVD always involves all attributes of the table.
3. An MVD always introduces data redundancy in the table.

The normal form of a table is 4NF if and only if the table is in BCNF and has no MVD. To eliminate the data redundancy caused by MVD, further normalization is needed for a table in BCNF with MVD. In the example in Figure 5.9, to eliminate the MVD, the STUDENT table must be decomposed into two tables, say, MAJORS which contains the StudentID and Major attributes as the combination key of the table, and MINORS which contains the StudentID and Minor attributes as the combination key of the table. These two tables are in 4NF, as shown in Figure 5.10.

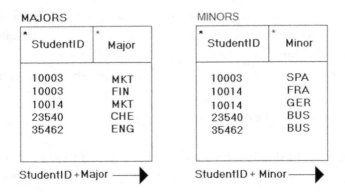

Figure 5.10. Tables in 4NF without Multivalued Dependency

5.3.12. Normalize BCNF table with multivalued dependency into 4NF
The procedure of normalizing a BCNF table with MVD into 4NF tables includes the following steps.

Step 1. Identify any MVD in the table which is in BCNF. In the example of Figure 5.9, StudentID $\to\to$ Major and StudentID $\to\to$ Minor are MVD.

Step 2. Create a new table (e.g., MAJORS in the Figure 5.10 example) for the attributes involved in the MVD (StudentID and Major in this example), and assign the combination primary key for this new table ([StudentID+Major] in this example).

Step 3. Delete the multivalued attribute involved in the MVD (i.e., the right hand side of the MVD, Major in this example) from the original table (STUDENT in this example), and rename the table (e.g., to MINORS in this example).

Step 4. Repeat Step 1 through Step 3 for the table resulted in Step 3 (e.g., MINORS in this example) until no MVD exists in all resulting tables. Revise all functional dependencies in the resulting tables.

5.4. The Nature of Normalization and Higher-Level Normal Forms

If you consider Figure 5.8 and Figure 5.10 at once and try to consolidate all attributes StudentID, StudentName, Advisor, Major, MajorProject, etc. for the database in a complicated business environment, you may conclude that once tables are normalized into 4NF, the data redundancy is eliminated completely in this example, but, at the same time, the number of tables expands and the data become less integrated. Consequently, normalization purity is often difficult to sustain in a large database because data processing could be prohibitively slow. Nevertheless, many database design experts argue that database tables should be in 4NF.

Our position is clear that the normalization process must be consistent with the clearly defined business rules (functional dependencies) for the database being designed. In principle, a large database for commercial use should be in 4NF. However, the decision on the normal form for each table should take the pertinent business rules of the business environment into account. The example of normalization in Technical Guide B in this textbook explains this fine point further.

In fact, even higher-level normal forms such as 5NF and DKNF (Domain Key Normal Form) exist. However, these normal forms mainly fit theoretical purposes such as information science research, but are not practically useful for the databases in the business environment.

5.5. Logical Database Design

Logical database design is the process that defines the databases structures to meet the data requirements of the business. Generally, logical database design includes the following steps.

> **Step 1.** Generate an initial (or trial) ER model for the database through interviews, surveys, observations, and data samples based on the business requirements.
>
> **Step 2.** Convert the trial ER model into a preliminary set of tables.
>
> **Step 3.** Perform normalization on the preliminary set of tables into normalized tables (see the procedure in the previous section) based on the assumptions of functional dependencies for the business environment and the practical

requirements for the database. Determine the final normalized tables, incorporating the consideration of the level of normal forms (3NF, BCNF, or 4NF) for the business environment.

Step 4. Based on the normalized tables, revised the initial ERD to obtain the approved ERD for the database.

Step 5. Convert the normalized tables into the DBMS internal model in the selected DBMS (e.g., Oracle, DB2, Microsoft Access, etc.).

Step 6. Attach pertinent constraints to applicable tables.

Step 7. Verify that the internal model for the selected DBMS is consistent with the approved ER model.

The steps of logical database design are depicted in Figure 5.11.

Figure 5.11. Logical Database Design

Three points are important to learn.

(1) The logical database design for a database is an iterative process. It refines the ER model and a set of tables for the database through the analysis of business requirements and the normalization process. If the logical design process starts with data samples, Step 1 might be skipped and a preliminary set of tables could be derived directly from the data samples without a trial ERD, as explained by the example in Technical Guide B in this textbook. However, having a trial ERD before the normalization process would make the logical database design less problematic for a large database.

(2) The ERD of a database is a blueprint for the database. It is used for human communication among the database designers, the DBA, and the users to understand the structure of the database. More importantly, because it is difficult for human to verify whether the computer internal model is consistent with the normalized tables with appropriate relationships, the ERD must be used as the blueprint for the design. Most CASE (Computer Aided Software Engineering) tools can support mapping from an ERD onto a computer internal model to some extent. As shown in Technical Guide A in this textbook, some DBMS, such as Microsoft Access, can show its computer internal model of the normalized tables in a form of relationships which allows the DBA to verify the computer internal model against the approved ERD.

(3) Logical database design ensures the data needs for the business, but does not take the performance of database into account. As data are normalized into 3NF, or even BCNF and 4NF, the data in tables become more and more detached from each other, and become less and less integrated for the user. The ultimate consequence of data in higher-level normal forms is the inefficiency of data retrieval. To solve this problem in a large database, physical database design must be applied, as discussed in Chapter 7.

Chapter 5 Exercises

1. Given the following table, define commonsensical functional dependencies between the attributes.

GreenPlant Auction House Disclosure

Auction Date	Auction Sponsor	Contact	VIN	Make	Model	Year	Miles	Price	Buyer	Buyer Address	Down Payment	Loan Number
09/04/10	N.B.City	j@nbcity.com	AQ122	Ford	Mustang	2010	43k	$25000	Brown	Westport	$500	A-321
09/04/10	N.B.City	j@nbcity.com	B2344	Toyota	Corolla	2009	12k	$13000	Smith	Northport	$280	B-432
09/04/10	RedBank	r@redbank.com	D34R2	Ford	F-250	2011	50k	$35000	Sousa	Eastport	$1000	B-456
09/12/10	RedBank	r@redbank.com	AT343	GMC	Sierra	2010	23k	$34000	Jones	Southport	$750	C-489
09/12/10	YellowBank	s@ybank.com	F45E3	Honda	Accord	2009	19k	$27700	Smith	Northport	$345	A-380
09/23/10	YellowBank	s@ybank.com	P36Y8	Ford	Focus	2009	23k	$10999	Lee	Newport	$210	B-541
09/23/10	BlueCar	t@bluecar.org	K39L9	Toyota	Camry	2010	68k	$29950	Shaw	Oldport	$450	C-543
09/23/10	BlueCar	t@bluecar.org	N2345	Volvo	C90	2010	71k	$32000	O'Neil	Greenport	$621	C-567

2. Given the table in Question 1, provide examples of data insertion anomaly, data deletion anomaly, and data update anomaly.

3. Is each of the following statements true or false?

a) A table with no non-key dependency might have partial key dependency.

b) The normal form of a normal table (non-0NF) with no combination key can't be 1NF.

c) The normal form of a normal table with no non-key attribute can't be 2NF.

d) The normal form of a normal table with no non-key attribute must be BCNF.

e) The normal form of a normal table with no combination key and just one non-key attribute must be 4NF.

f) A multivalued dependency occurs only when the table has at least 3 attributes.

4.* GreenBook library maintains data on the books. Some of the attributes and functional dependencies are described as follows:

Attributes	Functional Dependencies
BookNumber	BookNumber → BookTitle
PublishDate	BookNumber → FirstAuthor
BookTitle	BookNumber → PublishDate
FirstAuthor	BookTitle → FirstAuthor
Length (in pages)	BookTitle → Length
ClientNumber	ClientNumber → ClientName
ClientName	ClientNumber → ClientAddress
ClientAddress	[BookNumber+ClientNumber+RentalDate]→
RentalDate	ReturnDate, RentalFee
ReturnDate	
RentalFee	

For each of the following tables, first write the table's current normal form (as 1NF, 2NF, or 3NF), and explain why. Then, for those tables that are currently in 1NF or 2NF, reconstruct them to be 3NF tables. Primary key attributes are marked with *. Do not assume any functional dependencies other than those shown.

a. *BookTitle, FirstAuthor, Length

b. *BookNumber, PublishDate, BookTitle, FirstAuthor

c. [*BookNumber+*ClientNumber+*RentalDate], ReturnDate, RentalFee

d. [*BookNumber+*ClientNumber+*RentalDate], ClientName, ReturnDate, RentalFee

e. [*BookTitle+*ClientNumber], FirstAuthor, Length, ClientName, ClientAddress

5.* GreenSales keeps track of data about products, orders, customers. Each order can include many product items ordered by the same customer. Each ordered product item is specified by sale price and order quantity. The attributes and functional dependencies at GreenSales are assumed as follows. Do not assume any functional dependencies other than those shown.

Attributes	Functional Dependencies
ProductID	ProductID → ProductName
ProductName	CustomerID → CustomerName
CustomerID	CustomerID → CustomerAddress
CustomerName	OrderID → CustomerID
CustomerAddress	OrderID → OrderDate
OrderID	OrderID → ShippingDate
OrderDate	[OrderID+ProductID] → ProductSalePrice
ShippingDate	[OrderID+ProductID] → OrderQuantity
ProductSalePrice	
OrderQuantity	

For each of the following independent tables (primary key attributes are marked with "*", and combination primary key is connected with "+"), explain the table's current normal form (as 1NF, 2NF, or 3NF, and why). Then, for the tables that are currently in 1NF or 2NF, decompose them into 3NF tables, and mark the primary key with "*" for the 3NF tables.

a) *OrderID, OrderDate, ShippingDate, CustomerID, CustomerName, CustomerAddress

b) [*OrderID+*ProductID+*CustomerID], CustomerAddress, ProductName, ProductSalePrice, OrderQuantity

6.* GreenClinic is a medical clinic. It keeps track of data about patients, patient's insurance, doctors, and medical treatments. The attributes and functional dependencies at GreenClinic are assumed as follows.

DoctorID → DoctorName

DoctorID → DoctorTelephone

PatientID → PatientName

PatientID → InsuranceName

DoctorID+PatientID+TreatmentDate → TreatmentType

TreatmentType → TreatmentCost

TreatmentType+InsuranceName → InsuranceBenefit

Given the above functional dependencies and following table, explain the table's current normal form (as 1NF, 2NF, or 3NF, and why). If the table is currently in 1NF or 2NF, normalize it into 3NF, preserving functional dependencies.

[*DoctorID+*PatientID+*TreatmentDate],
    DoctorName, InsuranceName, TreatmentType, TreatmentCost, InsuranceBenefit

7. GreenPlace is an apartment rental business. It wants to keep track of data of apartment units, parking units, clients, superintendents, and leases. Explain why the following assumptions of functional dependencies of the apartment management system are commonsensical.

ApartmentUnitID → ParkingUnitID

ApartmentUnitID → ApartmentAddress

ApartmentUnitID → ApartmentType

ApartmentUnitID → MonthlyRental

ApartmentUnitID → Superintendent

ParkingUnitID → ParkingMonthlyFee

ClientID → ClientName

ClientID $\to \to$ ClientEmployer

ClientID $\to \to$ ClientPhone

[ApartmentUnitID+ClientID] $\to$ LeaseStartDate

[ApartmentUnitID+ClientID] $\to$ LeaseEndDate

[ClientID+SpecialNeedType] $\to$ SpecialFacilityID

SpecialFacilityID $\to$ SpecialNeedType

Given the above functional dependencies, for each of the following tables,

(1) explain why the attribute or a combination of attributes marked with * is the primary key of the table;

(2) tell the current normal form (0NF, 1NF, 2NF, 3NF, BCNF, or 4NF), and explain why;

(3) if the table is not in 3NF, normalize it into tables in 3NF;

(4) if the current table is in 3NF, explain whether the table is in BCNF or 4NF; if the current table is not in BCNF/4NF, normalize it into tables in BCNF/4NF.

Note that, do not make your own assumptions of functional dependency. Each question is independent.

a) *ApartmentUnitID, ApartmentAddress, ApartmentType, Superintendent

b) [*ParkingUnitID+*ClientID], ClientName, ParkingMonthlyFee

c) *ApartmentUnitID, MonthlyRental, ParkingUnitID, ParkingMonthlyFee

d) [*ApartmentUnitID+*ClientID], ClientName, Superintendent, MonthlyRental, LeaseEndDate

e) [*ApartmentUnitID+*ClientID+*ParkingUnitID], MonthlyRental, ParkingMonthlyFee

f) [*ClientID+*SpecialNeedType], ClientName, SpecialFacilityID

g) ClientID, ClientName, ClientEmployer

h) ApartmentUnitID, ClientID, ClientEmployer

i) ApartmentUnitID, ClientID, ClientName, ClientEmployer,
LeaseStartDate, LeaseEndDate

j) [*ClientID+*ClientEmployer+*ClientPhone], ClientName

Minicase: *GreenJetNB (Chapter 5)*

Follow the GreenJetNB minicase in Chapter 3 and Chapter 4. Perform normalization for the tables you generated for the database, and/or justify why the tables are normalized. Re-define or verify the constraints for each normalized table.

CHAPTER 6. DATABASE PROCESSING AND SQL

6.1. Introduction to SQL

SQL (Structured Query Language) is a universal language for creating, updating and querying databases. As SQL is a small language, SQL program is often called SQL script. SQL can be used for all database management systems (DB2, Access, Oracle, etc.) as well as all computer language platforms (Java, .NET, etc.). SQL was developed under the name SEQUEL by IBM in the mid-1970s. That is why people pronounce SQL as "sequel" more often than "ess-que-ell". SQL has been standardized by ANSI (American National Standard Institute).

A particular database management system can have its query development environment, so-called QBE (Query By Examples, to create queries without using SQL. In the query development environments of QBE, the database management system generates the query code in SQL. This gives an impression that one might not need to write SQL code. In fact, there are two major reasons for using SQL.

(1) SQL integrates features of data definition languages (DDL) and data manipulation languages (DML). QBE itself does not possess any features of DDL, such as CREATE and DELETE tables. Also, QBE is unable to implement sophisticated features of DML. Thus, complicated queries are always implemented by SQL.

(2) QBE relies on the particular DBMS environment (e.g., Microsoft Access). When using a large computer language (such as COBOL, C++, Java, .NET) to develop a business application program that is connected to databases (Oracle, DB2, etc.), one must write SQL code that is embedded into the program in the large computer language to access and update the databases.

The syntax of SQL is quite simple. A SQL script contains a command along with needed clauses, and ends with a semicolon. This section explains how SQL scripts can be used to define and create tables, to insert and update instances of records, retrieve data, and manipulate the data. To explain SQL examples, we use the design of a tiny database with 4NF tables as shown in Figure 6.1.

Figure 6.1. The 4NF Tables for SQL Examples in This Chapter

6.2. CREATE and DROP

CREATE TABLE is used to create a table with all attributes and their **data types**. For example, the SQL script in Listing 6.1 creates a table named tblStudent with its four attributes, including the primary key.

```
CREATE TABLE tblStudent
(StudentID CHAR(8),
 StudentName CHAR(20),
 StudentAddress CHAR(20),
 StudentEnrolYear INT,
 PRIMARY KEY (StudentID));
```

Listing 6.1. CREATE TABLE

Common data types used in the standard SQL are:
- CHAR(*n*) – Character string (text), at most *n* characters long;
- DATE – Date data;
- DECIMAL(*p*,*q*) – Decimal number *p* digits long and *q* digits after the decimal point;
- INT – Integer.

The PRIMARY KEY clause is used to define the **primary key** of the table. A **combination primary key** could have more than one attribute, e.g.,

```
PRIMARY KEY (StudentID, CourseID)
```

defines the two-attribute combination key.

DROP TABLE is used to delete a table. The SQL script in Listing 6.2 deletes tblStudent.

```
DROP TABLE tblStudent;
```

Listing 6.2. DROP TABLE

6.3. INSERT, UPDATE, DELETE

INSERT is used to add one record to the table. The SQL script in Listing 6.3 appends one student record to tblStudent.

```
INSERT INTO tblStudent
VALUES ('01234567', 'John', '285 Westport', 2018);
```

Listing 6.3. INSERT a Record

UPDATE is used to change the value(s) of the record with a certain key value. The SQL script in Listing 6.4 changes the address of the student record with key '01234567'.

```
UPDATE tblStudent
SET StudentAddress = '300 Eastport'
WHERE StudentID='01234567';
```

Listing 6.4. UPDATE a Record

DELETE is used to delete a record with a certain key value. The SQL script in Listing 6.5 deletes the student record with key '01234567'.

```
DELETE FROM tblStudent
WHERE StudentID='01234567';
```

Listing 6.5. DELETE a Record

In the above two examples, condition of the query is defined in the WHERE clause. We will discuss the WHERE clause in more detail later in this chapter.

The above SQL commands we have learned are used for database construction and maintenance. These SQL commands fit in the category of database DDL. The SQL scripts with these commands can be embedded in the large computer programs to allow the user to update the database. Apparently, it is not convenient to use these SQL commands to build a database from scratch. Practically, a DBMS can have a user-friendly interface that allows the database designer to create tables and to maintain the tables without using tedious SQL scripts. Microsoft Access is a good example of DMBS with a user friendly interface for building a database, as illustrated in Technical Guide A in this textbook.

Suppose we use the above SQL commands to create the database as modeled in Figure 6.1 that contains the three tables with their instances as shown in Figure 6.2. We use these data for demonstrating the rest examples of SQL scripts that fit in the category of DML or query.

StudentID	StudentName	StudentAddress	StudentEnrolYear
01234567	John	285 Westport	2018
02345678	Anne	287 Eastport	2020
03456789	Robert	324 Northport	2019

CourseID	CourseName	CourseEnroll
ACT211	Financial Accounting	35
ACT212	Cost Accounting	28
MIS315	Information Systems	40
MIS322	Systems Analysis & Design	38
MIS432	Database Design	30
MKT311	Principles of Marketing	25
MGT490	Special Topics	20

StudentID	CourseID	Grade
01234567	ACT211	A+
01234567	ACT212	A
01234567	MIS315	B
02345678	ACT211	B+
02345678	MIS322	C
03456789	ACT212	B
03456789	MIS432	A
03456789	MKT311	A

Figure 6.2. Sample Database

6.4. Query - SELECT

A **query** is a piece of script that commands the DBMS to retrieve needed data from the database. Queries can generate integrated data from the normalized tables.

In SQL, the SELECT command is used to implement queries. The general structure of SELECT query is

```
SELECT      [attributes] [built-in functions]
FROM        [tables]
WHERE       [conditions]
AND         [conditions];
```

Listing 6.6 is an example of a simple query that *"finds the student's name and address of student ID 01234567 from the student table."*

```
SELECT StudentName, StudentAddress
FROM    tblStudent
WHERE   StudentID = '01234567';
```

StudentName	StudentAddress
John	285 Westport

Listing 6.6. Select Specified Data from a Table

Listing 6.7 is a query that *"finds the student's entire record of student ID 01234567 from the student table."* The "*" sign represents all attributes of the table.

```
SELECT *
FROM tblStudent
WHERE StudentID = '01234567';
```

StudentID	StudentName	StudentAddress	StudentEnrolYear
01234567	John	285 Westport	2018

Listing 6.7. Select an Entire Record from a Table

The WHERE clause is used to define the conditions. If it is omitted, the query is to retrieve the entire table.

In some cases, the result of a query may contain duplicated data items. To screen

118

out duplicated data items, DISTINCT is used. Consider query: *"Find distinctive student enrollment years from the student table."*

```
SELECT DISTINCT StudentEnrolYear
FROM tblStudent;
```

StudentEnrolYear
2018
2019
2020

Listing 6.8. DISTINCT Eliminates Duplications

6.5. WHERE Clause and Comparison

As shown in the above examples, the WHERE clause defines the conditions for data selection. In addition to "=" (equal), comparison operations ">" (greater than), "<" (less than), ">=" (greater than or equal to), "<=" (less than or equal to), and "<>" (not equal to) can be applied in the WHERE clause. Listing 6.9 is query that *"lists the names of those students who enroll to the program after 2017."*

```
SELECT StudentName
FROM tblStudent
WHERE StudentEnrolYear > 2017;
```

StudentName
John
Anne
Robert

Listing 6.9. Comparison - Greater Than

A WHERE clause can have a combination of multiple conditions connected through the **Boolean operators** AND and OR. If the AND operator is applied, the two conditions must be true in order for the combination condition to be true. If the OR operator is applied, at least one of the two conditions must be true in order for the combination condition to be true. When ANDs and ORs are used in the same WHERE clause, ANDs are considered before ORs are considered. To avoid mistakes, it is recommended to use pairs of parenthesis to indicate the consideration priorities. Listing 6.10 is query that *"lists the names of those students whose ID numbers are greater than 00234567 and who enroll to the program after 2017 or before 2005."*

```
SELECT StudentName
FROM tblStudent
WHERE StudentID > '00234567'
AND (StudentEnrolYear > 2017 OR
     StudentEnrolYear < 2005);
```

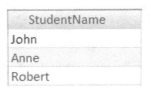

StudentName
John
Anne
Robert

Listing 6.10. AND and OR Operators

Character strings can also be compared using unequal signs because they are represented by internal code (e.g., ASCII code).

For strings of characters (text), the LIKE operator and a "wildcard" are used to test for a pattern match. Listing 6.11 is a query that *"finds the student records for those students whose street names contain 'Westport'."* Here, the percent sign "%" is a wildcard to represent any collection of characters. Note that, Microsoft Access uses "*" for this type of wildcard.

```
SELECT *
FROM tblStudent
WHERE StudentAddress LIKE '%Westport%';
```

StudentID	StudentName	StudentAddress	StudentEnrolYear
01234567	John	285 Westport	2018

Listing 6.11. LIKE Operator and Wildcard "%"

Listing 6.12 is a query that *"finds the student record for each student whose name has the letter 'o' as the second letter of the name."* Here, the wildcard sign "_" represents any one character. Note that, Microsoft Access uses "?" for this type of wildcard.

```
SELECT *
FROM tblStudent
WHERE StudentName LIKE '_o%';
```

StudentID	StudentName	StudentAddress	StudentEnrolYear
01234567	John	285 Westport	2018
03456789	Robert	324 Northport	2019

Listing 6.12. LIKE Operator and Wildcard "_"

The IN operator allows you to specify a list of character strings to be included in a search. Listing 6.13 is a query that *"finds the student whose ID is '01234567', '00234567', or '00034567'."*

```
SELECT StudentName
FROM tblStudent
WHERE StudentID IN ('01234567',
     '00234567', '00034567');
```

StudentName
John

Listing 6.13. IN Operator

6.6. User Input Request

SQL is mainly embedded into large **host computer programming languages** (e.g., C++, COBOL, Java, .NET, etc.) for database processing on servers. Database manipulation is performed through interactions between SQL and the host language. Direct **SQL-user interaction** is not a main concern of standard SQL because a program in the host programming languages can implement the user interface. Nevertheless, many versions of SQL (especially PC versions of SQL) provide means for the user to interact with SQL directly. The user is allowed to input a value directly through SQL that is used to complete the condition in the WHERE clause. For example, one might want to search the student data based on the user's input of student ID which is not determined by the query itself. In Microsoft Access, this can be done by including user input request, such as:

```
SELECT StudentName
FROM tblStudent
WHERE StudentID=[Please input student ID:];
```

User input request features are commonly available in SQL for the PC environment, and the syntaxes vary depending on the versions.

6.7. ORDER BY Clause

The ORDER BY clause is used to list the data in a particular order based on the values of an attribute. The default order is ascending. The ASC operator makes ascending explicit. The DESC operator is used to sort data in the descending order. Listing 6.14 is a query that *"lists all student records in the reverse alphabetic order by student name."*

```
SELECT *
FROM tblStudent
ORDER BY StudentName DESC;
```

StudentID	StudentName	StudentAddress	StudentEnrolYear
03456789	Robert	324 Northport	2019
01234567	John	285 Westport	2018
02345678	Anne	287 Eastport	2020

Listing 6.14. ORDER BY Clause

6.8. Aggregate Functions

Database stores raw data, not secondary (or processed) data such as average, total, etc. to avoid data redundancy. One of the important roles of queries is to provide secondary data as information for the user. SQL uses **aggregate functions** to calculate sums (SUM), averages (AVG), counts (COUNT), maximum values (MAX), and minimum values (MIN). Listing 6.15(a) is a query that *"finds the total number of student records in the student table."*

```
SELECT COUNT(*)
FROM tblStudent;
```

Expr1000
3

Listing 6.15(a). COUNT Function

In the query result in Listing 6.15(a), a default name assigned by the DMBS (e.g., Expr1000 in Microsoft Access) is used for the query result of aggregation function. If you want to name the result, e.g., CountOfStudents, you use AS keyword, as shown in Listing 6.15(b).

```
SELECT COUNT(*) AS CountOfStudents
FROM tblStudent;
```

CountOfStudents
3

Listing 6.15(b). Use AS Keyword to Define Result Name

Listing 6.16 answers the query *"what are the smallest enrollment number, largest enrollment number, total enrollment number, and average enrollment number in the course table?"*

```
SELECT MIN(CourseEnrollment), MAX(CourseEnrollment),
       SUM(CourseEnrollment), AVG(CourseEnrollment)
FROM tblCourse;
```

Expr1000	Expr1001	Expr1002	Expr1003
20	40	216	30.8571428571429

Listing 6.16. MIN, MAX, SUM, and AVG Functions

Note that, aggregate functions is not allowed to be used in WHERE clause directly. For instance, a clause such like WHERE COUNT(*)>1000 is not allowed.

6.9. GROUP BY Clause and HAVING Clause

When an aggregate function is used, one might want to find the calculated value for **each** group. GROUP BY clause is used to calculate results based on each group. If a condition on the calculated results is needed, the HAVING clause can be added.   Listing 6.17 is a query to *"find the total number of courses taken by **each** student, and only include students who have taken at least 2 courses."* Two points are worth noting in this query. First, the query with the GROUP BY clause matches "each" in English.   Second, the HAVING clause is different from the condition in the WHERE clause in that the HAVING clause goes with the GROUP BY clause and must use an aggregate function.

```
SELECT StudentID, COUNT(*)
FROM tblGrading
GROUP BY StudentID
HAVING COUNT(*) > 1;
```

StudentID	Expr1001
01234567	3
02345678	2
03456789	3

Listing 6.17. GROUP BY Clause and HAVING Clause

It is possible to add a WHERE clause before GROUP BY. The SQL standard specifies that when WHERE and GROUP BY occur together, the WHERE condition will be applied first. Listing 6.18 is a query to *"find the total number of courses taken by **each** student, and* *only include students whose ID are greater than '01234600' and have taken at least 2 courses."*

```
SELECT StudentID, COUNT(*)
FROM tblGrading
WHERE StudentID>'01234600'
GROUP BY StudentID
HAVING COUNT(*)>1;
```

StudentID	Expr1001
02345678	2
03456789	3

Listing 6.18. Apply WHERE Clause before GROUP BY Clause

6.10. Arithmetic Operations

The major purpose of SQL is data retrieval from the database together with simple data manipulations. Complicated manipulations on the retrieved data and information presentations shall be implemented by the application programs (e.g., Java and ASP.NET) that host SQL scripts. Nevertheless, SQL provides **arithmetic operations**. Addition (+), subtraction (-), multiplication (*), and division (/) can be used in the SELECT clause. The query in Listing 6.19 is to *"list the course ID, course enrollment, and seats available for each course, assuming that the normal cap for each course is 30."* Here, 30-CourseEnrollment is the difference (subtraction) between the cap and the actual enrollment of the course.

```
SELECT CourseID, CourseEnrollment,
       30-CourseEnrollment AS SeatsAvailable
FROM tblCourse;
```

CourseID	CourseEnrollment	SeatsAvailable
ACT211	35	-5
ACT212	28	2
MGT490	20	10
MIS315	40	-10
MIS322	38	-8
MIS432	30	0
MKT311	25	5

Listing 6.19. Arithmetic Operations

6.11. Joining Tables

The queries we have examined thus far deal with a single table. If two or more tables are involved in a query, the **join** operation can be applied. Suppose we are going to "*list the names of those students who receive "A" or "A+" in any course.*" Apparently, two tables, namely, tblStudent and tblGrading, are involved. To process the query, the query processor must do the following steps.

(1) Marge the two tables, tblStudent and tblGrading, into a single large table by matching the values of StudentID in tblStudent and the values of StudentID in tblGrading for all students and for all grade records. The merged table contains all data of tblStudent and tblGrading.
(3) Find the value of StudentName in the merged large table so that the student receives at least one "A" or "A+".

Listing 6.20 shows the query.

```
SELECT DISTINCT tblStudent.StudentName
FROM tblGrading, tblStudent
WHERE tblStudent.StudentID=tblGrading.StudentID
AND (tblGrading.Grade='A+' OR
        tblGrading.Grade='A');
```

StudentName
John
Robert

Listing 6.20. Join Two Tables

The SQL script in Listing 6.21 joins the three normalized tables, tblStudent, tblCourse, and tblGrading to integrate all related data in a denormalized form for the user to view.

```
SELECT   *
FROM tblStudent, tblCourse, tblGrading
WHERE tblStudent.StudentID = tblGrading.StudentID
AND tblCourse.CourseID = tblGrading.CourseID;
```

tblStudent.St	StudentNar	StudentAddre	StudentEnr	tblCourse.(	CourseName	CourseEnr	tblGrading.	tblGrading	Grade
01234567	John	285 Westport	2018	ACT211	Financial Accou	35	01234567	ACT211	A+
01234567	John	285 Westport	2018	MIS315	Information Sys	40	01234567	MIS315	B
02345678	Anne	287 Eastport	2020	ACT211	Financial Accou	35	02345678	ACT211	B+
02345678	Anne	287 Eastport	2020	MIS322	Systems Analysi	38	02345678	MIS322	C
03456789	Robert	324 Northport	2019	MIS432	Database Desigi	30	03456789	MIS432	A
03456789	Robert	324 Northport	2019	ACT212	Cost Accountinε	28	03456789	ACT212	B
03456789	Robert	324 Northport	2019	MKT311	Principles of Ma	25	03456789	MKT311	A
01234567	John	285 Westport	2018	ACT212	Cost Accountinε	28	01234567	ACT212	A

Listing 6.21. Join Multiple Tables to Integrate Related Data

In the above examples of join operation, tables are joined by using the WHERE clause with conditions. Three general rules are applied in a query with joining tables. (1) The general formation of a condition that associates two tables is:

$[TableOn-1-Side].[PrimaryKey] = [TableOn-M-Side].[ForeignKey]$

(2) If n tables are joined in the query, then n-1 conditions are needed, and these n-1 conditions are tied by the AND operator.

(3) To differentiate the same names in different tables, the table name followed by a period sign is used for an attribute name (e.g., tblStudent.StudentID) to **qualify** the attribute name. That is, the table name must be quoted as **qualifier** to specify which table the attribute belongs to if the query involves multiple tables.

Listing 6.22 shows another example of query with multiple tables: *"Who (student ID and name) receives "A+" or "A" grade in which course (course ID and course name)? List the results in order of student ID."*

```
SELECT tblGrading.StudentID, tblStudent.StudentName,
       tblGrading.CourseID, tblCourse.CourseName,
       tblGrading.Grade
FROM tblGrading, tblStudent, tblCourse
WHERE tblStudent.StudentID=tblGrading.StudentID
AND tblCourse.CourseID=tblGrading.CourseID
AND (tblGrading.Grade='A+' OR tblGrading.Grade='A')
ORDER BY tblStudent.StudentID;
```

StudentID	StudentName	CourseID	CourseName	Grade
01234567	John	ACT212	Cost Accounting	A
01234567	John	ACT211	Financial Accounting	A+
03456789	Robert	MKT311	Principles of Marketing	A
03456789	Robert	MIS432	Database Design	A

Listing 6.22. Query with Multiple Tables

6.12. Alternative Format of Inner Join and Outer Join

6.12.1. Explicit inner join clause

The join approach discussed in the previous examples is called **inner join** which lists only those rows that satisfy the conditions in the WHERE clause. SQL-92 (SQL Standard 1992) provides an alternative format of inner join as shown in the example of Listing 6.23.

```
SELECT DISTINCT tblStudent.StudentName
FROM tblStudent
INNER JOIN tblGrading
ON tblStudent.StudentID=tblGrading.StudentID
WHERE (tblGrading.Grade='A+' OR
       tblGrading.Grade='A');
```

StudentName
John
Robert

Listing 6.23. Explicit Format of Inner Join

In this format, the FROM clause includes the first table, the INNER JOIN clause includes the second table, and then ON clause specifies the join condition. Apparently, this format could be confusing if three or more tables are involved, and thus is not recommended for beginners.

6.12.2. Outer join

Outer join is to list all the rows from one of the tables in a join, regardless whether or not they match any rows in a second table. There are three types of outer join: **left outer join** (all rows from the first table are included, but only the matched rows from the second table are included), **right outer join** (only the matched rows from the first table are included, but all rows from the second table are included), and **full outer join** (all rows from both tables are included). Practically, outer join is not used often. Listing 6.24 shows an example of left outer join that is to "*list the course ID and course name for all grades. Include all courses in the results. For courses that do not have grade records, omit the grade.*" The execution result of this example of left outer join shows that the course MGT490 without matching grades is also included.

```
SELECT tblCourse.CourseID, tblCourse.CourseName, tblGrading.Grade
FROM tblCourse LEFT JOIN tblGrading
    ON tblCourse.CourseID=tblGrading.CourseID;
```

CourseID	CourseName	Grade
MIS315	Information Systems	B
MIS322	Systems Analysis & Design	C
ACT211	Financial Accounting	A+
ACT211	Financial Accounting	B+
MKT311	Principles of Marketing	A
ACT212	Cost Accounting	B
ACT212	Cost Accounting	A
MIS432	Database Design	A
MGT490	Special Topics	

Listing 6.24. Query with Left Outer Join Clause

6.13. Subquery

A SELECT query can embed another SELECT query which is called **subquery**. A subquery can have its subquery, and go on.

6.13.1. Subquery - reducing computational workload of join operation

A subquery can be used as an alternative to a join operation in a simple situation when the retrieved data are not integrated. Revisit the query in Listing 6.20 which is to *"list all students who receive "A" or "A+" in any course."* One can follow the following logic and write a subquery as shown in Listing 6.25.

(1) Find the values of StudentID in tblGrading for those students who receive "A+" or "A".

(2) Using the found values of StudentID as the key to search tblStudent to find all relevant records in tblStudent.

(3) Find the values of StudentName in the found records.

```
SELECT  tblStudent.StudentName
FROM    tblStudent
WHERE   tblStudent.StudentID IN
            (SELECT tblGrading.StudentID
             FROM tblGrading
             WHERE(tblGrading.Grade='A+'
               OR tblGrading.Grade='A'));
```

StudentName
John
Robert

Listing 6.25. An Example of Subquery that Avoids Join Operation

In Listing 6.25, there are two SELECT commands. The second SELECT command finds the student IDs who receive "A" or "A+" from tblGrading. The query processor then matches the student IDs in tblStudent (by the first WHERE clause). Finally, the top SELECT command finds the corresponding student names.

The SQL query with a subquery in Listing 6.25 finds the same data as the query in Listing 6.20 does, but avoids the join operation which takes significantly more computation resource than a subquery does. However, in cases where integrated data from two or more tables are going to display concurrently, this type of subquery becomes incapable, and a join operation must be applied.

If the joining tables are large, and the needed data from the joining tables do not involve all attributes, a subquery in the FROM clause can generate a smaller table to reduce the computational workload of the join operation. For example, the query in Listing 6.26 is to *"list all student grade records, including only the student numbers, the student names, the course numbers, and the grades."* As StudentAddress, StudentYear, CourseName, and CourseEnrollment are not involved in the query and can be excluded from the join operation, the sub-queries are applied in the first (top-level) FROM clause to make the joined tables smaller by including needed attributes only. Note the new table names in the first FROM clause (i.e., **tblStudentSmall** and **tblCourseSmall**) and these table names in the WHERE clause for the join operation.

```
SELECT tblStudent.StudentID, tblStudent.StudentName,
       tblCourse.CourseID, tblGrading.Grade
FROM
    (SELECT tblStudent.StudentID, tblStudent.StudentName
    FROM tblStudent) tblStudentSmall,
    (SELECT tblCourse.CourseID
    FROM tblCourse) tblCourseSmall, tblGrading
WHERE tblStudentSmall.StudentID=tblGrading.StudentID
AND tblCourseSmall.CourseID=tblGrading.CourseID;
```

StudentID	StudentName	CourseID	Grade
01234567	John	ACT211	A+
01234567	John	MIS315	B
02345678	Anne	ACT211	B+
02345678	Anne	MIS322	C
03456789	Robert	MIS432	A
03456789	Robert	ACT212	B
03456789	Robert	MKT311	A
01234567	John	ACT212	A

Listing 6.26. An Example of Subquery in the FROM Clause

6.13.2. Subquery as an alternative to *GROUP BY*

A subquery can be used as an alternative to the GROUP BY clause. For example, the query in Listing 6.27(a) is to *"show each student's name along with the number of courses she/he has taken"* using a subquery.

```
SELECT tblStudent.StudentName,
    (SELECT COUNT(*)
    FROM tblGrading
    WHERE tblStudent.StudentID=tblGrading.StudentID)
    AS NumberOfCourses
FROM tblStudent;
```

StudentName	NumberOfCourses
John	3
Anne	2
Robert	3

Listing 6.27(a). Subquery for Groups

The subquery does the similar job as GROUP BY clause which is shown in Listing 6.27(b).

```
SELECT tblStudent.StudentName, COUNT(*) AS NumberOfCourses
FROM tblStudent, tblGrading
WHERE tblStudent.StudentID=tblGrading.StudentID
GROUP BY tblStudent.StudentName;
```

Listing 6.27(b). GROUP BY Clause for Groups

The use of subquery for groups could cause confusion if the design of the subquery is incorrect. For beginners, the GROUP BY clause would be better than this type of subquery.

6.13.3. Subquery - representing a variable

In many cases subquery is necessary. Suppose we want to *"find the percentage of the enrollment of MIS432 out of the total enrollment of all courses."* Beginners of SQL might have the following wrong answer.

```
(SELECT SUM(CourseEnrollment)
FROM    tblCourse
WHERE   CourseID = 'MIS432')/
(SELECT SUM(CourseEnrollment)
FROM    tblCourse);
```

This query does not work. The fact is that a SQL script can have only one top-level SELECT statement. In the above wrong SQL script, there are two parallel top-level SELECT statements. The correct SQL script for the query is listed in Listing 6.28 which has one top-level SELECT statement and a subquery.

```
SELECT SUM(CourseEnrollment)/
(SELECT SUM(CourseEnrollment) FROM tblCourse)*100
 AS MIS432EnrollmentPercent
FROM    tblCourse
WHERE   CourseID = 'MIS432';
```

MIS432EnrollmentPercent
13.8888888888889

Listing 6.28. An Example of Subquery as a Variable

6.13.4. Subquery - determining an uncertain criterion

A subquery is used to determine an uncertain criterion. Suppose we want to know *"which students with ID numbers greater than '02000000' have the earliest enrollment year of such students?"* Beginners of SQL often have the following wrong answer.

```
SELECT StudentName
FROM    tblStudent
WHERE   StudentID > '02000000'
AND StudentEnrolYear = MIN(StudentEnrolYear);
```

This query does not work. The fact is that SQL does not allow an uncertain term on the right side in the WHERE clause because of its ambiguity. In the above wrong SQL, the WHERE clause is equivalent to

```
WHERE StudentEnrolYear=?
```

because MIN(StudentEnrolYear) is unknown in terms of its specific condition. To make a correct WHERE clause, you need to put either a certain value or a subquery on the right side of the WHERE clause. Thus, the correct SQL for the above query is Listing 6.29.

```
SELECT StudentName
FROM    tblStudent
WHERE   StudentID > '02000000'
AND StudentEnrolYear=
        (SELECT MIN(StudentEnrolYear)
         FROM tblStudent
         WHERE   StudentID > '02000000');
```

StudentName
Robert

Listing 6.29. An Example of Subquery for Uncertain Condition

Two points in writing subquery, which determines uncertain criteria in the WHERE clause, are worth noting.

(1) When the right side of the WHERE clause is uncertain (e.g., MIN, MAX, SUM, AVG, COUNT), you must use a subquery to replace the uncertain condition.

(2) In Listing 6.29, you can see that the condition StudentID>'02000000' in the host WHERE clause repeats in the condition in the subquery WHERE clause. If this condition is not repeated in the two WHERE clauses, then the meaning of the query is quite different. For example, if the first WHERE clause is omitted, the query represents *"which students (in the entire population) have the earliest enrollment year of those students with ID number greater than '02000000'?"* On the other hand, if the second WHERE clause is omitted, the query represents *"which students with ID numbers greater than '02000000' have the earliest enrollment year of all students?"*

A query can have join operations as well as subquery. Listing 6.30 is a query: *"List student names, course names, and grades of those students whose ID numbers are greater than '02000000' and have the earliest enrollment year of such students."*

```
SELECT tblStudent.StudentName,
        tblCourse.CourseName, tblGrading.Grade
FROM tblStudent, tblCourse, tblGrading
WHERE tblStudent.StudentID=tblGrading.StudentID
AND tblCourse.CourseID=tblGrading.CourseID
AND tblStudent.StudentID > '02000000'
AND tblStudent.StudentEnrolYear=
        (SELECT MIN(tblStudent.StudentEnrolYear)
         FROM tblStudent
         WHERE tblStudent.StudentID > '02000000');
```

StudentName	CourseName	Grade
Robert	Database Design	A
Robert	Cost Accounting	B
Robert	Principles of Marketing	A

Listing 6.30. An Example of Join and Subquery

Again, when you use multiple tables, qualifiers (i.e., the table names) must be applied to specify the attribute names.

6.14. UNION Operator

The UNION operator connects two SELECT statements to produce all the rows that would be in the query results of the first SELECT statement and the second SELECT statement. The UNION operator is commonly used to create a virtual table. As an illustrative example, the query in Listing 6.31 is to *"list the course ID and course enrollment for each course that has enrollment greater than 35, or the student name and student ID for each student who enrolled after 2019."* In fact, the UNION operator is a kind of OR operator between the two SELECT statements. This example is merely to demonstrate how the UNION operator works. As shown in this example, if the attributes listed in the two SELECT statements are not comparable, the query result of the UNION operator would not be particularly meaningful.

```
SELECT CourseID AS Name, CourseEnrollment AS Data
FROM tblCourse
WHERE CourseEnrollment>35
UNION
SELECT StudentName AS Name, StudentID AS Data
FROM tblStudent
WHERE StudentEnrolYear>2019;
```

Name	Data
Anne	02345678
MIS315	40
MIS322	38

Listing 6.31. UNION Operator

6.15. Tactics for Writing Queries

The following is general tactics for writing SQL scripts in SELECT statements.

(1) Read the query carefully. Determine what data are to be retrieved and what attributes are to be included in the SELECT command.

(2) If a variable is needed, use a subquery as the variable.

(3) Determine what tables are will be used in the FROM clause.

(4) If two or more tables are involved, use a join operation(s) (match the

primary key in one table with the foreign key in another table) in the WHERE clause.

(5) Construct the WHERE clause by including all conditions that are linked by AND or OR. Never use any aggregate function in the WHERE clause directly.

(6) If a condition has an uncertain criterion (MAX, MIN, AVG, SUM, COUNT) on the right side of the condition, use a subquery.

(7) Consider GROUP BY (for each group) with HAVING condition, ORDER BY clauses, and other operators (e.g., DISTINCT) if needed.

(8) For hands-on practices, you may construct test tables with a limited number of test samples to test the SQL script to see if it generates the expected result.

6.16. SQL Embedded in Host Computer Programming Languages

Computer application programs in large languages (e.g., COBOL, C++, Java, and .NET) often host SQL scripts to deal with relational databases directly. These programs, typically called middleware, implement the user interface, retrieve the needed data through the SQL scripts, and then perform manipulations on the retrieved data for the business applications.

To make a connection to the databases and to process the embedded SQL in the host language, specific database connection software must be integrated into the system, as further discussed in Chapter 9. Listing 6.32 is an example of Web application that uses SQL to access a Microsoft Access database in the ADO.NET environment. In this example, the Access database is named TestDB.accdb, the data of which is shown in Figure 6.2 and is stored in the same folder with the ASP.NET program on the server. The code in bold is relevant to the use of SQL to search the data of tblStudent by the user on the client side on the Internet. Figure 6.3 shows the execution result of this example in the Microsoft Visual Studio environment.

```
<%@ Page Language="VB" %>
<%@ import Namespace="System.Data.OleDb" %>
<script runat="server">
    Public Sub Page_Load()
    End Sub
    Public Sub abc(sender As Object, e As EventArgs)
```

```
label1.text="The inquired record for " + textbox1.value + " is:"
dim dbconn,sql,dbcomm,dbread
dim var1 as String
var1=textbox1.value
dbconn=New OleDbConnection("Provider=Microsoft.ACE.OLEDB.12.0; _
        data source=" & server.mappath("TestDB.accdb"))
dbconn.Open()
sql="SELECT * FROM tblStudent WHERE StudentID=" & "'" & var1 & "'"
dbcomm=New OleDbCommand(sql,dbconn)
dbread=dbcomm.ExecuteReader()
tblStudent.DataSource=dbread
tblStudent.DataBind()
dbread.Close()
dbconn.Close()
End Sub
</script>
<html><body><form runat="server">
        Type the student number for inquiry:
        <input id="textbox1" type="text" runat="server" /><br />
        <input id="submit1" type="submit" value="Search"
                runat="server" onserverclick="abc" /><br /><br />
        <asp:Label id="label1" runat="server"></asp:Label>
        <asp:Repeater id="tblStudent" runat="server">
            <HeaderTemplate><table border="1" width="100%">
                    <tr><th>Student ID</th>
                        <th>Student Name</th>
                        <th>Student Address</th>
                        <th>Student Enrollment Year</th></tr>
            </HeaderTemplate>
            <ItemTemplate>
             <tr><td><%#Container.DataItem("StudentID")%></td>
                 <td><%#Container.DataItem("StudentName")%></td>
                 <td><%#Container.DataItem("StudentAddress")%></td>
                 <td><%#Container.DataItem("StudentEnrolYear")%></td></tr>
            </ItemTemplate>
            <FooterTemplate></table></FooterTemplate>
        </asp:Repeater>
    </form>
</body></html>
```

Listing 6.32. SQL Is Used in ADO.NET

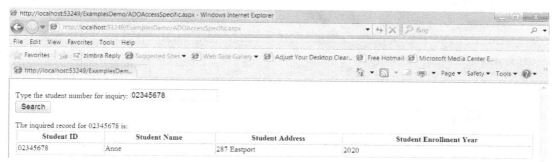

Figure 6.3. Search Access Database in the Internet Environment

The format of SQL scripts in a host computer programming language depends on the syntax of the host language. As you can see in Listing 6.32, in the .NET environment, a SQL script is a text string, and is placed between the double quotation mark pairs which are linked by "&" signs. Note that an unnecessary space sign in the SQL script could cause problems in compiling the program. Also, each database connection open and close cycle can execute only one SQL script. In other words, if there are multiple SQL scripts in a program, the server must open and close the database connection multiple times.

Chapter 6 Exercises

1.* Consider the following tables in the GreenHeating database in exercise question 2 of chapter 3.

HOUSE

*HouseAddress	HouseOwner	Insurance

HEATINGUNIT

*HeathingUnitID	UnitName	UnitType	Manufactory
	DateOfBuilt	Capacity	*HouseAddress*

TECHNICIAN

*EmployeeNumber	EmployeeName	Title	YearHired

SERVICE

HeatingUnitID	*EmployeeNumber*	ServiceType	*Date	*Time

a) Find the owner of the house "285 Westport Rd".

b) List the heating unit names and numbers of the gas heating units which was built in the "285 Westport Rd" house.

c) The unit types of heating units include gas, electric, solar, and several hybrid models. List the heating unit number, date of built, and manufactory of all heating units other than hybrid models with capacity between 3000 and 4000 cubic feet from largest to smallest.

d) List the names of technicians who maintained a heating unit in "285 Westport Rd" along with the service type performed.

e) Find the name and number of the largest Gas heating unit.

f) What percent is the total capacity of Gas heating units out of the total capacity of all types of heating units?

Minicase: *GreenJetNB (Chapter 6)*

Follow the GreenJetNB minicase in Chapter 3. Suppose that the following tables are included in the GreenJetNB database.

AIRCRAFT

*AircraftID	AircraftModel	Capacity	DateOfBuilt	MaxFlyDistance

PILOT

*PilotID	PilotName	Gender	DateOfBirth			
			DateOfHire	CellPhone	Salary	

PASSENGER

*PassengerID	PassengerName	PassengerAddress	PassengerPhone

FLIGHT

*FlightID	*FlightDate	DepartureAirport	DepartureTime		
	ArrivalAirport	ArrivalTime	*AircraftID*	*PilotID*	

TRIP

PassengerID	*FlightID*	*FlightDate*	Airfare	
	ReservationDate	SatisfactionRating		

Write SQL for the following queries.

a) Create the PASSENGER table using the assumed data types for the attributes.

b) Follow Question a. Insert a record into the PASSENGER table using assumed values of these attributes.

c) Follow Question b. Change the passenger name of the record you have inserted to the table.

d) Follow Question b. Delete the record you have inserted to the table.

e) Delete the PASSENGER table.

f) List the names and telephone numbers of all of the pilots.

g) List the aircrafts that have at least 30 passenger seats and were built after 2005. Order the results from smallest to largest.

h) Find the aircraft records (including all available data) for those aircrafts in which the model names begin with 'Wind'.

i) List the names of the female pilots who were hired after 2005 and whose salaries are greater than 100000.

j) How many pilots are working for the company?

k) Find the total number of trips for each passenger, and only list passengers (PassengerID) who have had at least 3 trips.

l) Find the total number of trips for each passenger, and only list passengers (PassengerID) who have a satisfaction rating of 3 or lower.

m) List the names of the pilots who have taken to the air between New Bedford and Providence.

n) List the names of the passengers who have commuted between New Bedford and Providence.

o) List the names of the pilots who were hired after 2005 and have the highest salary in such a group of pilots.

p) List the names of the pilots who were hired after 2005 and have the highest salary of all pilots.

q) What percent is the total salary of female pilots out of the total salary of all pilots?

CHAPTER 7. PHYSICAL DATABASE DESIGN

7.1. Physical Design

The normalization process and the database logical design ensure that the database contains no redundant data, and maintain the data consistency and integrity. However, a database with a logical design only can have disadvantages of poor performance. For instance, in the database represented by Figure 3.13, suppose students access the STUDENT table and the TEACH table together frequently during the final examination period, the join operations might take place frequently. As a result, the database would have slow response to the concurrent accesses of hundreds or even thousands users. To improve the performance of the database, one might design the database to perform the following operations so that the database would have quick response to the users' requests without scarifying the data accuracy to a certain degree.

(1) Select the currently registered students' records from the huge STUDENT table, and temporarily store them as a separate table, say, STUDENT-CURRENT.
(2) Join the STUDENT-CURRENT table and the TEACH table, and temporarily store the joined table on the disk as a separate table, say STUDENT-CURRENT-TEACH.
(3) Use the STUDENT-CURRENT-TEACH table for the final examination period, so that repeating join operations can be eliminated. After the period, discharge these two temporary tables.

The above example indicates that techniques are needed in addition to the logical database design for a large database to improve the database processing performance. **Physical database design** is to supplement the logical database design and to improve the database performance in the following aspects.

- **Response time** – the time delay from the database access request to the result appears;
- **Throughput volume** – the volume of data access output in a given time period;
- **Security** – the data protection.

In the early years of database (1970s and 1980s), physical database design mainly deals with the data structure of the database at the physical storage level. In the context of contemporary databases, physical database design has a broad range of techniques. In many cases, a physical database design alters the logical database design. Note that those modifications to the logical database design should be well controlled by the DBMS. The data integrity, accuracy, and timeliness might be compromised due to the physical design (e.g., temporary data redundancy), but such drawbacks should not have any serious consequence in the specific business environment.

Unlike logical database design, physical database design is more or less artistic and depends upon the specific situations of applications of the database. The support functions for physical database design vary depending on the DBMS. Large DBMS such as Oracle and DB2 have rich functionalities for physical database design, but end user oriented DBMS for tiny databases, such as Microsoft Access, have few physical design features. In this chapter, ten important physical database design techniques are discussed.

7.2. Adding Index

As explained in Chapter 2, a large database has massive B-trees so that random searches would be fast. All primary keys are automatically indexed by B-trees by the DBMS. However, if the values of a non-key attribute (or a combination of attributes) are often used for random search, then this attribute should be also indexed. For example, if the user searches students from the STUDENT table often by StudentName as well, then StudentName should be indexed although it is not the primary key. The downside of adding indexes is the increase of computation overhead for the maintenance of B-trees.

7.3. Adding Subschema

An ER diagram represents the database's **schema** which is the conceptual semantic structure of the entire database. A **subschema** is a virtual part of the database which is created for a particular purpose (e.g., for a user or a group of users). Using a subschema, the user is only allowed to use the part of the database within her/his subschema, and is not even aware of the existence of the other part of the database. A subschema is an important device to protect the security and privacy of data. It can also improve the performance of query processing. Figure 7.1 illustrates subschema. The downside of adding subschemata is the increase of computation resources consumption.

A **view** is a special case of subschema with one virtual table which is a saved query result. The virtual table assembles parts from the database tables in response to the frequent query.

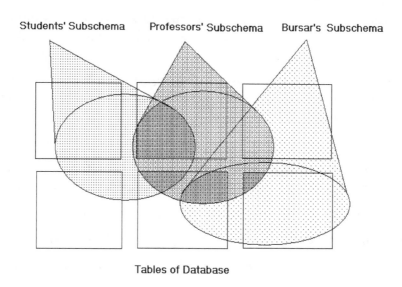

Figure 7.1. Subschemata

7.4. Clustering Tables

If two or more tables are used together so often, these tables should be clustered; that is, are placed close to each other (e.g., on the same disk cylinder) so that the computer access device can retrieve the data from these tables together quickly. For instance, if the STUDENT table is often accessed together with the COURSE table, then the two tables should be physically placed closely (e.g., on the adjacent cylinders). The downside of clustering is that it might increase the "distances" between one of the clustered tables and other tables which are not in the cluster because it is impossible to cluster all tables together.

7.5. Merging Tables

If two or more tables are repeatedly joined through the join operations, then **merging** these tables into a large table might be necessary to reduce the valuable computing time spent on the repeating join operations. The example in the first section of this chapter explains this technique. The **combined table** becomes a **denormalized** table and usually contains data redundancy. In principle, the DBMS should keep the original copies of the normalized tables, and use the combined table for only a period. To keep the data sufficiently accurate, re-merging could take place from time to time. In comparison with clustering tables, merging tables is a short-lived means to ease repeating join operations.

7.6. Horizontal Partitioning Table

In **horizontal partitioning**, the rows of a table are divided into parts, and the parts are stored separately for reasons, such as they are accessed at different access frequencies, or they have different security requirements. Horizontal partitioning is done based on the value of an attribute of the records of the table. For instance, if the STUDENT table is huge, it can be divided into two parts based on the values of StudentYear: one sub-table contains records of active students (e.g., >=2010) and the other sub-table contains records of inactive students (e.g., <2010) (see Figure 7.2). The sub-table of active students is used more often. Because of the smaller size, the join operations are less time consuming. The downside of partitioning is that the computation overhead would be increase when the entire table is used.

STUDENT Table

*StudentID	StudentName	StudentAddress	StudentYear
0101	Mark Sousa	12 Northport Ave.	1964
0211	Susan Bush	43 Wood St.	1967
⋮	⋮	⋮	⋮
1201	Chris Smith	23 William St.	2016
1334	Anne Riley	38 Union Ave.	2017
1432	John Kerry	17 Wood Lane	2016
2874	Doug Dale	6 Lake Rd.	2018
⋮	⋮	⋮	⋮

ACTIVE-STUDENT Table

*StudentID	StudentName	StudentAddress	StudentYear
1201	Chris Smith	23 William St.	2016
1334	Anne Riley	38 Union Ave.	2017
1432	John Kerry	17 Wood Lane	2016
2874	Doug Dale	6 Lake Rd.	2018

Figure 7.2. Horizontal Partitioning Table

7.7. Vertical Partitioning Table

In **vertical partitioning**, the columns of a table are divided into parts (or sub-tables), and the parts are stored separately for the different applications, and each part is accessed for different types of applications. Vertical partitioning is done by selecting the specific attributes for each part. For example, suppose the STUDENT table is often used by academic advisors as well as the Residence Office. Advisors access StudentID, StudentName, and StudentYear frequently, but do not access StudentAddress often. On the other hand, the Residence Office accesses StudentName and StudentAddress frequently, but do not really use other data. In the new academic seasons, the database might divide the huge STUDENT table into two sub-tables, and each sub-table has its own attributes in response to the high usage of the STUDENT data for the two applications. Note that, when creating vertical partitioning, each part must have the primary key. In this example, one sub-table contains StudentID, StudentName, and StudentYear; and the other sub-table contains StudentID, StudentName, and StudentAddress (see Figure 7.3).

The concepts of vertical partitioning and adding indexes are different, although both involve attributes. The adding index technique is applied to situations of quick search by a value of a specific attribute, while the vertical partitioning technique is applied to situations of retrieving all values of specific attributes together.

Figure 7.3. Vertical Partitioning Table

7.8. Creating New Primary Key

A combination primary key makes data retrieval process slow, especially when the combination key involves too many attributes. For example, in Figure 3.13 [StudentID+CourseID+ProfessorID] is a combination key for the associative entity TEACH. Such a combination key makes the indexing in the B-trees tedious. It is preferred to create a new single attribute as the primary key for the table to replace the combination primary key to make the indexing simple. Note that the table still keeps the attributes of the original combination key because they are either foreign keys or intersection data. For instance, one may create a new artificial primary key, say, OccurrenceID, to replace [StudentID+CourseID+ProfessorID]. However, StudentID, CourseID, and ProfessorID will stay in the associative entity as the foreign keys from other tables.

7.9. Substituting Foreign Key

A foreign key of the table on the M-side is usually the primary key of the table on the 1-side. However, if an alternative key of the table on the 1-side is more often used for data retrieval than the primary key, this alternative key could be used as the foreign key of the table on the M-side. For instance, in the database represented by Figure 3.13, ProfessorID is the foreign key in the TEACH relation. Considering ProfessorName is an alternative key of the PROFESSOR relation, and is used more frequently than ProfessorID, ProfessorName can substitute ProfessorID as the foreign key in the TEACH relation. In such a way, the preferred combination data of ProfessorName, CourseID, and Responsibility can be retrieved quickly from the single TEACH table without involving the PROFESSOR table.

7.10. Duplicating Table or Duplicating Part of Partitioned Table

When multiple users try to access the same table, the response time of the database will be slow. To reduce the bottleneck effect (traffic jam), the technique of **duplicating** a table(s), or duplicating a part of partitioned table, is used to route different queries to the different copies. For instance, if the STUDENT table is accessed intensively during a certain period, it can have duplicated copies to response numerous queries at the same time. Apparently, duplication creates the risk of overt data redundancy. The duplication should be temporary only for the access peak period, and should be fully managed by the DBMS.

7.11. Storing Information (Processed Data)

As discussed earlier in this book, a database is not an information base and it stores raw data only. In principle, the computer processes the raw data to provide the needed information (or processed data, or derived data), such as summation and trend, upon the user's request. However, if a piece of information is requested frequently and/or by many users in a short period, the system would waste much computation resource to reproduce needed information. **Storing information** (or **processed data**) is to reduce the unnecessarily repeating computation. Apparently, the stored piece of information should be of short life to keep the information updated. For example, a GPA value is not supposed to be stored in the database, because the GPA is redundant if all grades for a student are already recorded in the database. However, during the advising period, the GPA of a student is frequently needed. To avoid the repeating calculation of the GPA, the database might store the GPA values. Clearly, the GPA data are redundant, and must be re-calculated from time to time to keep the accuracy.

7.12. Implementation of Physical Database Design

The implementation of physical database design highly depends on the DBMS. A sophisticated DBMS has **DBMS performance tuning**, a set of algorithms and procedures designed to improve the database performance. Generally, several methods available in many DBMSs can be used for the implementation of physical database design.

(1) **Storage-related construction**. Many large DBMSs allow the DBA to define storage groups for tables when constructing the database. This makes it possible to cluster tables.

(2) **SQL-related construction**. Many large DBMSs support advanced SQL for physical database design. These DBMSs allows the DBA or users of the database to implement the physical database design through commands such as CREATE INDEX, CREATE TABLE, ALTER TABLE, CREATE VIEW, and CREATE SCHEMA. These SQL-related constructions make a physical design possible to add indexes, to change the structure of tables, to make duplications or partitions, and to create views or subschemata.

(3) **Query optimizer**. Many DBMSs support the SQL ANALYZE command to analyze the database performance statistics. Also, a sophisticated DBMS has its own algorithms for determine the most efficient way to execute SQL. The DBA can define the mode of the query optimization: either rule-based or cost-based.

Chapter 7 Exercises

1.* Consider the following tables in the GreenHeating database in exercise question 2 of Chapter 3.

HOUSE

*HouseAddress	HouseOwner	Insurance

HEATINGUNIT

*HeathingUnitID	UnitName	UnitType	Manufactory	
	DateOfBuilt	Capacity	HouseAddress	

TECHNICIAN

*EmployeeNumber	EmployeeName	Title	YearHired

SERVICE

*HeatingUnitID	*EmployeeNumber	ServiceType	*Date	*Time

Analyze each of the following situations, and state what physical database design technique you would like to apply to improve the data retrieval performance. Specify the technique.

a) There is a critical need to quickly list the heating units with a particular type.

b) There is a frequent need to list all heating unit numbers along with their unit types and house addresses.

c) There is a frequent need to retrieve detailed data about a heating unit together with detailed data about the house in which it locates.

d) There is a much more frequent and high priority need to access the records for Gas heating units than for the other types.

e) Due to large numbers of access activity, the HEATINGUNIT relation has become a bottleneck.

Minicase: *GreenJetNB (Chapter 7)*

Follow the GreenJetNB minicase in Chapter 3. Suppose the following tables are included in the GreenJetNB database.

AIRCRAFT

*AircraftID	AircraftModel	Capacity	DateOfBuilt	MaxFlyDistance

PILOT

*PilotID	PilotName	Gender	DateOfBirth

		DateOfHire	CellPhone	Salary

PASSENGER

*PassengerID	PassengerName	PassengerAddress	PassengerPhone

FLIGHT

*FlightID	*FlightDate	DepartureAirport	DepartureTime

	ArrivalAirport	ArrivalTime	*AircraftID*	*PilotID*

TRIP

PassengerID	*FlightID*	*FlightDate*	Airfare

	ReservationDate	SatisfactionRating

Analyze each of the following independent situations, and apply physical database design techniques to improve the data retrieval performance.

a) There is a critical need to quickly list the flights that uses a particular airport.

b) The users of the operation department are not allowed to access pilots' private data which are used by the human resource department only.

c) There is a frequent need to be able to retrieve detailed data about a flight together with detailed data about its passengers.

d) There is a frequent need to get a list of the names and phone numbers of the passengers together with the data of their trips including flight number, flight date, and satisfaction ratings.

e) There is a much more frequent and high priority need to access the records of the flights on holidays than the flight records of other days.

f) In the TRIP table, there is a frequent need with strict response time requirements for accessing the flight number together with the passenger number and satisfaction rating than for accessing the rest of the data in the table.

g) In the TRIP table, there is a frequent need with strict response time requirements for accessing the record(s) of a particular combination of flight number, passenger number, and satisfaction rating.

h) Consider the TRIP table. The database designer wants to create a table called SATISFACTION that records more passengers' satisfaction data beyond just SatisfactionRating, such as suggestions.

i) Assume that the PassengerName attribute in the PASSENGER table is unique. There is a frequent need to quickly retrieve the following data from the TRIP table: passenger name, flight number, flight date, airfare, and reservation date.

j) Due to a large number of users, the FLIGHT relation has become a bottleneck of the database access traffic.

k) Due to a large number of users, the records of the flights on holidays have become a bottleneck of the database access traffic.

l) There is a frequent need to quickly find the total number of trips that any particular passenger has traveled with GreenJetNB.

CHAPTER 8. DATABASE ADMINISTRATION

This chapter describes the major functions of database administration, and the major responsibilities and tasks of the DBA.

8.1. Data Planning and Database Design

Data are valuable assets for the organization. It is crucial for the organization to plan what data are needed for the time being, as well as in the future. The DBA should play a leading role in data planning, database design, as well as choosing the DBMS.

8.2. Data Coordination

Data are the shared corporate resource. Whether and how **centralize** or **decentralize** the data in the organization are always questions without clear-cut answers. The DBA should coordinate the use of data as well as the distribution of the computational costs for the organization.

8.3. Data Security, Access Policies, and Data Ownership

Data security, data privacy, and data ethics become more and more important for the society. The DBA plays key role in designing the **access policies** for the organization, and monitors the execution of these policies to maintain the standards in data security, data privacy, and data ethics. The database administration acts as the custodian of the data of the organization, and should clarify the **ownerships** of the data.

8.4. Data Quality

Data quality is evaluated by accuracy, objectivity, believability, reputation, access, security, relevancy, value-added, timeliness, completeness, amount of data, interpretability, ease of understanding, concise representation, and consistent representation. The DBA should apply the concepts and tools of **total data quality control** in the data resource management.

8.5. Database Performance

The DBA should monitor the performance of the database and should lead the specialist team of the organization to improve the database performance.

8.6. User Training

User training is another important task for the DBA to lead. All users of the database, including programmers and end users, need to know the policies, procedures, design, standards, and utilities of the database.

8.7. Data Standards, Data Dictionary, and Documentation

A database has its **standards** to regulate the names of tables and attributes, data types of attributes, and procedures/methods of the use of the database. If the company becomes a member of an EDI group or a business association, the database might have to adopt new data standards.

A tool for enforcing the data standards for databases is **data dictionary**. A data dictionary stores **metadata**, namely data about the data in the database. For instance, suppose a database has two tables as shown in the upper part of Figure 8.1. A simple hypothetical data dictionary of this database could be similar to the table in the lower part of Figure 8.1.

There is no universal standard for data dictionary. Individual DBMS has the data dictionary in its own way. A **passive data dictionary** is used for **documentation** purposes. The passive data dictionary is simply a small-scale database for the administration of the "mother database". An **active data dictionary** is a sophisticated one that interacts with the "mother database" in a real-time fashion. If the "mother database" has a change, the data dictionary is automatically changed correspondingly, and also might provide consulting information to the administration regarding the change. On the other hand, if the data dictionary has a change, the change will trigger changes to the "mother database".

As shown in Technical Guide A of this textbook, you can find a way to retrieve the DMBS generated data dictionary for the database in Microsoft Access. If you build a database for your course project, you can learn a variety of metadata that are useful for the database management.

"Mother Database"

CLASSROOM   Relation
* ClassroomID   ClassroomLocation   ClassroomType   ClassroomSize

COURSE   Relation
* CourseID   CourseName   CourseEnrollment   CourseTime   *ClassroomID*

Data Dictionary

Relations Metadata

Table Name	Number of Records	Disk Cylinder	Access Permission code
CLASSROOM	232	A234	103
COURSE	568	M467	347

Attributes Metadata

Attribute Name	Data Type	Attribute Length	Indexed	Validation Rule Code
ClassroomID	Text	6	Key / FK	12
ClassroomLocation	Text	10	No	23
ClassroomType	Text	10	No	23
ClassroomSize	Number	3	No	35
CourseID	Text	6	Key	12
CourseName	Text	30	Yes	23
CourseEnrollment	Number	3	No	35
CourseTime	Date/Time	16	No	11

Figure 8.1. Example of Data Dictionary

8.8. Database Backup and Recovery

A database can be destroyed by a disaster, can be corrupted after a failure of hardware or software, or can have errors caused by human mistakes. The DBA should have a database **backup and recovery** strategy and conduct disaster planning for the database. There have been many backup and recovery techniques that are commonly supported by DBMS. Three major backup and recovery methods are described below.

8.8.1. Mirrored databases

The easiest backup and recovery strategy is to use of **mirrored** (or **duplicated**) databases for the database system. Two or even three copies of the entire database are maintained concurrently. Physically, the duplicated copies of database should be placed in different places. If any of the duplicated databases goes wrong, simply use the undamaged one as the backup copy to recover the database. Apparently, this backup and recovery method is prohibitively expensive if the database is huge. It might be useful in military or space projects, but is rarely used in business.

8.8.2. Re-do transactions

In the **re-do transactions** approach, the database is taken a "snapshot" periodically to have a backup copy. After the backup, the database system keeps all **logs** (or **journals**) that record every transaction occurred after the backup. Once the database is damaged, the last database backup copy and the logs after the last backup are used to re-produce a new database. This process is illustrated in Figure 8.2. The backup and recovery processes can be done automatically by the DBMS. Usually, at least three generations of backup copies along with the logs are reserved for the database system.

8.8.3. Un-do transactions

A damage in the database can be caused by an erroneous operation (e.g., human mistakes), or by an incompletely processed transaction (e.g., due to an interruption of network connection). In such cases, the scope of the damage is small, and the re-do transactions method is too expensive for fixing a small scope error. The **un-do transactions** method is designed to solve those situations. In the un-do transactions method, the system keeps logs as backup. Once an error occurs, the logs and the erroneous database are used by the DBMS to un-do the incomplete/flawed transaction to correct the database. The invalid erroneous or incomplete transaction is then reviewed manually to detect the real cause of the error. The un-do transactions method is illustrated in Figure 8.3.

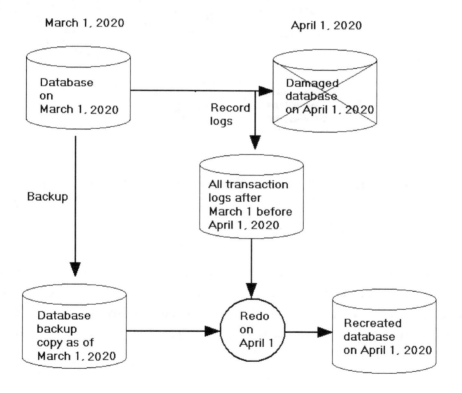

Figure 8.2. Re-Do Transactions for Recovery

Figure 8.3. Un-Do Transactions for Recovery

8.9. Data Archiving

The organization needs data retention for particular needs and/or legal reasons. There have been many business laws or government laws that specify the data retention requirements. One solution to data retention is **data archiving**. A data archive is a place where a set of certain data is kept. Typically, the archive does not belong to the database itself, but should be traceable from the database.

8.10. Database Maintenance

The database of the organization needs maintenance due to hardware and software upgrading and/or other changes of the environment. The DBA should have long-term maintenance policies as well as short-term maintenance plans, and have the responsibility of dealing with the cost issues and the relationships with the vendors for database maintenance.

8.11. Managing Business Rules Related to the Database Design

A **business rule** is a statement that aims to influence or guide business in the organization. Business rule management is critical for business success, but is under-researched in the IT field because it involves so many areas including business regulation, organization structure, job responsibility, business procedure, security, database, and others. One of the DBA roles is to manage the business rules related to the database design. We have learned three major types of business rules for database design.

(1) Functional dependencies between the attributes of entities.

(2) Cardinalities and modalities attached to the relationships between the entities.

(3) Referential integrity rules for record insertion and deletion.

Chapter 8 Exercises

Minicase: *GreenJetNB (Chapter 8)*

Follow the GreenJetNB minicase described in Chapter 3.

1. Write a simple data dictionary (similar to Figure 8.1) for the following three tables of the GreenJetNB database.

AIRCRAFT

*AircraftID	AircraftModel	Capacity	DateOfBuilt	MaxFlyDistance

PILOT

*PilotID	PilotName	Gender	DateOfBirth			
			DateOfHire	CellPhone	Salary	

FLIGHT

*FlightID	*FlightDate	DepartureAirport	DepartureTime		
	ArrivalAirport	ArrivalTime	*AircraftID*	*PilotID*	

2*. Describe a scenario that the re-do transactions method is applicable for backup and recovery of the GreenJetNB database.

3. Describe a scenario that the un-do transactions method is applicable for backup and recovery of the GreenJetNB database.

CHAPTER 9. DATABASE IN COMPUTER NETWORKS

9.1. Centralized Database in the Local Area Network Environment

A **local area network** (**LAN**) is a network that links computers and printers together. Typically, a computer with a larger computational capacity, called **server**, holds a **centralized database**, and other smaller PCs, called **clients**, use the centralized database, as illustrated in Figure 9.1. A centralized database is easy to manage, but causes busy data access traffic on the network if many clients use the centralized database. The DBMS of the centralized database on LAN has interface with the LAN operating system.

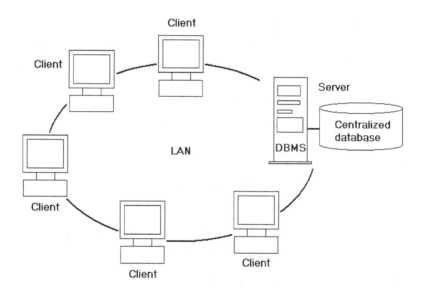

Figure 9.1. Centralized Database on LAN

9.2. Centralized Database in the Internet Environment

Massive client-server networks are connected and build the **Internet** (or **World Wide Web**). The access to a database on the Internet becomes complicated because of so many different computer hardware/software platforms and so many types of DBMS.

163

Also, the data security issues become extremely important. A general architecture of the entire system for accessing centralized database on the Internet is illustrated in Figure 9.2. The major components of the general architecture that are relevant to database are described below.

• **Firewall** is a computer with special software to protect the Web server, database server, and the database from unauthorized access, viruses, and other suspicious incoming code.

• **Web server** stores the Web portal, processes all applications (e.g., order process and payment), and makes all responses to the Internet users' requests. To support applications, a Web server has three important software components: API, middleware, and ODBC.

• **API** (**Application Program Interface**) is a set of functions that allow data exchange between the application software and the database.

• **Middleware** is specialized software to access the database. The application program in Listing 6.32 is an example of middleware with ADO.NET.

• **ODBC** (**Open Database Connectivity**) is the software interface to the relational database. On a Windows platform computer, you can set ODBC to connect the computer system to a particular data source provider(s) (e.g., SQL Server database or Excel tabular files) through [**Administrative Tools**] in the [**Control Panel**] of [**Settings**] (see Figure 9.3). In the Java platform, **JDBC** (**Java Database Connectivity**) plays the similar role.

• **Database server** is the dedicated server for data retrieval and maintenance of the database.

Figure 9.2. System Architecture for Accessing Database on the Internet

Figure 9.3. Set ODBC in Windows

9.3. Distributed Databases

A centralized database has disadvantages. First, it leads to busy network traffic. Second, the database server can never be fast enough if many users access it, and can become a bottleneck site. Third, if the centralized database goes down, all users have to wait. **Distributed databases** (see Figure 9.4) overcome these problems, and have many advantages including local autonomy, communication cost saving, and 24/7 service. However, a distributed database needs a sophisticated **distributed DBMS** (**DDBMS**) to support the complex functions.

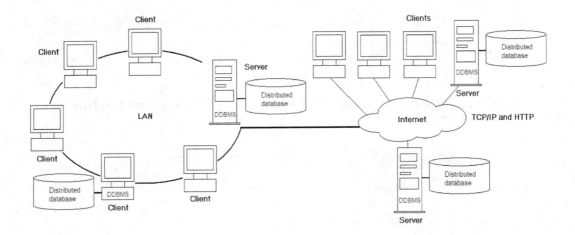

Figure 9.4. Distributed Database

9.3.1. Location transparency

The users of the distributed database just want to obtain needed data from the database, but are not interested in where the data are stored. The DDBMS manages the data physical locations and data migration, and makes the users feel as if the database is centralized in somewhere. This property of distributed databases is called **location transparency**.

9.3.2. Data deployment

In the distributed database environment, physical database design becomes more important and, at the same time, more artistic. Three data **table organization schemes** of **data deployment** must be considered for a distributed database: partitioning, placement, and duplication, as discussed below.

(1) **Partitioning** – A table may be split up into **fragments** through **horizontal partitioning**, **vertical partitioning**, or the combination of horizontal and vertical partitioning. Each **fragment** is subject to placement, as explained next.

(2) **Placement** – A table or a fragment of table should be placed at the site where the table or the fragment is used most frequently, and the site takes the major responsibility for its data integrity control as well as backup and recovery. This data deployment scheme is called local autonomy.

(3) **Duplication** – A table or a fragment of table may have a replicated copy at the site where the table or the fragment is used frequently. The site does not take the responsibility of maintenance.

The following example illustrates the concept of data deployment.

> *GreenAppliance Retail Company has the database as described in Figure 9.5. Its headquarters is set in Boston. There are four region offices: Providence, Toronto, New York, and Seattle. Each region office manages dozens branches in the region. Each region sells unique products. The CEOs of the company monitor the sales across the company on the daily basis, and also make decisions on the selection of suppliers regularly. The senior managers of each region office take the responsibility of sales and the performance of its branches, but do not deal with the suppliers directly. What is your strategy of data deployment for the distributed database?*

The database design is shown in Figure 9.5. First of all, you must make assumptions because the provided information of the situation may be incomplete. Then, you need to apply the data deployment schemes to each table for each site of the network to address the situations of the distributed database. Two tools can be useful for articulating data deployment strategies: data deployment matrix and data deployment graph. Table 9.1 shows a data deployment matrix for the above example, and Figure 9.6 shows a data deployment graph for this distributed database.

Figure 9.5. The Database of the Example

Locations Tables	Headquarters Boston	Region Offices Toronto, Miami, Seattle, Providence
MANUFACTORY	The table is placed in Boston.	
BRANCH	The table is placed in Boston.	
REGION	The table is placed in Boston.	
SALES	A duplicated table is placed in Boston which merges the four segments of the horizontally partitioned parts of the four regions.	A horizontally partitioned part is placed in each region. The H.P. is based on the values of BranchName that are related to the region (the value of RegionName) through BRANCH.
PRODUCT	The table is placed in Boston.	A duplicated horizontally partitioned part is placed in each region. The H.P. is based on the values of ProductNumber that are related to the region (the value of RegionName) through SALES and BRANCH.

Table 9.1. Data Deployment Matrix for Distributed Database

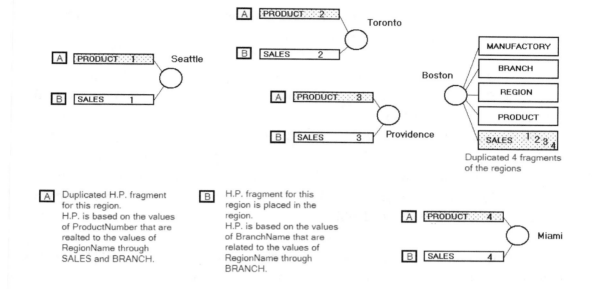

Figure 9.6. Data Deployment Graph for Distributed Database

The following is the justification of the data deployment in the above example.

(1) As the headquarters makes decisions on suppliers, the MANUFACTORY table is placed in Boston. Region offices might access the MANUFACTORY table occasionally, but the usage is low since they do not assume the responsibility of selection of suppliers.

(2) The REGION and BRANCH tables are mainly used by the headquarters and are rarely used by any region office. Thus, these two tables are placed in Boston.

(3) As each region office takes the responsibility of sales of the branch, the SALES table should be horizontally partitioned for each region office based on the values of BranchName that are related to the values of RegionName through the BRANCH table. The individual sub-table is placed to the corresponding region office. The headquarters also needs to access the SALES table on the daily basis but not in the

real-time mode. Thus, a duplication SALES table, which merges the four sub-tables for the four region offices, is placed in Boston.

(4) As the headquarters takes the responsibility of selection of suppliers, the PRODUCT table is placed in Boston. However, each region office must access the PRODUCT table as well for monitoring sales activities. As each region sells unique products, the PRODUCT table is duplicated for each region office for only a horizontally partitioned part which is relevant to the products for that region. The horizontal partition of the PRODUCT table for each region office is based on the values of ProductNumber that are related to the values of RegionName though the SALES table and the BRANCH table.

Note the statements of horizontal partitioning criteria in the above example. The criterion for the horizontal partitioning of PRODUCT and SALES is the region name (i.e., the values of RegionName in BRANCH). However, a record in PRODUCT or SALES does not have a value of RegionName. Thus, each record of these two tables needs to be related to a particular value of RegionName by tracing the relationship chain represented in the ERD.

9.3.3. Data integrity control and concurrency control

As duplicated data spread in many places, data integrity control becomes complicated. Also, **concurrency control** in distributed databases becomes especially important and difficult. Additional layers of concurrency control procedures, which include complex concurrency control algorithms, are implemented in DDBMS. Further discussion on concurrency control is beyond the scope of this book.

9.3.4. Distributed join operations

Join operations in distributed databases would become more time consuming because the joined tables may not be located in the same place. Many heuristic algorithms are employed to "optimize" **distributed join operations**.

9.4. XML for Databases

XML (**Extensible Markup Language**) is a computer language designed to provide a standard information description framework used for data exchanges on the Internet. XML is derived from the **Standard Generalized Markup language** (**SGML**) which was defined in 1986 as an international standard for document markup. XML was completed in early 1998 by **Word Wide Web Consortium** (W3C). However, the implementation of the XML standard is far from over and depends upon the progress of the entire information technology industry. Also, the XML technology is somehow more complicated than any other computer language because the XML language alone is not sufficient for effective Web applications.

The major motivation of the use of XML is the need for uniform data format for data exchanges among different databases on the Internet. There have been many database systems commonly used in the information industry. Although SQL is a standard language for databases, the data formats are all platform-dependent. To transfer data from one database to another, usually one needs an interface implemented by computer programs to describe the specific data formats (see Figure 9.7).

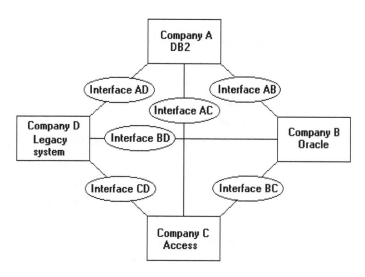

Figure 9.7. Data Exchanges between Databases Could Be Complicated

To make data transfers on the Internet efficient, we need a common data format description framework so that an application can understand exactly what is requested or what is received. The price for this is that each database must support the XML standard (so called XML-enabled database) in order to exchange data in the common XML format (see Figure 9.8).

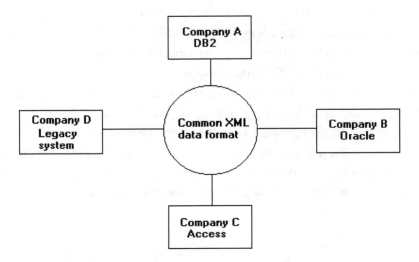

Figure 9.8. The Common XML Data Format Makes Data Exchanges Efficient

Furthermore, the traditional relational databases are typically used for processing numerical data and character data. However, the data types available on the Internet are rich, including image, audio, video, complex documents, and international characters. Using XML, these rich data formats can be easily handled.

Listing 9.1 shows an example of an XML document for the STUDENT table in Figure 6.2. As you can see from this example, the user can search the data in the XML document by using the names of tables and attributes which are specified in the XML tags.

It is worth noting several important points about XML and its companion tools. (1) The XML data model is hierarchical, not relational. The conversion of data from a relational database into the XML format might not be as straightforward as thought.

(2) An XML document is actually a datasheet that can be used for data search because each piece of data is described by tags. However, an XML document cannot be used for data presentation directly. To present data in an XML document, one must use another computer language, such as XSLT or CSS, for data retrieval and presentation.

(3) An XML document contains the data that can be shared by a group of users on the Internet. Thus, the structure of the XML document must be well-formatted, otherwise it could be misinterpreted. Thus, one must use another computer language, such as XML Schema or DTD, to validate the structure of the XML document.

In summary, to fully use XML, one must apply at least two XML companion computer languages: one for data retrieval and presentation, and the other for validation.

```xml
<?xml version="1.0" standalone="yes"?>
<StudentTable>
 <Student
      StudentID="01234567"
      StudentName="John"
      StudentAddress="285 Westport"
      StudentEnrolYear="2018" >
 </Student>
 <Student
      StudentID="02345678"
      StudentName="Anne"
      StudentAddress="287 Eastport"
      StudentEnrolYear="2020" >
 </Student>
 <Student
      StudentID="03456789"
      StudentName="Robert"
      StudentAddress="324 Northport"
      StudentEnrolYear="2019" >
 </Student>
</StudentTable>
```

Listing 9.1. XML Document for the STUDENT Table in Figure 6.2

Chapter 9 Exercises

1.* Follow exercise question 2 in Chapter 3. GreenHeating became a coast-to-coast service chain that operates heating units maintenance work across the North America. Its database has the following 4NF tables.

HOUSE

*HouseAddress	HouseOwner	Insurance

HEATINGUNIT

*HeathingUnitID	UnitName	UnitType	Manufactory
	DateOfBuilt	Capacity	*HouseAddress*

TECHNICIAN

*EmployeeNumber	EmployeeName	Title	YearHired

SERVICE

HeatingUnitID	*EmployeeNumber*	ServiceType	*Date	*Time

GreenHeating now has region offices in four cities: Halifax (also the headquarters), Montreal, Calgary, and Seattle, to manage the operations in the respective four regions. The HouseAddress attribute of the HEATINGUNIT relation indicates in which of the four regions the heating unit is located. GreenHeating has decided to reconfigure its database as a distributed database among its four regions, and to make the five tables distributed and replicated among these four cities. The situation has the following characteristics:

HOUSE consists of 100,000 records. It is used most heavily by the headquarters for centralized customer surveys, advertising, and promotion of new heating technologies.

HEATINGUNIT consists of more than 100,000 records. The heating unit data are used most heavily in the regions in which the individual heating units are located. The TECHNICIAN table consists of 10,000 records with a situation similar to the HEATINGUNIT table. The SERVICE data have a huge volume, and are used and updated with the data of HEATINGUNIT and TECHNICIAN by the regions. In other words, the three tables are treated in the similar way.

Design a distributed relational database for GreenHeating. Specify the data deployment schemes for each of the tables: placement, partitioning (horizontal or vertical), replication, and/or any combination of these methods using a data deployment matrix.

Minicase: *GreenJetNB (Chapter 9)*

Recall the GreenJetNB minicase in Chapter 3, and the tables you developed for the GreenJetNB database for Chapter 4 and Chapter 5.

GreenJetNB is a regional airline. It has several aircrafts and various commute itineraries between hubs and small cities. The GreenJetNB's database keeps data of aircraft, pilots, past and future flights, passengers who traveled with GreenJetNB, aircraft maintenance work, and sales of airtickets.

1. GreenJetNB has decided to reconfigure the database as a distributed database, and to deploy the data in four major airports: New Bedford (MA) (also GreenJetNB's headquarters), New Haven (CT), Burlington (VT), and Bangor (ME). Data are supposed to be distributed and replicated among these four locations. The data have the following main characteristics:

(1) The data of aircrafts, pilots, schedules, and airticket sales are processed in the headquarters.

(2) The regular maintenance jobs for each aircraft are performed at a major airport except for emergency situations.

(3) The passenger data are available at the four major airports so that the adjacent small airports access the data for passenger check-in and check-out.

Design a distributed relational database for GreenJetNB by showing the data deployment using a data deployment matrix or a data deployment graph. Specify the data deployment schemes for each table.

2. Follow the previous question. Describe hardware and software components involved in accessing the database at the New Bedford headquarters from the Internet (e.g., for online flight reservations).

CHAPTER 10. DATA WAREHOUSE

10.1. Data Warehouse

In a large organization, it is unlikely to have just one database. Also, the database we have discussed thus far is normalized and is current. On the other hand, people need a variety of types of data which may not be normalized or may not be current. For example, if a student changes her name, the database keeps the new name, but where is the old name placed in the database for search?

A **Data warehouse** holds all kinds of data for supporting decision making activities. A data warehouse can be divided into **data marts**, and each data mart serves a particular functional division (e.g., finance, accounting, human resource management, etc.).

Unlike DMBS, data warehouse management systems are rather artistic. There is no matured system for data warehouse management.

10.2. Multidimensional Data and Data Cube

Dimensions are perspectives of data. For example, sales data can be viewed in the perspectives of time, location, type of product, sales team, etc. Technically, such dimensions are described by dimension tables, as explained later in this section.

Data warehouse typically deals with **multidimensional** data, called **data cube**, to describe facts of *what, who, where, how, when*, and/or *why*. For example, Sales can have three dimensions such as Product, Branch, and Time, as illustrated in Figure 10.1 in 3D vision. Apparently, there is no way to illustrate hyper-space with more than 3 dimensions graphically, but the concept of high-dimensional data for data warehouses is basically the same as the data cube in Figure 10.1.

The volume of data in data warehouse is usually large. You can imagine when the data set has a high dimensionality (e.g., 10 dimensions), and each dimension has a high number of levels (e.g., 100), the volume of data would be huge (e.g., 100^{10}).

Figure 10.1. High-Dimensional Data and Data Cube

10.3. Creating Data Cube from Relational Database

The concept of data warehouse was developed in the 1990s during the information technology wave. For the time being, almost every data warehouse is built based on relational databases, although relational DBMS have been with us for longer than three decades. In a relational database, as we have learned, the unit of data for an entity is a two-dimensional table. In principle, any data cube can be represented by a set of normalized (i.e., without data redundancy) two-dimensional tables, and a data warehouse can then be represented by a set of data cubes. A typical method to describe high-dimensional data through two-dimensional data tables using ERD is **star schema**. Figure 10.2 shows an example of star schema for the sales data in the high-dimensional perspective.

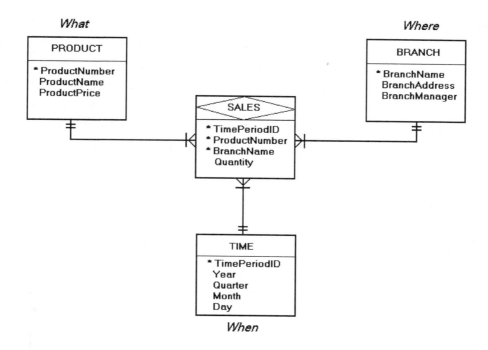

Figure 10.2. Star Schema for Generating High-dimensional Data Cube

As shown in Figure 10.2, the Sales data cube involves three dimensions: Product (*what*), Branch (*who*), and Time (*when*). The attributes and their data of each dimension are stored in a table, called **dimensional table** in the present context. The values of the key of the table represent the levels of this dimension. The center of the star is called the **fact table**. The fact table represents a data cube without redundant data. In this example, the fact table (SALES) keeps the sales data for the three-dimensional data cube as illustrated in Figure 10.1. A relational DBMS supports queries. A query can pull out needed data from each dimensional table to generate a data cube that integrates all data needed from the dimensional tables. For example, give a database modeled in Figure 10.2, the query *"Find all monthly sales which are generated by every branch for every existing product within the past four months"* will generate an integrated data cube.

A data warehouse can have many fact tables. For instance, in addition to the SALES fact table, one can develop other fact tables, such as INVENTORY and

SHIPPING.

Snowflake design is an extension of star schema design of multidimensional data for data warehouses. In the snowflake design, tables have 1:M relationships chains towards the fact table, the center of the star schema. Figure 10.3 is an example of snowflake design which shows the shape of snowflake. Since the relationships between tables are always 1:M towards the fact table, the snowflake design makes it possible to generate meaningful very high dimensional data cubes.

Figure 10.3. Snowflake Design

10.4. Definition of OLAP

OLAP (**Online Analytical Processing**) is one of the most popular **business intelligence** techniques in organizations. The word "**online**" means data availability. The volume of data for business intelligence is usually huge. To perform analytical processing, one must retrieve data from the data warehouse dynamically in the online fashion. A sophisticated OLAP tool makes the huge data warehouse **transparent** to the user, which means that the user is not required to be aware of the location of data. After the data are downloaded to the user's PC side, an elementary analysis process is always offline. The phrase "analytical processing" means all activities involved in data analysis, including queries, statistical analysis, data visualization, and reporting. Thus, OLAP is a variety of data analysis techniques that are applied to very large data sets for organizations to discover interesting information.

10.5. Analytical Processing Techniques of OLAP

There are many techniques of OLAP data manipulation for discover useful information. Here we discuss major OLAP elemental techniques: query, OLAP cube operations, statistical analysis, and data visualization. People often use combinations of these methods for business intelligence.

(1) A **query** is a set of instructions for processing the data with any dimensionality to extract useful information. One can create queries using SQL, or QBE (Query By Example) if the computation environment is end-user oriented (such as Microsoft Office). Using queries, one can find whatever needed data from databases through defining the query criteria. Simple functions of queries include SELECT, ORDER, GROUP, etc. Sophisticated queries can provide information of the correlations among data (e.g., *"how many customers buy beer and diaper together"* in a well-known data mining story.)

(2) OLAP cube operations include slicing, dicing, and drill-down. **Slicing** is to reduce the dimensionality of data by fixing the level(s) of one or more dimensions to create **slices**. Figure 10.4 illustrates slicing.

Dicing is to divide the data cube into sub-cubes (called **dice**) for comparison, (e.g., *"actual vs. plan"*, *"this year vs. last year"* etc.). Figure 10.5 shows dicing.

Combinations of slicing and dicing with other methods, such as queries, statistical analysis, and data visualization, are also called **drill-down**, which means investigating information in increasing details.

Figure 10.4. Slicing

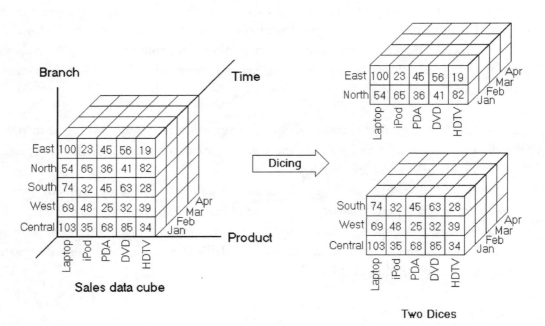

Figure 10.5. Dicing

(3) OLAP is supported by traditional **statistical analysis**. Simple statistical analysis includes descriptive statistics (Sum, Min, Max, Average), t-test, z-test, ANOVA, MANOVA, regression, etc. Advanced statistical analysis includes classification, clustering analysis, etc.

(4) **Data visualization** is the approach of the visual representation of data. In the business field, business graphics (line chart, bar chart, pie chart, etc.) are used to support human cognitive activities in analytical processing for comparison, trends tracing, pattern discovery, and exception detection. Color is usually used for business graphics.

Microsoft Excel is a useful tool for OLAP in the Windows environment. In fact, many OLAP software products use Microsoft Excel as the front interface with the user. Technical Guide C in this textbook provides detailed instructions of OLAP in the Microsoft Office environment.

10.6. Business Intelligence and Data Mining

Business intelligence is a broad category of applications and technologies of gathering, accessing, and analyzing a large amount of data for the organization to make effective business decisions. Typical business intelligence technologies include business rule modeling, data profiling, data warehousing and OLAP, and data mining. The central theme of business intelligence is to fully utilize massive data to help business gain competitive advantages.

In the information era, the capability of analyzing and utilizing massive data lags far behind the capability of gathering and storing the data. New generation of computational techniques and tools are required to support information discovery in databases. This is the subject of **data mining**. Data mining is the process of trawling through data to discover the interesting patterns of the data. Data mining is different from traditional data analysis in that it is aimed at finding unsuspected relationships which are of interest or value to the databases owners.

There is a well-known data mining story. A supermarket found that consumers who purchase diaper were more likely to purchase beer at the same time in that supermarket. This story sounds interesting because such a purchase pattern is unsuspected. Apparently, these consumers may not be the typical ones. This story is an example to demonstrate to people how data mining could help the business to catch opportunities although such an unsuspected fact might be regional or short-lived. Clearly, data mining does not make good decisions automatically. In this story, the data mining result does not tell the supermarket manager whether beer and diaper should be placed close to each other (for the customer's convenience) or far away (to let customers browse more goods).

Due to the large number of dimensionality and the huge volume of available data, the traditional statistical methods have their limitations in data mining. To meet the challenge of data mining, many artificial intelligence techniques such as neural networks, genetic algorithms, and other special data mining algorithms have been developed for data mining.

10.7. Data Resource for Organizational Knowledge Development

Data mining is a growing field in business. More often, information is used for decision making based on the data miner's *a priori* knowledge of the business context and creativity. Thus, the concept of data mining goes beyond the data and algorithms themselves, and data mining should be carried out through human-computer collaboration to demystify the information discovery models and to validate the information discovery results.

Because of overlaps between business intelligence and knowledge development, many people do not fully understand the fundamental differences between business intelligence and knowledge management. Knowledge management is a set of practices of the creation, development, and application of human knowledge to enhance performance of the organization. Generally, knowledge management is concerned with human subjective knowledge flows, not data or objective information.

As the closing episode, we return the point about data, information, and knowledge we discussed in Chapter 1. There have been many myths and great confusion about the concepts of data, information, and knowledge these years. The true propositions are (a) databases organize structured data in the scientific way, and they are the foundation of data resources of the organization; (b) all structured data and unstructured data provide the data source for OLAP and data mining to generate interesting and useful information for the users; (c) the users learn from the instances of information and create knowledge which can be explicit or tacit, and the users can share and exchange their knowledge; (d) the users apply their existing knowledge to conduct OLAP and data mining through a trial-and-error search process in order to obtain more information. This framework is depicted in Figure 10.6.

Figure 10.6. Data, Information, and Knowledge

Chapter 10 Exercises

1.* Recall the case of GreenHeating exercise question 2 of chapter 3. The GreenHeating database has the following tables that include a SERVICE-SPECS table for specifications of service activities.

HOUSE

*HouseAddress	HouseOwner	Insurance

HEATINGUNIT

*HeathingUnitID	UnitName	UnitType	Manufactory
	DateOfBuilt	Capacity	*HouseAddress*

TECHNICIAN

*EmployeeNumber	EmployeeName	Title	YearHired

SERVICE-SPECS

*ServiceSpecsID	ServiceSpecsName	ServiceDuration	RequiredFrequency

SERVICE

HeatingUnitID	*EmployeeNumber*	*ServiceSpecsID*	*Date*	*Time*

Design a multidimensional database using a star schema for a data warehouse for GreenHeating. The fact table will be SERVICE. Include snowflake features as appropriate.

2. Read Technical Guide C in this textbook before working on this assignment. Start Microsoft Access. Click on [Sample Templates], you will see a sample called [Northwind]. Click on it, you are now allowed to create the sample database called Northwind Traders on your PC. You may choose the folder you want to work on the sample database, and then click on the button [Create]. You will see the following window.

Click on [Enable Content] when you see Security Warning sign on the top of the window. Follow the instructions to open the Northwind Traders database, and review the queries and their datasheets.

Suppose you are the new CEO of Northwind Traders. You have an overview of the fictional data set, and understand the nature of the business of this company. Your assignment is to find interesting facts from the database using the OLAP and data mining concepts.

Minicase: *GreenJetNB (Chapter 10)*

Recall the GreenJetNB minicase in Chapter 3. GreenJetNB is a regional airline. It has several aircrafts and various commute itineraries between hubs and small cities. GreenJetNB's database keeps data of aircraft, pilots, past and future flights, passengers who traveled with GreenJetNB, aircraft maintenance work, and sales of airtickets.

1. Design the following multidimensional databases using a star schema or snowflake design for a data warehouse.

a) The subject is "maintenance" that keeps track of maintenance records of aircrafts, operation pilots, maintenance jobs, and responsible maintenance companies over time periods.

b) The subject is "trip" that keeps track of the airfares and passengers' satisfaction ratings of trips over time periods.

2. Read Technical Guide C. Design an OLAP plan to find interesting facts.

TECHNICAL GUIDE A. CONSTRUCTING DATABASE USING MICROSOFT ACCESS

Typeset Convention

UPPERCASE - name of entity; e.g., STUDENT
ITALIC - name associative entity between two entities; e.g., *GRADING*

MonoSpace   - name of file, table, attribute, query, form, report, of the database.

[**Note:** It is a good practice to use a single Camel Style word (without a space) (i.e., UpperCaseLowerCase style) for any name of table, attribute, query, form, and report; e.g., StudentName.]

> tbl – prefix of table name (e.g., tblStudent)
> qry – prefix of QBE query name (e.g., qryStudent2020)
> sql – prefix of SQL query name (e.g., sqlStudentMIS)
> frm – prefix of form name (e.g., frmStudent)
> rpt – prefix of report name (e.g., rptStudent)

* indicates the primary key; e.g., *StudentID

Italic indicates foreign key; e.g., *StudentID*

[Monospace] – menu item or icon for clicking on; e.g., [Start]

An Example for Hands-On Practice

This tutorial provides detailed instructions to build a toy database that implements the following ERD.

1. Overview of Microsoft Access DBMS

Microsoft Access is an end-user oriented DBMS, and has limited capacity. For instance, Microsoft Access provides no function for physical design of the database, and limited utilities for relationships of tables. Before we learn how Microsoft Access can be applied to create and use your own database, we give an overview of database construction and manipulation that available in the Microsoft Access environment.

1.1. Table

The first thing for database construction is to create tables using Microsoft Access. You are allowed to perform the following processing on table.

(1) Give a name to the table you are creating. For example, you can name `tblStudent` for the STUDENT entity. Here, we use common conventions: `tbl` means table.

(2) Define the attributes of the table. For example, you can create `StudentID`, `StudentName`, `StudentAddress`, `StudentYear` as the attributes of `tblStudent`.

(3) Declare the key of the table. For example, you are allowed to declare that `StudentID` is the key of table `tblStudent`. Key ensures unique record and makes the database manipulation efficient.

(4) Declare the data type for each attribute. For example, you may use **Text** for `StudentID`, `StudentName`, `StudentAddress`, and use **Number** for `StudentYear`.

(5) Display the table you created.

(6) Add records to the table.

(7) Delete records from the table.

1.2. Relationship

One of the major functions of relational DBMS is to define relationships between tables and maintain the data in accordance with these relationships. Microsoft Access has limited utilities in defining relationships. For instance, unary relationship and modality are not supported in Microsoft Access. Nevertheless, Microsoft Access supports major functionalities for relationship, as described below.

(1) Create one-to-one relationship between two tables.

(2) Create one-to-many relationship between two tables. Many-to-many relationship must be convert to two one-to-many relationships using a junction (associative) table.

(3) Choose the option of enforce referential integrity.

(4) Choose the option of cascade update related attributes of the two tables.

(5) Choose the option of cascade delete related records of the two tables.

(6) Define join properties.

(7) Delete a relationship.

1.3. Query

The major purpose of database is to use the data stored in tables for particular process or decision making. A **query** is a function that retrieves data from the database. Using Access, you are allowed to create queries and other operations as described below.

(1) Create a query. For example, you may want to create a query that displays names of all students who are enrolled in the 2016 class. In this example, only `tblStudent` is used for this query. You are allowed to create queries using **multiple tables**. For instance, you may want to create a query that displays names of all students who are

enrolled in the 2016 class and have grade "A" in "MGT311". In this case, `tblStudent` and `tblGrading` must be used concurrently.

(2) Give a name to the query you created. For example, you may name the query `qryStudent2016` that displays students in the 2016 class. Here, `qry` means QBE (Query-By-Examples) query. You can also write a SQL script, say, `sqlStudent2016` for the query. `sql` means SQL query.

(3) Use the queries you created. You are allowed to click on the icon of query and retrieve the needed data from the database.

1.4. Form

Data of tables and queries can be displayed in different format. A **form** is used to display data from a table or query in a particular format on the screen. If you do not use forms, all data are displayed in a default format which is less user-friendly. In this sense, form is a secondary application of Microsoft Access. Major functions of Access for form are summarized below.

(1) Create and design a form. For example, you may want to create and design a form for table `tblStudent` to display the student data in a user-friendly way.

(2) Give a name to the form you created. For example, you may name the form `frmStudent` that displays student data. Here, `frm` means form.

(3) Use the form you created. You are allowed to click on the icon of form and display the data in the designed from.

Switchboard is a special type of form that allows you to implement a user-computer interface for the database. We will further discuss on switchboard in the next section.

1.5. Report

Data of tables and queries can be printed on paper in different format. A **report** is used to print data from a table or query in a particular format to fit the size of the paper. You can also add logos and images to a report for printing. In this sense, report is also a secondary application of Access. Major functions of Access for report are summarized below.

(1) Create and design a report. For example, you may want to create and design a report for table `tblStudent` to print the student data in an organized format on paper.

(2) Give a name to the report you created. For example, you may name the report `rptStudent` that prints student data. Here, `rpt` means report.

(3) Use the report you created. You are allowed to click on the icon of report and print the data on the printer.

There are other end-user oriented utilities in Microsoft Access for database construction and manipulation as you can learn from your project.

2. Hands-On of Microsoft Access: Step-by-Step Basics

This section provides basics of step-by-step hands-on of Microsoft Access for you to practice. Remember, in Microsoft Access one thing can be done in a variety of different ways. However, if you are confused in the middle of practice of this step-by-step hands-on, you'd better start over again from the point where you are lost. If you have difficulties in using Microsoft Access, please refer to section 2.13 of this tutorial to find possible solutions. Students are encouraged to further use Microsoft Access online help to learn more about Access for the database project.

2.1. Start Access and Prepare to Create a Database

Find Microsoft Access on your PC, depending on the installation setting, and load it (see Figure T-A-1).

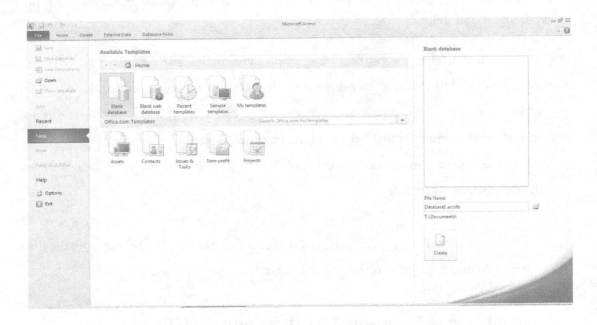

Figure T-A-1. Load Microsoft Access

Click on [Blank Database] icon. You will have [Blank Database] pane on the right side (see Figure T-A-2). You are requested to choose the folder you want store your database, and type your database name (e.g., Student.accdb) for the new database. Next time you can click on [File] on the ribbon to open this database using this name. Note that the Access environment often gives you **Security Warning** when you open an existing database, and you need to click on [Enable Content] on the top [Security Warning] banner to enable all contents.

To create a new blank database, you click on [Create].

Figure T-A-2. Create a New Database

Figure T-A-3 shows the typical screen you will work on. On the top menu, you can see [File] (for [Open], [Save], [Print], etc.), [Home], [Create], ... [Database Tools]. Click on a top menu item, you can see a **Ribbon** which contains a variety of commands for the menu item. The left side of the screen is the **Navigation Pane**.

In Figure T-A-3 you can see the **Table Tools** and **Datasheet** ribbon, as well as the working pane for a table. Now it is ready to create a new table.

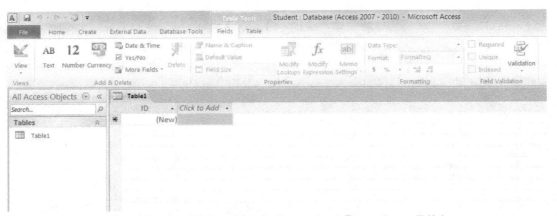

Figure T-A-3. Table Tools Pane and Datasheet Ribbon

2.2. Create a New Table and Design It

On the **Datasheet Ribbon**, click on [View] icon and you will enter the **Design View**. You are requested to give a table name. In the [Save As] pane, you type the name for the table tblStudent (see Figure T-A-4), and click on [OK]. You will see the design pane of the table (see Figure T-A-5).

Figure T-A-4. Save a Table

Figure T-A-5. The Design View of the Table

You type StudentID for Attribute Name. To declare StudentID as the **primary key** if the system does not assign it automatically, highlight it and then click on [Primary Key] on the top menu. Note a small key icon marked on StudentID.

It is recommended to choose [Text] for the Data Type of keys, but not to use the default type AutoNumber. You design other attributes for the table as shown in Figure T-A-6. When you complete the design, right click on the [tblStudent] tag, and click on [Save] to save the design.

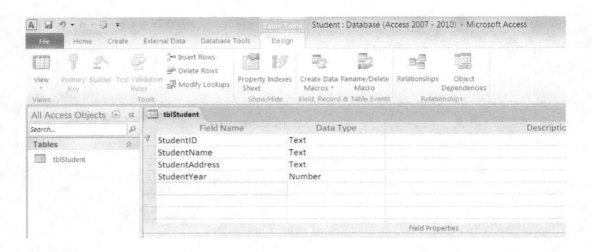

Figure T-A-6. Design Table tblStudent

2.3. Create More Tables

On the top menu click on [Create] and then choose [Table] on the ribbon (see Figure T-A-7). You will create another table (see Figure T-A-8).

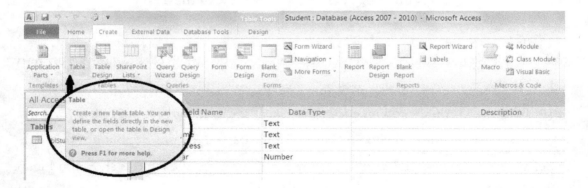

Figure T-A-7. Create a New Table

Figure T-A-8. New Table

You crate the second table tblCourse with attributes CourseID, CourseName, CourseEnrol. Note that you need to use "Text" type for CourseID, and "Number" for CourseEnrol.

Similarly, you create the third table tblGrading with attributes StudentID, CourseID, Grade. Note that you need to declare a **combination key** for tblGrading, because the grade is functionally dependent on both StudentID and CourseID. To do so, in the design view, you hold the [Ctrl] key down and highlight both StudentID and CourseID, and click on the Primary Key icon on the ribbon, as shown in Figure T-A-9. Note that each attribute of the combination key is a foreign key, and should have the same **domain of values** (the same data type) as its corresponding primary key.

Figure T-A-9. Declare Combination Key

2.4. Define Relationships between the Tables

Close all tables by right clicking the table tabs and then [Close All]. Click on top menu [Database Tools] and [Relationships] icon, you will see **Relationship Tools** pane. You are now allowed to create relationships and edit relationships by yourself. On the top menu, click on [Design] and then the [Show Table] icon. You will see the **Show Table** pane (Figure T-A-10). You choose tables needed for the relationships. If the relationships represented by connections are not shown up, click on the key attribute on one table and drag to the corresponding key of the other table as a **foreign key**. You will have a connection between the two tables. Right-click on the connection, and you will see the **Edit Relationships** pane and are allowed to define the relationship and its **referential integrity** rules (see Figure T-A-11). Check the [Enforce Referential Integrity] checkbox in the Edit Relationships pane, and you will see that the "One-To-Many" type relationship has been created. The rationale of these operations is to establish the relationship between the entities and to enforce the data integrity. For example, when you input data to the database, the database will not allow you to give a grade to a student who is not on the student list.

You are not allowed to change `Relationship Types` (1:1 or 1:M) in the relationship pane. To define a "one-to-one" type relationship instead of "one-to-many", you must go back to table design, find the foreign key which associates with the relationship, in its **Field Properties** pane define [`Indexed`] by choosing [`Yes (No Duplicates)`] for the 1:1 relationship.

Note that the relationship diagram displayed in Access is not really an ER diagram, as the relationships are not shown as explicit as an ER diagram.

Figure T-A-10. Relationship Tools and Show-Table Pane

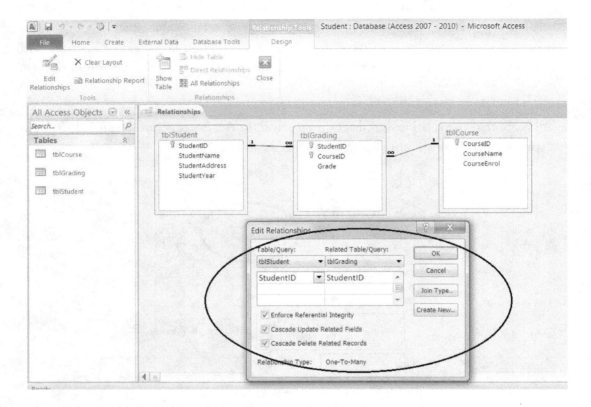

Figure T-A-11. Edit the Relationships between Tables

For your database project, you need to check over all relationships before you can input data to all tables. Make sure the relationships implemented by the DBMS are identical with the approved ERD.

2.5. Input Data to a Table

You should never input data to tables before you complete the ERD, design all tables, define all relationships, and make sure all relationships are correct. Otherwise, your database might become a collection of garbage data.

To input data to a table, click on the [View] icon on the ribbon again and you enter the **Datasheet View**. You type the sample data. You check the datasheets of the three tables, as suggested in Figures T-A-12, T-A-13, and T-A-14.

Figure T-A-12. Datasheet of Table tblStudent

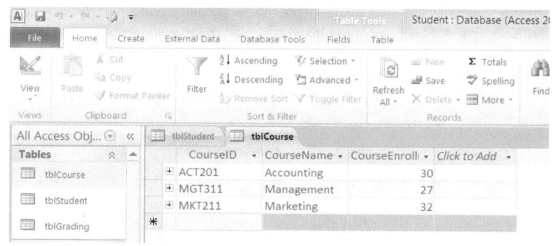

Figure T-A-13. Datasheet of Table tblCourse

Figure T-A-14. Datasheet of Table tblGrading

At this point of hands-on, you must pay attention on the sample data that do not violate data integrity. For instance, you must not input a grade in tblGrading for a student who does not exist in tblStudent. Similarly, you must not input a grade in tblGrading for a course which does not exist in tblCourse. The rule is that the inputted value of a foreign key in one table (e.g., 1334 of *StudentID* in tblGrading) must exist already in the primary key of another table (e.g., 1334 of *StudentID* in tblStudent).

2.6. Create a Query for a Single Table Using QBE

Before you create queries, you must make sure all tables are normalized and all relationships are correctly defined, or you would have many problems with queries. In the MS Access environment, you can create queries by using either **Query Wizard**, or so called the **Query By Examples** (QBE) technique through **Query Design**, or **SQL**. Query Wizard is easy to use, and you can learn it by yourself. Query Wizard can implement simple queries. QBE and SQL can be used for more sophisticated queries. We discuss SQL later in this section. In this sub-section we learn QBE. QBE allow us to view tables, attributes, and relationships when you design queries.

Close the tables and relationships you have worked on. Click on [Create] on the top menu and click on [Query Design]. You will see the **Query Design** and **Show Table** pane (Figure T-A-15). On the Show Table pane, click on the [Table] tab, and you will see a list of tables. You choose tblStudent, and click on the [Add] button. After you close the Show Table pane, you will have the design pane like Figure T-A-16.

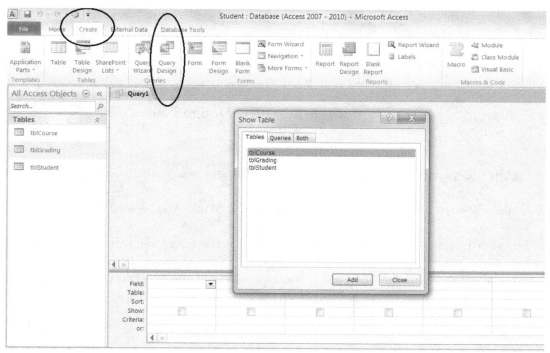

Figure T-A-15. Design a Query

Figure T-A-16. Query Design Pane

On the query design pane, click on the attributes you want to include in the query on the shown tblStudent table, say StudentID, StudentName, and StudentYear. In the lower pane, you are allowed to set **criteria** for the query. In this example, we want to see all students of the 2016 class, and type =2016 in the StudentYear column in the criteria cell, as shown in Figure T-A-17.

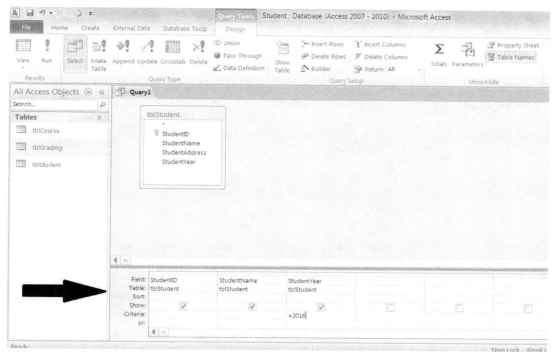

Figure T-A-17. Design a Single-Table Query

Right click on the query tag, and click on [Save]. You will be requested to give the name of the query you created. You type qryStudent2016 for the name, and click on [OK] (see Figure T-A-18). You click on the [! Run] icon on the upper left corner of the ribbon, and will see the query result (see Figure T-A-19).

You close the query design pane and quite the design mode. On the **Navigation Pane** (the left side of the screen), you can view and run the tables and queries you have created.

Figure T-A-18. Save a Query

Figure T-A-19. The Query Result of the Single-Table Query

2.7. Create a Query on Multiple Tables Using QBE

The procedure to create a query on multiple tables is not much different from that for a single-table query if you have defined the relationships of tables for your database. If you have defined the relationships between the involved tables correctly before creating a multiple-table query, the first thing you need to do is selecting more than one table when you work on Show Table pane (Figure T-A-15). If the relationships between the tables have not been defined or defined incorrectly, queries on multiple tables often give unpredictable wrong results.

As an example, we choose tblStudent and tblGrading. Make sure that shown the relationship between the two tables is correct. Set the criteria for the query that is to find the students who receive "A" in MGT311, as shown in Figure T-A-20 of the working Query Design pane. Figure T-A-21 shows the query result.

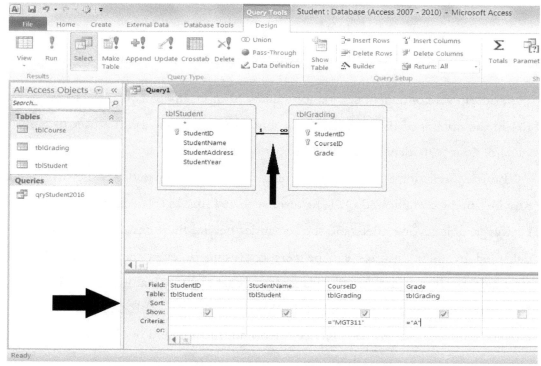

Figure T-A-20. Design a Multiple-Table Query

Figure T-A-21. Query Result of the Multiple-Table Query

You can set contingent criteria for a query. For instance, if you set [Input Course ID] in the criteria of the CourseID attribute, the query will ask the user to input the value of CourseID depending on the user's needs.

Before discussing SQL behind the queries, we clarify a paradox. Microsoft Access provides many complicated QBE features such as [Totals], [Crosstab], [Union], etc. However, unless you understand the semantics behind these features, the query results delivered by these features can be very confusing or even meaningless. The best approach to understanding the semantics behind these features is to learn SQL. However, once you have learned SQL, these complicated QBE features would be no longer "simple to use" to you. Hence, we do not recommend over-using QBE.

2.8. SQL in Microsoft Access

2.8.1. View SQL of a query created by QBE in Access

Recall the query you have created, qryStudent2016 as shown Figure T-A-18. Click on the query on the Navigation Pane, you can view the query result. Right-click on the query tab, and choose [SQL View] on the menu (see Figure T-A-22), you can view the SQL code generated by the Access database management system when the qryStudent2016 was created (see Listing T-A-1 and Figure T-A-23).

```
SELECT  tblStudent.StudentID,
        tblStudent.StudentName,
        tblStudent.StudentYear
FROM    tblStudent
WHERE   (((tblStudent.StudentYear)=2016));
```

Listing T-A-1. An Example SQL Code for Query

The SQL in Listing T-A-1 means: select the data of StudentID, StudentName, and StudentYear from table tblStudent where StudentYear is equal to 2016. We will describe SQL syntax later in this section.

Note: You may find that the style of SQL code generated by Access through QBE is little bit different from the normal style as shown in the textbook. For the course project, you need to write SQL by yourself as instructed in the next sub-section. Do not use QBE generated SQL code to substitute your own SQL for your project. Also, if you write a SQL script for a query, the SQL script is not supposed to be viewed in QBE ([Design View]); otherwise, QBE will change the style and will make it impossible to differentiate whether the SQL script is QBE generated or written by yourself.

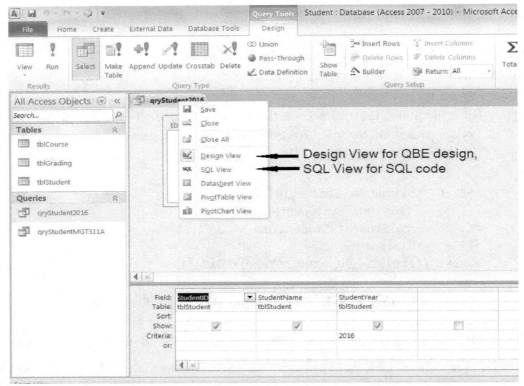

Figure T-A-22. View the SQL Code for a Query

Figure T-A-23. The SQL Code of qryStudent2016

2.8.2. Write and run SQL in Access

To edit SQL in Access,

● Open the database.

● Click on [Create] on the top menu, and choose [Query Design] in the ribbon.

● Close the Show Table pane.

● Right-click on the query tab and choose [SQL View]. Or, you can click on [SQL View] on the ribbon. Now you have the SQL edit window (similar to Figure T-A-23 except for that it has word "SELECT;" only), and you are ready to write SQL code here.

● After editing SQL, you can save it as a SQL query by using the sql prefix, say, sqlStudent2016. To run the SQL, you click on the button marked with   !   on the ribbon.

The SQL code in Listing T-A-2 joins the two normalized tables tblStudent and tblGrading to show the denormalized data for users.

```
SELECT   tblStudent.StudentID, StudentName,
            CourseID, Grade
FROM     tblStudent, tblGrading
WHERE    tblStudent.StudentID = tblGrading.StudentID;
```

Listing T-A-2. SQL of Joining Tables

It will display all students' number, names, the numbers of the courses they have taken, and their grades, as shown in Figure T-A-24. Note that, since the same attribute name StudentID are used in the two different tables, you must quote the table name to specify which table StudentID refers to.

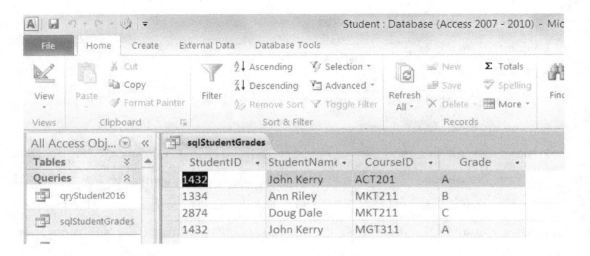

Figure T-A-24. Execution Result of Joining Tables

Note: To learn SQL, you must write SQL queries without using QBE. Use [SQL View] (not [Design View]) for viewing and editing SQL scripts. If you modify QBE generated SQL code, Access always converts the modified SQL code back to the original style which indicates that the SQL code is not written by yourself. Also, for your course project, you need to use sql as the prefix for the name of queries, e.g., sqlStudentGrades, and test and run the SQL queries without contacting QBE.

2.9. Create a Form

Close all tables and queries you have worked on. As discussed earlier in this tutorial, Form and Report are secondary utilities of DBMS. Here we show how it is easy to use **Form Wizard**. Click on [Create]-[Form]-[More Forms]- [Form Wizard] on the ribbon, and you will see **Form Wizard** pane as shown in Figure T-A-25.

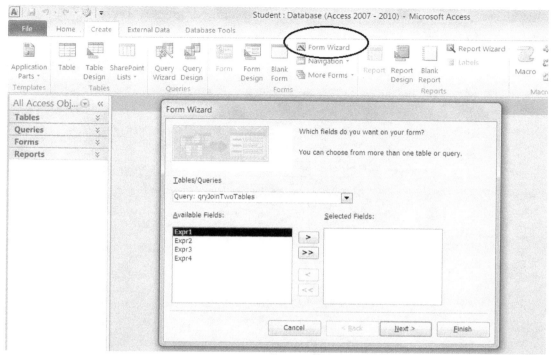

Figure T-A-25. Use Form Wizard to Design a Form

On the Form Wizard pane, click on the [Tables/Queries] drop-down menu, you will see all tables and queries you have created. As an example, choose table tblStudent, select all attributes for the form, and click on [Next] button. You will have many steps that allow you to specify the form in a variety of formats. You may try different options, and click on [Next] after every step. Finally, you click on the [Finish] button and give the name of the form, say, frmStudent. You return to Database pane, and can see the icon of the form. Click on the icon, and you will see the form (Figure T-A-26). You can view and update tblStudent data from this form. Compare Figure T-A-26 with Figure T-A-7, and you can see that tblStudent and frmStudent are virtually the same, but the form is more user friendly to read and edit.

To further customize the generated forms, you right-click on the form tab and click on [Design View] on the menu, and you will be allowed to redesign the form. For learning more about graphical user interface, which is not a major topic in this database course, students are encouraged to embed images, buttons, and combo menus into forms.

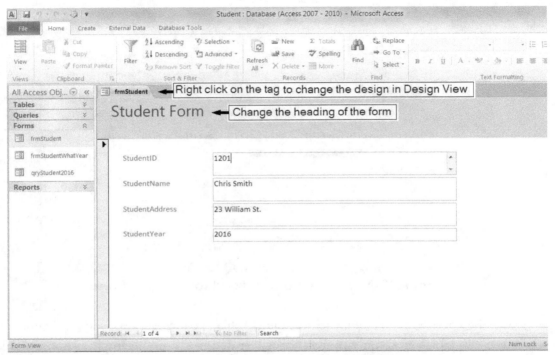

Figure T-A-26. An Example of Form

2.10. Create a Report

The procedure to create a report is almost the same as the procedure for creating a form. The only difference between the two is that you click on [Create]-[Report Wizard]. As an example, we choose tblStudent as the base for the report. The wizard allows you to specify the report in a variety of formats. After several steps, you can view the report you created. It is similar, but may not be identical, to Figure T-A-27 which has been polished through customization. To further customize the Wizard generated reports, you right-click on the report tab and select [Design View] on the menu, and you will be allowed to redesign the report. You can see that report allows you to print the data in a readable format on paper.

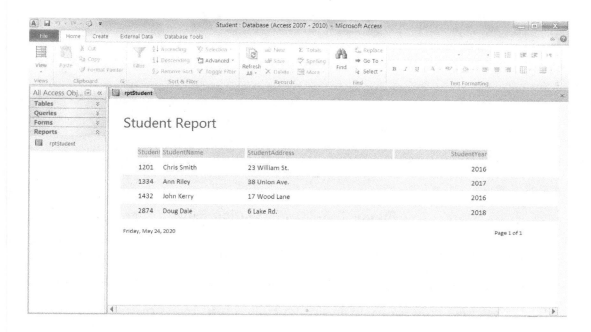

Figure T-A-27. An Example of Report

2.11. Additional Features of the Microsoft Access Environment

The Microsoft Access is an independent end-user oriented database development environment, and possesses many utilities for design of the user-computer interface as well as business applications of the database.

The Navigation Pane on the left side of the screen can help you to organize your database contents including tables, queries, forms, reports, macros, etc. Choose [Object Type] (see Figure T-A-28) to sort types of contents. You can also include [Search] in the Navigation Pane.

217

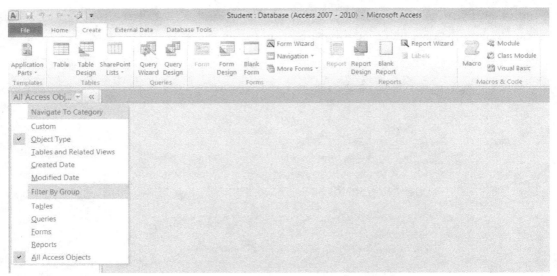

Figure T-A-28. Navigation Pane

Microsoft Access provides many other utilities for database development. Students are encouraged to learn them through [Access Help (F1)] and other Microsoft Access professional manuals. One Microsoft Access official example called Northwind Traders is an excellent example to learn. You can find it in [Sample Templates] of when you open Access (Figure T-A-1).

As a tutorial of the database textbook, this technical guide intends not to provide details of the instructions for secondary utilities of Microsoft Access. The authors believe that those technical skills are not essential for the database course at the present level but are important for students to learn on their own. Here, we summarize commonly used advanced features of Microsoft Access as follows.

(1) **Security** - You can include password protection for your database.

Figure T-A-29. Password Protection

(2) **Switchboard** – The Navigation Pane is used for the database designer to organize the database resources. However, from the user's view, the database would be better providing an application oriented user-computer interface. You can develop a well-organized user-computer interface for the database through designing a switchboard form(s) that is applicable to the specific business application.

Click on [Switchboard Manager]. If [Switchboard Manager] cannot be found on the Ribbon, you need to add it to the Ribbon. To do so, you start Access, click on [Options] on the left-side menu, and then click on [Customize Ribbon]. In the right side pane of Customize the Ribbon, choose commands from [Commands Not in the Ribbon], and you can add wanted commands to the Ribbon (see Figure T-A-30).

In **Switchboard Manager**, you can edit items for the switchboard. Figure T-A-31 through Figure T-A-33 show the major panes that are used in [Switchboard Manager] for editing sub-switchboard and menu items for the switchboard, and an example of switchboard. Note that, since Switchboard is a part of the user-database interface, Switchboard can only access forms (including other switchboards) and reports, but can't access tables and queries directly. Thus, you need to develop forms for any tables and queries that are linked to the switchboard.

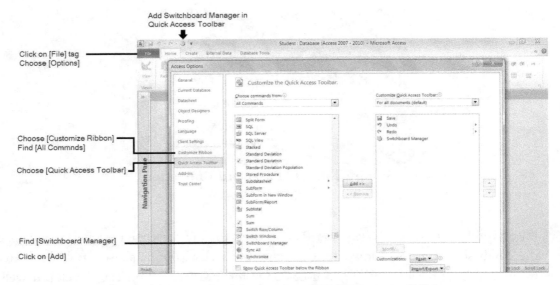

Figure T-A-30. Add Switchboard Manager to Ribbon

Figure T-A-31. Develop Multi-Level Switchboard

Figure T-A-32. Edit Switchboard Menu Items

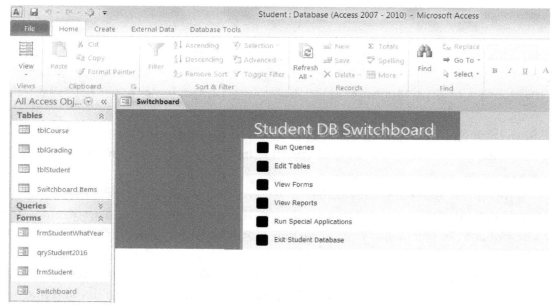

Figure T-A-33. Example of Switchboard

If you want to have sophisticated switchboard, you need to right-click on the switchboard tab and select [Design View] to design the switchboard.

The organization of switchboard items depends upon the designer's preference and the nature of the application. There is more than one way to design a good switchboard. Students are encouraged to develop multi-level and well-organized switchboards. For instance, you might want to have a top level switchboard to list all business areas for different types of users, and to have a second level switchboard for operations in each of these business areas, such as adding records and printing reports, and so on.

(3) **Macros** – Macros are programs/functions which can be executed repeatedly. There are two ways to create macros in Access. An easy way is to use [Create]-[Macro] to create macros without writing code. You may also use **Visual Basic for Applications** (**VBA**) (in [Database Tools]) to write code (or **Modules**) for relatively complicated business processes.

(4) **Startup** - The database can show a startup form with a logo through a macro named [AutoExec] or through the configuration of your database using [Access Options] and then [Current Database] to set [Display Form:]. You might also want to further develop macros and to design the command buttons on the startup form through its [Property Sheet] pane and then the [Event] pane so that the user can start the Switchboard from there. Figure T-A-34 shows a simple example of startup form for the database.

In general, there are many different ways of design of user friendly user-computer interfaces. For this database course, design of user-computer interfaces is not a core component. In fact, a university academic course like this course might provide guides for students to develop technical skills, but is not supposed to train students with practical details. On the other hand, those technical skills are important for students to possess for their jobs in the future. Thus, students are encouraged to develop practical skills on their own through the course project.

Figure T-A-34. An Example of Startup Logo

2.12. Data Dictionary

The final stage of a database project is to edit the **data dictionary** for the database. Microsoft Access can generate a data dictionary for the designer. Click on [Database Tools] on the ribbon and select [Database Documenter]. You will have the documenter pane (Figure T-A-35). You can generate a database document here based on your needs (Figure T-A-36), and meanwhile learn a variety of metadata for database management. To not over-document your data dictionary for your project report, you might have to edit a concise data dictionary based on your true understanding of computer generated documents.

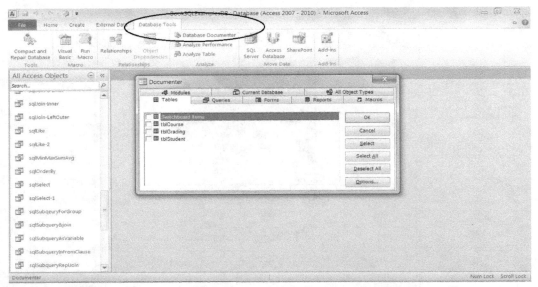

Figure T-A-35. Database Documenter for Generating Database Documents

Figure T-A-36. An Example of Database Document

2.13. Common Mistakes in Using Access and Possible Solutions

Access is an end-user oriented DBMS. It is easy to use. Nevertheless, beginners often make mistakes which Access can't fix by itself. The following table lists common mistakes and possible solutions.

Problem	Cause of the Problem	Solution
1. After open a database, Access does not response	Security protection	Click on [Enable Content] on the top of [Security Warning],
2. The key value of a table can't be changed	The default type of key values is set to AutoNumber	Change AutoNumber to Text
3. High digit 0 disappears in key value (e.g., 012 becomes 12)	The type of key values is set to Number	Change Number to Text
4. It does not allow to input data in table	The type of the values is set incorrectly; Or the data violate data integrity; Or the design of the table and the related tables is incorrect; Or the table is being used by other objects	Check the type of data. Check data consistency (e.g., do not try to input grade for a student who does not exist). Check the design of the table and related tables. CLOSE All tables, and reopen it
5. Being unable to set a combination primary key	You need to highlight the two or more attributes	Highlight the attributes of the combination key and then click on [Primary Key] button
6. It does not allow to change the design of a table when you are working on the table	You have already inputted data in the incorrectly designed table	Delete all data in the table before re-design. Or, CLOSE the table and delete it altogether and start a new table
7. It does not allow to switch to the Design View	Some objects are being used	CLOSE ALL tables, queries, forms, and reports that are being used
8. It does not allow to define relationships as desired in [Relationships Pane] (e.g., cannot show 1:M)	You have inputted data in the tables which have incorrect relationships, and/or the tables are open	Delete all data in the related tables, and redefine primary keys and relationships before inputting data, and CLOSE ALL tables
9. Query results are incorrect	The ER chart is incorrect, or the design of tables is incorrect	Check the ER chart, and then check the design of relevant tables and the relationships between the involved tables
10. The relationships type indicated in the relationships diagram is incorrect (e.g., it should be **1:1** instead of **1:M**, or *vice versa*)	The definition of the foreign key is set incorrectly	Go back to table design, find the foreign key which associates with the relationship, in its [Field Properties] pane, switch [Indexed] between [No Duplicates] and [Duplicates OK]
11. Previously successfully developed functions do not work this time	The contents might be disabled by the Security	Notice the security warning sign, click on [Enable Content]
12. Previous work has been lost	Wrong operations	Back up your work from time to time, and do not click on [Save] if you have made a wrong operation

3. Steps for Your Database Project

In conducting an Access database project, you need to follow the steps **strictly** as listed below in order to avoid generating a GIGO (garbage-in-garbage-out) database. To save time (trust me!), check each steps, do not skip steps, do not reverse steps, and do not mix steps.

☐ (1) Create a Learning-Test Zone (L-Zone) of Student Database which is exactly the same as the example in section 2 of this tutorial. Practice Access hands-on following section 2 step-by-step to fully understand the Access environment.

[**Note:** You'd better create a database that is exactly the same as the one in section 2 in this tutorial. You use this database for learning and test only. You must NOT use this hands-on database for your project. In other words, you must NOT mix L-Zone with your project (P-Zone). It would be a big mistake to use P-Zone as a hands-on tool for practicing Access because it would build-in errors in your project. Even during the development of your project, you might still want to return to the L-Zone to practice and learn new things without damaging the database of your project.]

L-Zone

Simple enough for
- learning
- testing new things
- re-building if start-over again

P-Zone

Your final product
- Error free
- Well organized
- Good looking

☐ (2) Generate an idea of database for your project. Write a transcript for the business, or collect sample datasheets from the business. The transcript or the datasheets is the start point of your database design.

[**Note:** Do not follow the textbook examples to model trivial entities for your project. Unary relationship is not supported by Microsoft Access.]

☐ (3) Develop an ERD for your project. Define the entities and the associative entities. Define the primary keys for the entities. Define the cardinalities and the modalities for the ERD. Pay attention to the foreign keys and the combination keys. Your ERD must be approved through a normalization process.

[**Note:** Before you finish your normalized tables and the relationships for your ERD, do not create a database for your project. Submit ERD to the instructor for approval before the next step.]

☐ (4) Create a Project Zone (P-Zone). Use Microsoft Access to create tables that implement all elements defined in your ERD.

[**Note:** For a 1:1 relationship, choose one of the two tables to include the foreign key. Make sure the 1:1 relationship is correctly implemented. For a 1:M relationship, place the foreign key from the 1 side to the many side. For an M:M relationship, you must create a table for the associative entity.]

☐ (5) Define the relationships for these tables in the Access environment (see subsection 2.4 of this technical guide). The relationships in Access and the approved ERD must be identical.

[**Note:** If you do not do this properly, you would have troubles later. If your ERD is incorrect, or the relationship does not match the approved ERD, your database will be GIGO. Watch all 1:M linkages and check all primary keys and foreign keys (see Figure

T-A-11).]

☐ (6) Input sample data to each of the tables.

[**Note:** Do not input sample data until this step. Otherwise, you would have troubles in defining the relationships between tables. When you input sample data, do not violate data integrity. For instance, do not try to input grade for a student who even does not exist in the student table.]

☐ (7) Develop queries for the database using QBE of the Access environment, and test them. For each QBE, write an English statement first to articulate the purpose of the query.

☐ (8) Write SQL and test them. For each SQL script, write an English statement first to articulate the purpose of the query.

[**Note:** When you write or test an SQL script, use [SQL View], and do not click on [Design View]. Otherwise, your SQL code will be converted into QBE generated code. Remember, do not use modified QBE generated SQL code for this part – Access always changes the modified QBE generated SQL code back to the original code with the strange style.]

☐ (9) Develop forms (except for switchboard) for selected tables and queries.

☐ (10) Develop reports for selected tables and queries.

☐ (11) If you want to develop macros, you may do this now.

☐ (12) Develop switchboard and sub-switchboards that link all things together for your project. If you like, develop a start-up window.

☐(13) Summarize the data dictionary for your database. Do not over-document the data dictionary.

☐(14) Write up and organize your project report. Include the following items.
- Transcript or datasheets for the database to describe the business environment
- Approved ERD
- Meaningful Data Dictionary
- English descriptions of queries, along with your own SQL code and QBE generated SQL code for the queries
- Important screenshots especially your favorite parts of the project to remind the user to use.
- Reflection of what you have learned from this project.

☐(15) Make a CD, or upload your whole package (report and the database artifact) to the instructor.

Suggested Time Frame for the Course Project

TECHNICAL GUIDE B. AN EXAMPLE OF NORMALIZATION

In this tutorial, we explain the normalization procedure through an example. In this example, we start with original datasheet samples, skip a trial ERD, and end up with the approved ERD which representing the normalized tables and their relationships. This example shows that it is possible, especially when the database is small, to carry out the logical database design without a trial ERD. It also shows interesting issues which are not discussed in the chapters such as denormalization and integration of tables derived from numerous datasheet samples. The learning objectives of this technical guide are:

- be able to generate 0NF tables from datasheet samples collected from the business operations;
- be able to normalize the tables to obtain 3NF tables;
- be able to combine tables derived from different sources of datasheet samples without compromising the normalization results;
- be able to perform denormalization without compromising the business rules;
- be able to generate a final version of ERD for the project.

Step 1. Generate 0NF table

To design a database, one needs to collect all of the business reports related to the data items which are supposed to be included into the computerized database. Any report containing original data samples could be rearranged in a two-dimensional table without missing values, called **relation** in relational database. Figure T-B-1 shows how to arrange a sales report for a sales management system into a relation. Before the table is assigned with its primary key, it is in unnormalized form or **0NF**.

Figure T-B-1. Generate Unnormalized Table (0NF) from Data Samples

Step 2. Establish primary key to generate 1NF tables

In the 0NF table, you identify a primary key so that if the value of the key is known, the value of each of the attributes of the table is determined. In this case, if you know the value of [ProductNumber+CustomerNumber+OrderDate], then you can know the value of each of the attributes of the table. Accordingly, [ProductNumber+CustomerNumber+OrderDate] is the primary key of this table. In this normal form, this table becomes 1NF. You make assumptions of functional dependencies based on "common sense" or the special situation of the business. As shown in Figure T-B-2.

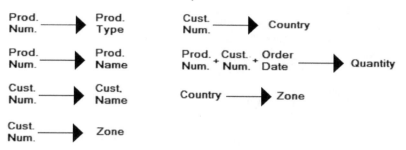

Figure T-B-2. Generate 1NF Tables from 0NF Table

The 1NF relation in this example has data redundancy caused by the partial key dependency. For example, the same fact that product number 100 is Red product appears in several places.

Step 3. Remove partial key dependency from the 1NF table

To remove this **partial key dependency**, the 1NF table is decomposed into three tables, as shown in Figure T-B-3.

Figure T-B-3. Normalize 1NF Table

Step 4. Remove non-key dependency to generate 3NF tables

Inspect the tables in Figure T-B-3 to see if there is non-key dependency. In the CUSTOMER table, Country is the determinant of Zone, and the two attributes are not keys. Thus, create a new table (AREA) with the two attributes, keep the determinant (Country) as the foreign key in the original table (CUSTOMER), and mark the determinant (Country) as the primary key of the new table. Figure T-B-4 shows the normalization results.

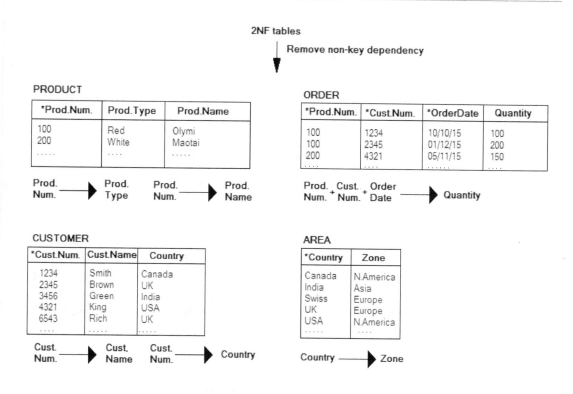

Figure T-B-4. Generate 3NF Tables through Normalization

3NF is not a perfect normalized form; however, it is commonly considered a "good enough" form for database, although higher-level normal forms could be considered.

Step 5. Combine tables with the common key for the entire database

The analysis listed above is based on one application data sample; namely sales reporting. In an organization, there usually are many applications. A result of analysis of other applications related to the tables being analyzed should be combined if they have the same primary key. Generally speaking, the database designer needs to check over all applications to generate 3NF tables for the entire organization. For instance, suppose another set of data samples related to the PRODUCT table deals with price, and the firm wants to incorporate the price data into the database. Then, the PRODUCT table would include the ProductPrice attribute as shown in Figure T-B-5. Clearly, such a process must not violate 3NF.

PRODUCT

*Prod.Num.	Prod.Type	Prod.Name	Prod.Price
100	Red	Olymi	1000
200	White	Maotai	2000
.....	....	.....	.....

Prod. ⟶ Prod. Prod. ⟶ Prod. Prod. ⟶ Prod.
Num.   Type   Num.   Name   Num.   Price

Figure T-B-5. Example of Combining Tables with the Common Key

Step 6. Draw ER diagram for the normalized tables

Once you obtain 3NF tables, you are ready to draw ERD for the database. Note that drawing an ERD and performing normalization are interactive and iterative processes. Here, we start with data samples (data sheets) used in the business, then go through normalization, and finally draw the ERD for the database. You can use an alternative approach; that is, start with an ERD based on verbal descriptions of the business, then convert the ERD to tables and normalize the tables, and finally revise the ERD if needed. You feel free to use either approach.

The ERD of the above example is shown in Figure T-B-6. Note the important features in our ERD format that can help you to avoid mistakes in building the database.

(1) Any M:M relationship is converted into 1:M relationships through an associative entity.

(2) Use detailed format for associative entities (e.g., *ORDER*), including combination

keys and intersection data (e.g., *CustomerNumber*, *ProductNumber*, and DateOfOrder).

(3) For each entity (including associative entity), mark the primary key with * clearly.

(4) For each 1:M relationship (or the special case 1:1), place the primary key in the 1-side (e.g., Country in AREA) into the M-side as the foreign key (e.g., *Country* in CUSTOMER), and use the Italic font for foreign keys.

(5) An ERD may show a pure relationship between entities (e.g., Locate in this example) that has no explicit table in the database. Note that, in this ERD format, except for these pure relationships in the diamond shapes, any notation must have its corresponding representative item in the database. In fact, those pure relationships are useful semantics for writing queries.

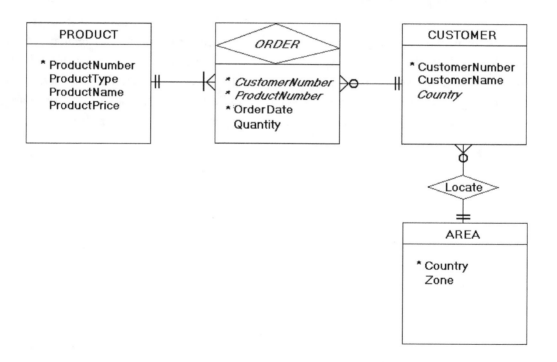

Figure T-B-6. Approved ER Diagram for the Database with 3NF Tables

Optional Step: Denormalization

For practical applications, denormalization is often useful for the efficiency of data access. Denormalization is an analysis procedure to build a certain amount of redundancy into the data base by merging normalized tables. Denormalization is acceptable as long as you do it for a good reason. For instance, let us consider the 2NF table CUSTOMER in Figure T-B-3. From a practical point of view, this 2NF table might have no serious negative consequence if the relationship between CUSTOMER and AREA is not a major concern in the organization which is not the postal office or a delivery company. Obviously, the 2NF table has better data integration than the 3NF tables in this case. We can view this issue in another perspective. Suppose this company is not concerned with the functional dependency County $\rightarrow$ Zone. Then, the CUSTOMER table with Country and Zone is in 3NF.

This example is similar to the classic example of argument against "over-normalization" in the database field that it would be a good practice to place all data items for the address in the same table (e.g., [... StreetNumber, Street, City, State, ZipCode ...]) instead of establishing a separate table (e.g., ZIP[*ZipCode, City, State]) for 3NF, if the database is not designed for a company with the delivery business.

TECHNICAL GUIDE C. OLAP USING MICROSOFT OFFICE

1. Introduction to OLAP

Business intelligence (BI) is a set of theories, methodologies, processes, technologies, and tools that transform raw data into information for business. While there have been a great variety of BI models, methods, techniques, and tools, Online Analytical Processing (OLAP) is the most important and the most commonly applied approach to BI in the industry. The concept of OLAP not only lays a foundation for students to learn other BI approaches (e.g., data mining using artificial intelligence), but also helps students to develop better understanding of the concept of BI for analyzing BI cases.

The major objective of this tutorial is to assist students to learn the concepts of OLAP through the hands-on OLAP exercises using Microsoft Office, and to learn the concepts of BI in general.

The prerequisite of this technical guide is basic computer skills in Microsoft Excel and Access which must be possessed by every business student.

The teaching guide is organized as follows. Section 1 is a brief overview of OLAP. Section 2 is a short introduction of Microsoft Office for OLAP. These two are mainly reading sections for students. Section 3 provides detailed step-by-step instructions of hands-on of Microsoft Office for OLAP. Students can download the OLAP example Access database from the instructor for the hands-on exercises, and follow the instructions in this section to practice OLAP. Section 4 lists the steps for an OLAP project.

1.1. Definition of OLAP

OLAP (Online Analytical Processing) is one of the most popular business intelligence techniques in organizations. The word "**online**" means data availability. The volume of data for business intelligence is usually huge. To perform analytical processing, one must retrieve data from the data warehouse dynamically in the online fashion. A sophisticated OLAP tool makes the huge data warehouse **transparent** to the user; but after the data are downloaded to the user's PC side, an elementary analysis process is always **offline**. The phrase "**analytical processing**" means activities of data analysis including **queries**, **drill-down operations**, **statistical analysis**, **data visualization**, and **reporting**. Thus, OLAP is a variety of data analysis techniques that are applied to very large data sets for organizations to discover interesting information.

1.2. Multidimensional data and data cube

Typical OLAP deals with **multidimensional** data, called **data cube**. For example, Sales can have three dimensions such as Product, Branch, and Time, as illustrated in Chapter 10 Figure 10.1 as a 3D vision. Apparently, there is no way to illustrate hyperspace with more than 3 dimensions visually, but the concept of high-dimensional data for OLAP is basically the same as the data cube in Chapter 10 Figure 10.1. A data cube used for OLAP is called **OLAP cube**.

You can imagine when the data set has a high dimensionality (e.g., 10 dimensions), and each dimension has a high number of levels (e.g., 100), the volume of data would be huge (e.g., 100^{10}).

1.3. Creating a data cube from a relational database

At the time being, almost every data warehouse is based on **relational databases**, although relational database management systems have been with us for longer than three decades. In a relational database, the unit of data for an entity is a two-dimensional **table**. In principle, a data cube can be represented by a set of **normalized** two-dimensional tables. A typical example of the representation of data cube through two-dimensional data tables is so-called **star schema**. Chapter 10 Figure 10.2 shows an example of star schema for a data cube of Sales.

As shown in Chapter 10 Figure 10.2, the Sales data cube involves three dimensions: Product, Branch, and Time. Level data and properties of a dimension are stored in a table for each dimension. The **star center** is Sales table that keeps sales data for the data cube. A **relational database management system** (such as Oracle, DB2, and SQL Server) supports **queries**. A **data cube generation query** can pull out the needed data from the tables to generate a data cube. For example, give a database modeled in Figure 10.2, the query *"Find all monthly sales which are generated by every branch for every existing product within the past four months"* will generate a sales data cube similar to Chapter 10 Figure 10.1. A data cube can contain an integrated data set.

1.4. View and analyzing high-dimensional data

A data cube is stored in the database as a two-dimensional table that arranges the high-dimensional data in a certain way. Because human brains have difficulties in processing high-dimensional data by using a flat two-dimensional table, OLAP tools employ pivot tables to represent high-dimensional data. A **pivot table** is a set of two-dimensional tables that are recursively embedded at each level of each of the dimensions, as illustrated in Figure T-C-1.

Sales						
		Product				
Branch	Month	Laptop	iPod	PDA	DVD	HDTV
East	Jan	100	23	45	56	19
	Feb	74	53	33	24	31
	Mar	28	38	26	54	29
	Apr	76	74	34	32	53
East Total		278	188	138	166	132
West	Jan	69	48	25	32	39
	Fab	49	23	43	26	38
	Mar	66	45	78	86	74
	Apr	63	13	15	47	23
West Total		247	129	161	191	174
North	Jan	54	65	36	41	82

Figure T-C-1. Pivot Table for a Data Cube

As shown in Figure T-C-1, the Sales related to Time and Product can be represented by a two-dimensional table that has the Time dimension for the rows and the Product dimension for the column. For the additional dimension of Branch, two-dimensional tables with Time and Product are generated at each branch, and a larger two-dimensional table with the Branch dimension for the column is created. The larger table is the pivot table representing the Time, Product, and Branch dimensions.

Apparently, the large two-dimensional pivot table embeds the smaller two-dimensional table for each branch. If there is an additional dimension (say, Chanel (how)), a pivot table can be generated for each level of Chanel (e.g., Online, Mailing, Phone, Store), and an even larger pivot table can be created to represent the four dimensions. Apparently, a pivot table can be arranged by the user depending on a specific need.

1.5. Elemental techniques of OLAP

OLAP is a trial-and-error search process to find interesting facts and information. An OLAP task can be accomplished by moving through different paths and by using various techniques. It is important for students to learn elemental techniques of OLAP. An elemental OLAP technique is a basic technique of OLAP that can be combined with other elemental OLAP techniques to become a more sophisticated OLAP method. Four elemental techniques of OLAP have been identified for this tutorial. They are: query, OLAP cube operation, statistical analysis, and data visualization. A complex OLAP task can be accomplished by using a combination of these elemental techniques.

1.5.1. Query

A **query** is a set of instructions for processing the data with any dimensionality to extract useful information. One can create queries using **SQL,** or **QBE** (Query By Example) if the computing environment is end-user oriented (such as Microsoft Office). Using queries, one can find whatever needed data from databases though defining query **criteria**. Simple functions of queries include **select**, **sort**, **group**, **filter**, etc. Sophisticated queries can provide information of the correlations among data (e.g., how many customers buy beer and diaper together.)

1.5.2. OLAP cube operation - Slicing, dicing and drill-down

To discover interesting facts and information from the data, one needs to manipulate the OLAP cube. **Slicing** is to reduce the dimensionality of data by fixing the level(s) of one or more dimensions to create **slices**. Chapter 10 Figure 10.4 illustrates slicing.

Dicing is to divide the data cube into sub-cubes (so called **dice**) for comparison, (e.g., actual vs. plan, this year vs. last year). Chapter 10 Figure 10.5 shows dicing.

Sophisticated OLAP tools support slicing and dicing on online data warehouses. Apparently, working on offline data cubes using pivot tables, one can still perform slicing and dicing operations through manipulation of pivot tables.

Combinations of slicing and dicing with other methods (such as queries) are also called **drill-down**, which means investigating information in increasing details.

1.5.3. Statistical analysis

OLAP is supported by traditional **statistical analysis**. Simple statistical analysis includes **descriptive statistics** (Sum, Min, Max, Average), **t-test, z-test, ANOVA, MANOVA, regression**, etc. Advanced statistical analysis includes **classification, clustering analysis**, etc.

1.5.4. Data visualization - Business graphics

Business graphics (line chart, bar chart, pie chart, etc.) are commonly used for human in OLAP for data visualization. Business graphics support human cognitive activities in analytical processing. The major purpose of the use of business graphics is to effectively support human for **comparison, trends tracing, pattern discovery**, and **exception detection**. Color is usually used for business graphics. While business graphics are widely used in OLAP for data visualization, users must take caution against illusion.

1.6. BI strategy of OLAP

Whereas there have been a great variety of BI models, methods, techniques, and tools, OLAP is the most important and the most commonly applied approach to BI in the industry. The OLAP techniques not only lays a foundation for students to learn other BI approaches (e.g., data mining using artificial intelligence), but also helps students develop a better understanding of the general concept of BI. We start with a framework of OLAP strategy for BI.

A key point that students must learn is that data and the BI tools, including OLAP, do not generate meaningful knowledge automatically without users' a priori knowledge of the business context and pertinent objectives of the analytical process. As a given data set can be viewed from many standpoints, an effective BI analysis must meet a clear business objective. Therefore, the first subject of OLAP is a user-centric framework of BI strategy development as illustrated in Figure T-C-2. This conceptual framework highlights the importance of OLAP strategy in several aspects for BI.

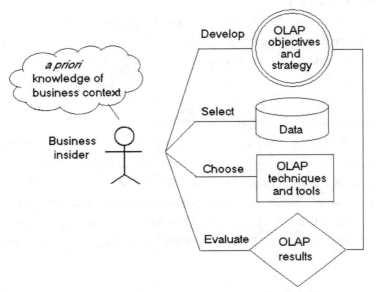

Figure T-C-2. Business Insider Sets Up OLAP Strategy

First, in order to effectively employ OLAP, the user must be a business insider who understands the specific context of business. The business users should have hypotheses about the type of information likely to be useful and how it might be employed in decision-making. Second, as there are virtually infinite ways to conduct OLAP, user's objectives for the specific analysis should be established prior to conducting OLAP. Third, as the data available for OLAP could be extremely large, it is crucial for the user to select a set of limited data and optimize the utility of the data set for the proposed OLAP analysis. Finally, as there are a variety of OLAP techniques, consideration should be given to the selection of techniques appropriate to the study objectives and the skills of the individuals who will be conducting the analysis. The emphasis of this tutorial presented below is to provide students with basic skills so they can participate in choosing appropriate techniques. Overall, OLAP is not a one-shot operation, but is a trial-and-error process.

Generally, an OLAP strategy is a set of generalized or coarse hypotheses in the user's mind that OLAP processes are used to verify or disprove. Clearly, an OLAP strategy highly depends upon the business context, and there is no single formula for setting up the OLAP strategies. Nevertheless, we provide a set of common guidelines for the OLAP strategy development, as listed below.

• Focus on the critical factors of the business, potential problems and possible opportunities;
• Focus on the key performance indicators;
• Find correlations or associations among data relating to critical factors and key indicators;
• Find exceptional facts;
• Detect abnormal observations;
• Detect time-dependent trends, short-term, medium-term, and long-term;
• Verify or disprove the outcome of a business decision or a business action; and
• Verify or disprove a novel idea.

2. Microsoft Office Environment for OLAP

Given the trial-and-error nature of OLAP, OLAP heavily relies on the human-computer interaction. Hence, user-computer interface is an important factor in OLAP. Many users are passionate about the features of spreadsheet integration in Microsoft Excel, leading to Microsoft Office becoming a widely-used BI tool. Many leading OLAP products, such as SAP Duet and SAS, use Excel as their user-computer interface. Microsoft Excel itself has essential OLAP functions to meet the challenge of BI. Microsoft Office is available at almost every educational institution as a necessary computing tool for business students, and thus is an ideal computational environment for us.

Microsoft Excel can be connected to various OLAP database systems (Oracle, DB2, SQL Server, etc.) through **ODBC**. Excel provides **OLAP tools** and commands (which may not be straightforward to business people) for the user to do OLAP. Alternatively, the user can download data from these database systems to the local PC.

Excel creates an **offline data cube** (in a .cub file) for the downloaded data set on your PC, and allows the user to perform OLAP-alike analytical processing as if "online". In the Excel environment, the user is allowed to use **PivotTable**, **Chart**, **Microsoft Query**, **Data Analysis Tools**, and a variety of built-in spreadsheet functions to perform OLAP-alike processing for BI.

In this tutorial, we take a simplified approach to learning the concepts of OLAP for BI through the use of Excel. Instead of using a large OLAP database system, we use Microsoft Access, which is a popular end-user oriented relational database management system without OLAP features, for generating high-dimensional data cubes. The connection between Excel and Access in the Microsoft Office environment is seamless and simple. The user can easily fill pivot tables created in Excel with high-dimensional data stored in the Microsoft Access databases and perform OLAP-alike analytical processing. Figure T-C-3 illustrates environment of Microsoft Office for OLAP. In this tutorial, we focus on the non-shaded parts in the figure, the core part of OLAP, without concerning "online database linkages".

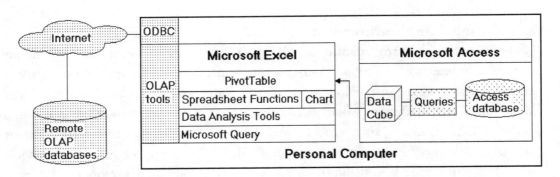

Figure T-C-3. Microsoft Office Environment for OLAP

3. Step-by-Step Hands-On of Microsoft Office for Analytical Processing

This section provides basics of step-by-step hands-on of Microsoft Office for you to practice OLAP analytical processing. Remember, in Microsoft Office, one thing can be done in a variety of different ways. However, if you are confused in the middle of practice of this step-by-step hands-on, you'd better start over again from the point where you are lost. Students must further use online help to learn more about Microsoft Office for BI.

3.1. Download sample database to your PC

You can download a small OLAP sample data set in the Microsoft Access format, named `OLAP.accdb`, from the instructor. The database contains 4 tables (3 dimensional table and 1 fact table) and 1 query. The fact table represents the data cube illustrated in Figure 10.1 (3D graph) and Figure T-C-1 (pivot table). The query generates a data cube with more integrated data from the other three tables.

Although you may go forward to the next step at this point, you might want to open the sample database in Access to have a look. When you open it, you might see a Security Warning on the top of the Window. If so, click on [`Enable Content`]. You may open the query that represents the sales data cube for the OLAP exercise, as shown in Figure T-C-4.

Figure T-C-4. The Sample Data Cube in the Access Format

3.2. Create a pivot table in Excel using Data from Access database

For perform OLAP in Excel, the OLAP cube is stored in the pivot table form. Start Excel, click on [Insert] on the ribbon, then click on [PivotTable], you will see Create Pivot Table pane. Choose [Use an external data source], click on [Choose Connection] button, you will see Existing Connection pane. Click on [Browse for More...] button, find OLAP.accdb you downloaded, and click on [Open] to connect the database (see Figure T-C-5).

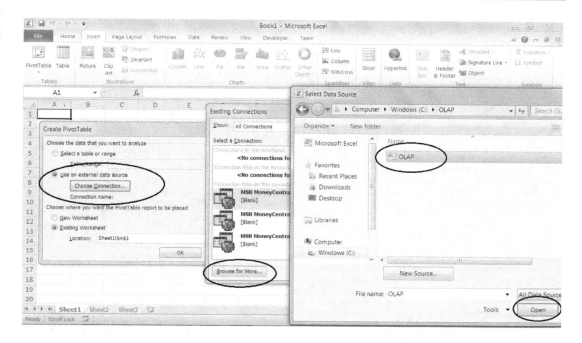

Figure T-C-5. Connect Access Database

After connecting to the database, you will see a Select Table pane as shown in Figure T-C-6. You choose query qrySalesDataCube for hands-on, click on [OK] in the Select Table pane and on [OK] in the Create Pivot Table pane, you will see the PivotTable Tools window that allows you to choose fields of the data set, as shown in Figure T-C-7.

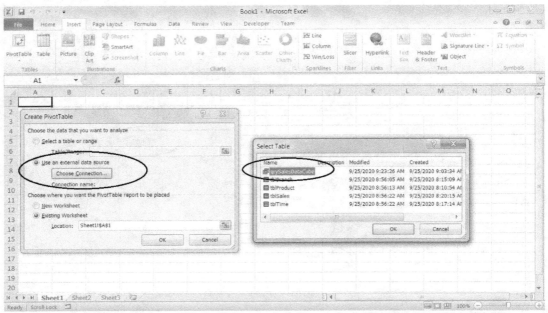

Figure T-C-6. Select High-Dimension Data Set (Query) for PivotTable

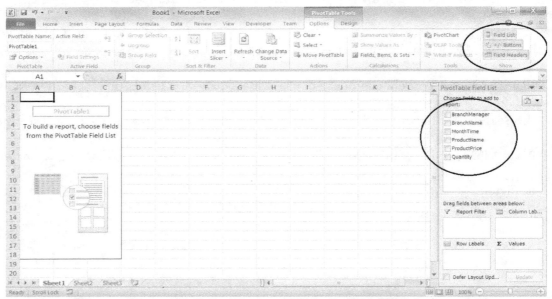

Figure T-C-7. Choose Fields for PivotTable

Choose BranchName, MonthTime, ProductName, and Quantity in the [PivotTable Field List] on the right side, you will see the created pivot table (i.e., the OLAP cube for this hands-on exercise), as shown in Figure T-C-8. If the [PivotTable Tools] menu does not show up, click on any part of the pivot table to bring it up. If [PivotTable Field List] does not show up, click on [Field List] on the [PivotTable Tools] menu.

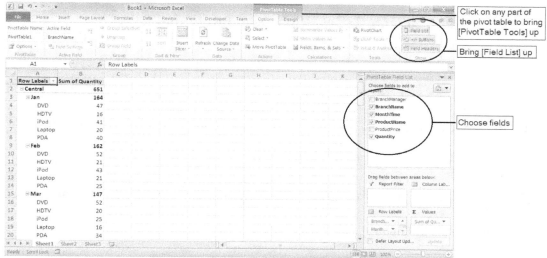

Figure T-C-8. Create a Pivot Table

To make the pivot table meaningful to yourself, you need to set parameters and re-design the pivot table using **Options** tab and **Design** tab in **PivotTable Tools** (see ribbons in Figure T-C-9). Functions **Filter**, **Column Labels**, **Row Labels**, Σ **Values** are important for your re-design.

Figure T-C-9. Ribbons of PivotTable Tools

You can redesign the pivot table layout as you like. For instance, if you consider the automatically generated grand totals and sub-totals of quantity are not used for this OLAP process, you may click on [Design] tab and click on [Subtotals] and on [Grand Totals] in the Layout group to delete these totals, as shown in Figure T-C-10. Click on [Report Layout] in the Layout group, you may change the layout of the pivot table as shown in Figure T-C-11. You may also choose ProductPrice if you would like to know the values of sales, or BranchManager if you would like to know the responsible person for each branch. You can find that the user plays significant role for her/his preferences.

Subtotals and
Grand Totals
can be deteted
if they are not
useful for OLAP

Figure T-C-10. Re-Design Pivot Table – Remove Totals

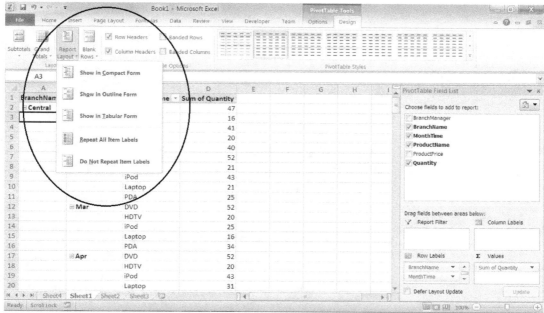

Figure T-C-11. Re-Design Pivot Table - Change the Layout

3.3. Query

You can develop your own queries in Excel based on the Access database, not limited to the pivot table you already created. It is clear that it does not matter whether you develop queries in Access or in Excel.

In this hands-on step of query, set aside the pivot table for a moment by clicking on any cell outside the pivot table. Click on [Data] on the ribbon, click on [From Other Sources] from the [Get External Data] group, choose [From Microsoft Query] from the pop-up menu, and you have the Choose Data Source dialog box, as shown in Figure T-C-12.

Select [MS Access Database*] and click on [OK], you will see Select Database dialog box. Select [OLAP.accdb] and click on [OK], you will see Query Wizard dialog box, as shown in Figure T-C-13. You can choose tables for develop queries, or choose queries for modification. As an exercise, you choose qrySalesDataCube and all its columns for further analysis.

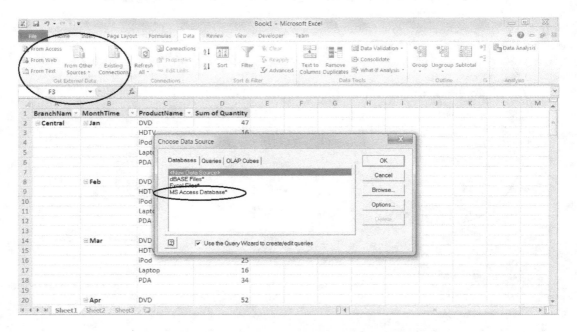

Figure T-C-12. Choose External Data Source

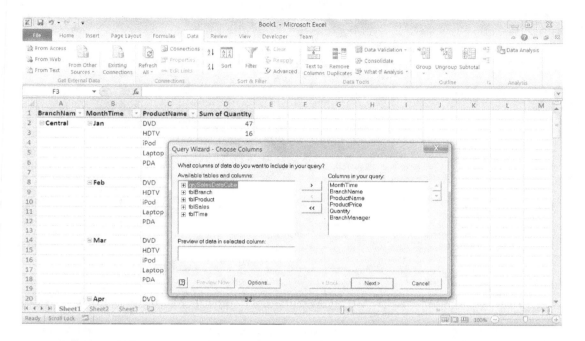

Figure T-C-13. Choose Tables or Queries and Columns for Your Own Queries

Click on [Next] buttons twice, and you will see the Query Wizard - Finish dialog box (Figure T-C-14). Choose [View data and edit query in Microsoft Query], and click on [Finish]. You will see the **Microsoft Query** pane, as shown in Figure T-C-15.

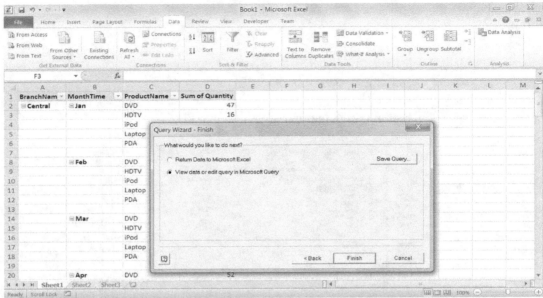

Figure T-C-14. Finish Query Wizard by Entering Microsoft Query Pane

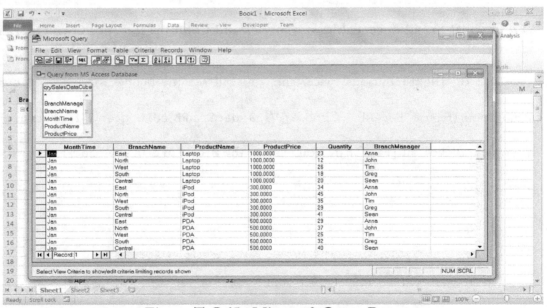

Figure T-C-15. Microsoft Query Pane

In the Microsoft Query pane you can develop your own queries. Click on [View] and check on [Criteria], you will see the **Criteria** pane. Suppose you try to "*Find Laptop top selling months and the responsible branch managers*". You may set criteria such as "ProductName = 'Laptop'" and "Quantity>30". Click on the ! button on the tool menu bar in Microsoft Query for running the new query, you will see the result, as shown in Figure T-C-16. This query reveals information for BI that

*"**Anna of East Branch was the number one Laptop sales manager in both Mar and Apr, although other branches (West and Central) had the same sales levels in one of the two months.**"*

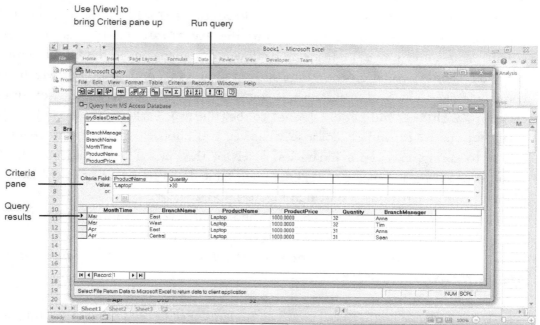

Figure T-C-16. The Result of a Sample Query

You may find that one can use Excel spreadsheet to do the same job, but Microsoft Query make the job much easier.

Through practicing the above exercise, students shall be able to meet the following three learning goals.

(1) Students shall be able to use the query technique in Excel for OLAP.

(2) Students shall understand the types of basic OLAP tasks as articulated in the prototype that can be accomplished by queries.

(3) Students shall be able to extend the OLAP prototype to add conceivable meaningful facts. For example, a student might want to extend the OLAP prototype to find out the lowest sales of products in alternative months.

3.4. OLAP cube operation - Slicing, dicing and drill-down

Slicing is much easier in Excel spreadsheet. Return back to the pivot table you have created. Click on the pivot table to bring **PivotTable Tools** ribbon up. Click on [Options] and on [Field List] and bring the **PivotTable Field List** up if it is hiding. You simply move the fields up or down (or dimensions in the OLAP term) in the **[Row Labels]** panel on the PivotTable Filed List, and figure out which slice you would like to view. For instance, if you want to obtain a slice of Apr, you simple click on MonthTime and choose [Move to beginning], click on those [+] or [-] small buttons to expand or collapse whatever you choose. A dicing procedure is similar to slicing, except for hiding less levels of the chosen field (dimension). An example of slicing and dicing to drill the pivot table down to details of East branch in Mar and Apr time periods is shown in Figure T-C-17.

This drill-down process through slicing and dicing reveals information for BI that

"East Branch has a significant increase of sales of DVD in Apr compared with Mar by ((73-57)/57=28%)."

Through practicing the above exercise, students shall be able to meet the following three learning goals.

(1) Students shall be able to perform slicing, dicing, and drill-down operations in Excel using a pivot table.

(2) Students shall understand the types of basic OLAP tasks as articulated in the prototype that can be accomplished by OLAP cube operations.

(3) Students shall be able to extend the OLAP prototype to add conceivable meaningful facts that can be revealed through OLAP cube operations.

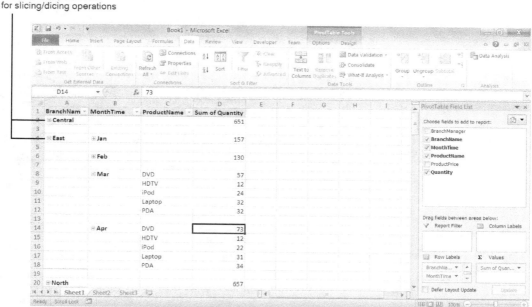

Expand/Collapse buttons
for slicing/dicing operations

Figure T-C-17. Slicing and Dicing in Pivot Table

3.5. Statistical analysis

Excel has common statistical analysis tools. Click on [Data] on the ribbon, and then [Data Analysis]. You can see the **Data Analysis** dialog box for choosing statistical analysis methods, including ANOVA, regression, descriptive statistics, *t*-test, z-test, etc., as shown in Figure T-C-18.

If the Data Analysis command is unavailable in the Analysis group on the Data tab, you need to **add-in** a supplement package called **Analysis ToolPak**. To do so, click on [File], and then click on the [Options]. In the Excel Options window, click on [Add-Ins], and then select [Excel Add-ins] in the Manage box. Click on [Go]. In the [Add-Ins available] box, select the [Analysis ToolPak] check box, and then click on [OK]. If the Analysis ToolPak is not listed in the [Add-Ins available] box, click on [Browse] to locate it. If you get prompted that the Analysis ToolPak is not currently installed on your computer, click on [Yes] to install it.

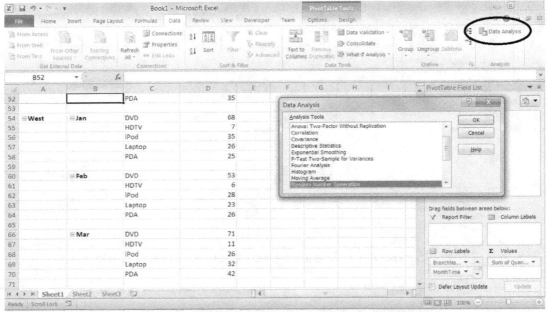

Figure T-C-18. Statistical Analysis Tools

It is hard to apply data analysis directly working on a pivot table. You need to take advantages of spreadsheet to generate ordinary tables through cut-paste operations before apply data analysis. The following is an example of statistical analysis for BI. Drag and copy all sales data of West Branch as well as South Branch, and paste them to Sheet2, as shown in Figure T-C-19. Start Data Analysis, and choose [t-Test: Paired Two Sample for Means]. Follow the instruction of the dialog box (not shown in Figure T-C-19), and define the two samples ranges (e.g., (D1:D23) and (I1:I23), depending on the format) as well as the output range (anywhere on the sheet you like to place the result). After click on [OK], you will see the statistical analysis result as shown in Figure T-C-19. The data analysis reveals information for BI that

"The difference of sales between West Branch and South Branch is insignificant, although the average sales of West Branch is slightly higher than sales of South Branch (by (30.5-29)/29=5%)."

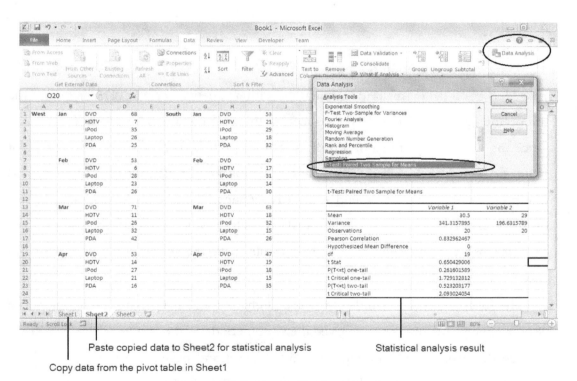

Paste copied data to Sheet2 for statistical analysis   Statistical analysis result

Copy data from the pivot table in Sheet1

Figure T-C-19. Statistical Analysis

Through practicing the above exercise, students shall be able to meet the following three learning goals.

(1) Students shall be able to use basic statistical analysis tools learned from the statistics course for OLAP.

(2) Students shall understand the types of basic OLAP tasks as articulated in the prototype that can be accomplished by statistical analysis.

(3) Students shall be able to extend the OLAP prototype to add more statistical analyses.

3.6. Data visualization and chart

Excel has good data visualization functions with a variety of charts. This is one of the important features of Excel spreadsheet as the user-computer interface for OLAP. Since the `PivotChart` function (in the `[Options]` tab) directly associates with a pivot table and generates so-called `PivotChart` which is awfully difficult to manipulate and interpret, we do not recommend using `PivotChart`. Instead, it is suggested to use ordinary **Chart** function working on ordinary tables which are derived from a pivot table through cut-paste operations. This would make the analysis easy to control and easy to understand.

The following is an example of the use of charts for analytical processing. Suppose you are going the analyze sales over the time period on the product basis. You re-arrange the pivot table, and copy relevant data set and paste it to a new data sheet. Click on the `[Insert]` tab and then click on `[Line]` in the Chart group to create a line chart. Usually, you will see a line chart that might not be what you want. Right-click on the displayed chart, and choose `[Select Data…]` in the pop-up menu, you will have the **Select Data Source** pane, as shown in Figure T-C-20. You are allowed to select data source, and, more importantly, to define the **legend entries** (**series**) and **axis labels** which make the chart meaningful.

Figure T-C-20. A Line Chart

The example line chart in Figure T-C-20 reveals information for BI that

*"**Over the time period, the fluctuation sales patterns of DVD and PDA are similar, while the sales of other three products are increasing after March.**"*

Through practicing the above exercise, students shall be able to meet the following three learning goals.

(1) Students shall be able to use data visualization methods in Excel for OLAP.

263

(2) Students shall understand the types of basic OLAP tasks as articulated in the prototype that can be accomplished by data visualization.

(3) Students shall be able to extend the OLAP prototype to display various data patterns and comparisons by using a variety of business graphics.

This tutorial has made it clear that how one can use OLAP to transform a huge amount of data into pertinent information. When demonstrating OLAP using the toy example, we have made implicit assumptions, or strategy, in performing the simple OLAP. The tutorial does not explain those implicit assumptions or strategy because the toy case is so simple. The tutorial does not go further to explain how the OLAP results (useful information) can be shared and transformed into knowledge because we can never go that far without a business reality including human and organization.

4. Steps for Your OLAP Project

Step 1. Get familiar with Microsoft Office for OLAP

Receive a tiny example of Microsoft Access database (OLAP.accdb) from the instructor. Practice analytical processing hands-on following Section 3 to fully understand the Microsoft Office environment for OLAP. Clearly, you need to do your project in a creative way.

Step 2. Obtain data for your OLAP project

In principle, you may use any large data set for your OLAP project. However, if you do not have a data set on hand, you may use a sample data set in Microsoft Access.

Open Microsoft Access. Click on [Sample Templates], you will see a sample called [Northwind]. Click on it, you are now allowed to create the sample on your PC. You may choose the folder you want to work on the sample database, and then click on the button [Create]. You will see the following window.

Click on [Enable Content] when you see Security Warning sign on the top of the window. Follow the instructions to open the Northwind Traders database.

Once you have the home page, click on left side of the window to bring up the Navigation Pane if it is hiding. On the Navigation pane, click on the small arrow button on the Northwind Traders title, bring up the pop-menu, and choose [Object Type]. Click on [Tables] and [Queries]. You may ignore other object types, and focus on queries (data cubes). Now you can bring needed data cubes up by clicking a query, as illustrated in the example in Figure T-C-4.

Step 3. Generate OLAP strategy

If you use the Northwind Traders data set, suppose you are the new CEO of Northwind Traders. You have an overview of the data set, and understand the nature of the business of this company based on your knowledge. You then generate ideas of OLAP strategy for the company. Write down your OLAP strategy by following the guidelines discussed in Section 1. Specifically, you need to articulate potential interesting information using techniques including queries, slicing, dicing, drill-down, statistical analysis, and data visualization.

Step 4. Develop more queries in Access to obtain more data cubes

This step is optional if you use the Northwind Traders data set. This is because the Northwind Traders Access database has generated many queries (data cubes) already, and these data cubes might be sufficient for you to practice OLAP in Excel. In this step, you can create data cubes (integrated queries) that are not available in the current database for your OLAP.

Step 5. Perform analytical processing using Excel

If you the Northwind Traders data set, open Excel and connect the Northwind Traders database. Apply and extend what you have learned from Step 1, and analyze the data set. Find interesting, meaningful, and significant facts to implement the OLAP strategy you identified.

To record the support of the OLAP results for your report and presentations, you might want to catch important screenshots (push the [PrtSc] key to catch the screenshots, and then [Paste] in Word or PPT), and/or keep relevant sheets and charts.

Step 6. Write a report
You write a report for the project to summarize the following items.

- An overview of the data used for this project.
- The OLAP strategies you used for the project. Explain you considerations.
- The specific data cubes and the OLAP techniques used to discover instances of useful information.
- Instances of interesting and useful information revealed through the OLAP.
- Explain how these instances of information meet your OLAP strategies.
- Lessons you have learned from this project about OLAP and BI in general.

ANSWERS TO EXERCISE QUESTIONS AND REVIEWS

Chapter 1, Question 1.

Master data: Student profile records
Transaction data: Course registrations
Historical data: Financial aids
Secondary data: Transfer credits and courses
Subjective data: Advisors' comments

Chapter 1, Question 3.

In Figure 1.2a, the same fact that "the customer holding the customer number 123456 is Smith with the address ..." is stored more than once. Thus, data redundancy occurs.

Chapter 1, Question 4.

In Figure 1.2b, 123456 in the CUSTOMER table represents the fact that "the customer holding customer number 123456 is Smith with the address ..." while 123456 in the PURCHASE table represents the fact that "the customer holding 123456 made a purchase." Thus, they are not redundant data.

In the PURCHASE table, the same number 123456 appears twice because the two 123456 represent two different facts: the two purchases on the different dates. Thus, they are not redundant data.

Chapter 2, Question 6(a).

There are several correct answers, as long as the rules are followed. One of the answers is:

To find the record with the key 5000, the computer

(1) starts with the root index record, and finds the pointer paired with key-value 7890;
(2) follows the pointer and finds the second index record at the next lower level;
(3) finds the pointer paired with 5678;
(4) follows the pointer and finds the record on Cylinder 5.

Chapter 2, Question 8.

a.

b.

OR

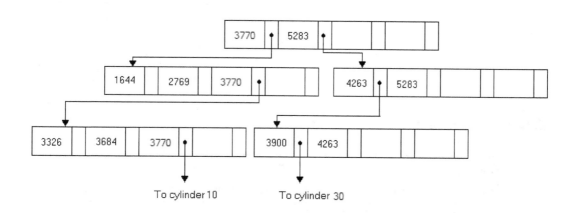

Chapter 3, Question 2.

Chapter 4, Question 1.

Chapter 4, Question 2.

Non-default constraints:
(1) 1:1 cardinality between INTENDANT and APARTMENT
APARTMENT {CONSTRAINT *EmployeeID* UNIQUE}

(2) 0 modality between INTENDANT and APARTMENT
APARTMENT {CONSTRAINT OPTIONAL TO INTENDANT}

(3) 0 modality between APARTMENT and TENANT
TENANT {CONSTRAINT OPTIONAL TO APARTMENT}

Chapter 5, Question 4.

a. *BookTitle, FirstAuthor, Length*
3NF

b. *BookNumber, PublishDate, BookTitle, FirstAuthor*
2NF because of non-key dependency: BookTitle→FirstAuthor

*BookNumber, PublishDate, BookTitle
*BookTitle, FirstAuthor

c. [*BookNumber+*ClientNumber+*RentalDate], ReturnDate, RentalFee
3NF

d. [*BookNumber+*ClientNumber+*RentalDate], ClientName,
   ReturnDate, RentalFee
1NF because of partial key dependency: ClientNumber→ClientName

*ClientNumber, ClientName
[*BookNumber+*ClientNumber+*RentalDate], ReturnDate, RentalFee

e. *[*BookTitle+*ClientNumber], FirstAuthor, Length, ClientName, ClientAddress*

1NF because of partial key dependency: BookTitle→FirstAuthor

*BookTitle, FirstAuthor, Length
*ClientNumber, ClientName, ClientAddress
[*BookTitle+*ClientNumber] (This table indicates who rents this book. Note that the table in question follows the business rule that "The combination [*BookTitle+*ClientNumber] is unique".)

Chapter 5, Question 5.

a) *Order ID, Order Date, Shipping Date, Customer ID, Customer Name, Customer Address*

2NF because of non-key dependency: CustomerID → CustomerName, CustomerAddress

Decompose it into 3NF tables:

*OrderID, OrderDate, ShippingDate, CustomerID
*CustomerID, CustomerName, CustomerAddress

b) *[*OrderID+*ProductID+*CustomerID], CustomerAddress, ProductName, ProductSalePrice, OrderQuantity*

1NF because of partial dependency: CustomerID → CustomerName ….

Decompose it into 3NF tables:

*OrderID, Customer ID

[*Order ID+*Product ID], ProductSalePrice, OrderQuantity

*ProductID, ProductName

*CustomerID, CustomerAddress

[*OrderID+*ProductID+*CustomerID]

(Note that one may have [*ProductID+*CustomerID] as a component of the original key and derive a table with this combination key but without a non-key attribute. It could be meaningful for "who bought what", but the business rule here is the combination [*ProductID+*CustomerID] is unique, which may or may not be true in general.)

Chapter 5, Question 6.

The normal form of the table is in 1NF, because of the partial key dependency DoctorID → DoctorName. The normalized tables in 3NF are:

*DoctorID, DoctorName

*PatientID, InsuranceName

[*DoctorID+*PatientID+*TreatmentDate], TreatmentType

*TreatmentType, TreatmentCost

[*TreatmentType+*InsuranceName], InsuranceBenefit

(Note that this question demonstrates the issue of revising and preserving functional dependencies in the normalization process. The original 1NF satisfies all given functional dependencies; that is, if you know the value of [DoctorID+PatientID+TreatmentDate], then you know the value of DoctorName, InsuranceName, TreatmentType, TreatmentCost, or InsuranceBenefit. However, as the normal form of the original table is 1NF, it must be normalized. When eliminating the partial key dependency PatientID→InsuranceName by creating a new table, the functional dependency TreatmentType+InsuranceName→ InsuranceBenefit is lost. To preserve this functional dependency, the last table must be added.)

Chapter 6, Question 1.

a) *Find the owner of the house "285 Westport Rd".*

```
SELECT HouseOwner
FROM HOUSE
WHERE HouseAddress='285 Westport Rd';
```

b) *List the heating unit names and numbers of the Gas heating units which was built in house "285 Westport Rd".*

```
SELECT HeatingUnitID, HeatingUnitName
FROM HEATINGUNIT
WHERE UnitType='Gas'
AND HouseAddress='285 Westport Rd';
```

c) *The unit types of heating units include gas, electric, solar, and several hybrid models. List the heating unit number, date of built, and manufactory of all heating units other than hybrid models with capacity between 3000 and 4000 cubic feet from largest to smallest.*

```
SELECT HeatingUnitID, DateOfBuilt, Manufactory, UnitType
FROM HEATINGUNIT
WHERE UnitType IN ('Gas', 'Electric', 'Solar')
AND Capacity BETWEEN 3000 AND 4000
ORDER BY Capacity DESC;
```

Or:
```
SELECT HeatingUnitID, DateOfBuilt, Manufactory, UnitType
FROM HEATINGUNIT
WHERE (UnitType='Gas' OR UnitType='Electric' OR UnitType='Solar')
AND (Capacity>=3000 AND Capacity<=4000)
ORDER BY Capacity DESC;
```

d) *List the names of technicians who maintained a heating unit in "285 Westport Rd" along with the service type performed.*

```
SELECT EmployeeName, ServiceType
FROM TECHNICIAN, SERVICE, HEATINGUNIT
WHERE TECHNICIAN.EmployeeNumber=SERVICE.EmployeeNumber
AND HEATINGUNIT.HeatingUnitID=SERVICE.HeatingUnitID
AND HEATINGUNIT.HouseAddress='285 Westport Rd';
```

e) *Find the name and number of the largest Gas heating unit.*

```
SELECT HeatingUnitID, UnitName
FROM HEATINGUNIT
WHERE UnitType='Gas'
AND Capacity=
        (SELECT MAX(Capacity)
                FROM HEATINGUNIT
                WHERE UnitType='Gas');
```

f) *What percent is the total capacity of Gas heating units out of the total capacity of all types of heating units?*

```
SELECT SUM(Capacity)/(SELECT SUM(Capacity) FROM HEATINGUNIT)
FROM HEATINGUNIT
WHERE UnitType='Gas';
```

Chapter 7, Question 1.

a) *There is a critical need to quickly list the heating units with a particular type.*

Build an index over the UnitType attribute of the HEATINGUNIT relation.

b) *There is a frequent need to list all heating unit numbers along with their unit types and house addresses.*

Make vertical partition of HeatingUnitID, UnitType, and HouseAddress in the HEATINGUNIT relation and separate them out physically.

c) *There is a frequent need to retrieve detailed data about a heating unit together with detailed data about the house in which it locates.*

One option is to use the clustering technique to bring HEATINGUNIT and HOUSE physically near each other on the disk.
Another option is to merge (denormalization) the HEATINGUNIT and HOUSE tables.

d) *There is a much more frequent and high priority need to access the records for Gas heating units than for the other types.*

Make horizontal partition of the records with Gas type in the HEATINGUNIT relation and separate them out physically.

e) *Due to large numbers of access activity, the HEATINGUNIT relation has become a bottleneck.*

Duplicating the HEATINGUNIT relation to route different queries to the different copies.

Chapter 8, Question 2.

2. Follow the GreenJetNB case in the exercise question of Chapter 3. Describe a scenario that the re-do transactions method is applicable for backup and recovery of the GreenJetNB database.

A: Highlight the typical situation of the re-do method:

(1) Backup, e.g., on the first day of each month.
(2) Keep logs.
(2) When a disaster occurs and the database is damaged, recover the database.

Then, use a graph similar to the following one, to explain a disaster recovery plan for a large-scale damage.

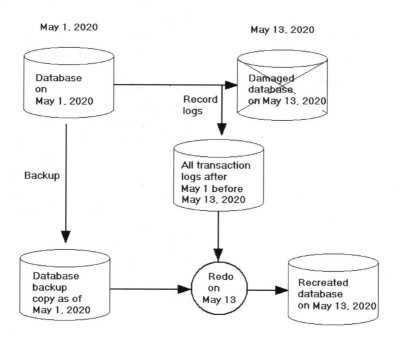

Chapter 9, Question 1.

A: The answer needs to include the design of placement, partitioning, replication, and their combinations for each table. The description for a horizontal partitioning must clarify the criterion used for the partitioning. The ER model is needed for this purpose.

Locations Tables	Boston Headquarters	Region Offices
HOUSE	*Placement* in Boston	H.P. based on the values of *HouseAddress* that related to each region office. *Replicate* the H.P. part for the region office.
HEATINGUNIT	*Replicate* the H.P. parts for the Boston headquarters.	H.P. based on the values of *HouseAddress*. *Place the* H.P. part to each region office.
TECHNICIAN	*Replicate* the H.P. parts for the Boston headquarters.	H.P. based on the values of *EmployeeNumber* that related to each region (i.e., *HouseAddress*) through the SERVICE and HEATINGUNIT tables. *Place the* H.P. part to each region office.
SERVICE	*Replicate* the H.P. parts for the Boston headquarters.	H.P. based on the values of *HeatingUnitID* that related to each region (i.e., *HouseAddress*) through the HEATINGUNIT table. *Place the* H.P. part to each region office.

Chapter 10, Question 1.

The question does not specify what dimension you need to include in the design. One common assumption is to include the time dimension (*when*), because almost every data warehouse has to keep the time dimension with few exceptions.

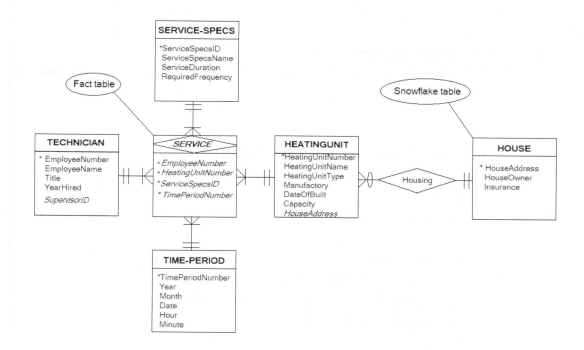

Review of Key Points of Problem Solving for Each Chapter

Chapter 1: Introduction - Data redundancy and data integration
- ◆ Given a table with redundant data
- ? Identify the data redundancy
- ? Use an intuitive method to eliminate the data redundancy without loss of data
- ? Discuss pros/cons of integrated data table vs. data tables with no redundancy

Chapter 2: File organizations
- ? Important concepts of sequential file, random file, and indexed file organizations

Chapter 2: B-tree
- ◆ Given the number of index-pointer pairs for each index record
- ◆ Given the maximum key values on cylinders
- ? Construct a B-tree
- ? B-tree maintenance (index record splitting) in response to an overfull cylinder

Chapter 3: Constructing ER diagram
- ◆ Given a transcript or sample datasheets
- ? Draw an ER diagram to map each sentence given in the transcript or every data item in the datasheets
- ? Primary keys
- ? Foreign keys
- ? Cardinality, modality
- ? Binary, unary, ternary
- ? For M:M relationship, define associative entity and intersection data, and convert the M:M relationship into 1:M relationships (using physical ERD).

Chapter 4: Converting ER diagram to tables

♦ Consider the ER diagram you have created.

? Convert the ER diagram you have created to relational database tables

? Mark CK, AK, PK, FK on each table based on common sense assumptions

? Define constraints for cardinalities and modalities

Chapter 4: Data retrieval and joining tables

♦ Given tables of relational database

? Identify FK for implementing 1:M relationship

♦ Consider a data retrieval situation

? Steps of data retrieval (must be specific on the particular data)

♦ Consider a situation of merge of two tables

? Merge tables, and discuss redundancy and integration

- You may want to show the merged table to discuss specifically.
  Pay attention on the way of merging tables (use the base table on the M-side)
- ? Data modification anomaly

Chapter 4: Referential integrity

♦ Given tables and deletion rules (restrict, cascade, set-to-null)

♦ Given independent situations of record deletion

? What will happen for each of the situations

Chapter 5: Normalization

♦ Given a table with its attributes and their functional dependencies

? Determine 1NF, 2NF, or 3NF for the table

? Explain why the table is 1NF, 2NF, or 3NF

? If the table is not 3NF, normalize it into 3NF tables

? Concepts of BCNF and 4NF

Chapter 6: SQL

♦ Given the relational database 3NF tables

♦ Given English descriptions of queries

? Write SQL for each query

- CREATE, DROP, INSERT, UPDATE, DELETE commands
- SELECT command
- Major clauses
  (WHERE, GROUP BY, etc.) and operators (AND, OR, etc.)
- Pay attention on join (not explicit inner join/outer join format)
- Subquery (especially, for the uncertain criteria in the WHERE clause)

Chapter 7: Physical database design

♦ Given 3NF tables of a relational database

♦ Given independent situations

? State a technique of physical database design to improve the performance for each situation (use the following key words and specify the techniques)

- Adding index (*on what attributes*)
- Cluster files (*of what tables*)
- Denormalization – merge tables (*what tables*)
- Horizontal partitioning (*what table based on what criteria*)
- Vertical partitioning (*what part of what table*)
- Duplication (*of what table*)
- Add subschema (*what tables for the subschema, and for who*)
- New primary key (*what new key to replace what old key*)
- Substitute foreign key (*what new foreign key for which old one*)
- Store information/processed data (*what information*)

Chapter 8: Data dictionary

♦ Given the relational database 3NF tables

? Write a simple data dictionary for tables and attributes

Chapters 8: Database backup and recovery

♦ Given the relational database

? Describe a re-do or un-do backup and recovery strategy for the database

Chapter 9: Database on networks

♦ Given the relational database

♦ Given situations

? Design distributed database to fit all of the situations

• Explain the deployment of each table about
placement, partitioning (H. P. or V.P.), replication,
and/or combinations of these methods using
a data deployment matrix or a data deployment graph

Chapter 10: Star schema

♦ Given the relational database, and a need for the time dimension
for data warehouse

? Design star schema for a data warehouse

• Draw an ER diagram for star schema similar to Figure 10.2

INDEX

POWERPOINT SLIDES

Preface Preface-1	**Importance of Database Technology** • Data is a valuable resource of the organization • Data resource management is a key part of business • Database is a key component of business Preface-2
Reality of Database Technology • Historically, there are several types of database models, as we discussed later in the course • Information technology is the fast innovative field. Ironically, after it was introduced in the late 1970s and the early 1980s, the relational database model is still "the only" database model practically used in business • It is unlikely that the relational database model will be replaced by someone any soon Preface-3	**Overview of the Book** • Ten chapters of fundamentals of database technology • Each chapter has sufficient problem solving exercise questions • Three technical guides as tutorials for applications of database technology • answers to representative exercise questions • key learning objectives of each chapter • PPT handouts of lectures Preface-4
Unique features of This Book • This book is designed for business students • A good balance between core components and secondary components • A good balance between core knowledge and practical skill • A huge amount of material in the database area is boiled down to a manageable volume – "no waste moisture" Preface-5	**Relation between Database Technology and Information System Development** • Database design is parallel with business process design for the information system development • Data modeling is parallel with process modeling for systems analysis and design • The focal point of database design is the generalized abstraction of data and their relationships Preface-6

Chapter 1. Introduction Ch1-1	**Database Technology** • Database technology includes theory and application methodologies for building information systems that manage, access, and process data. • Database technology supports the database development for information systems. • Database technology empowers organizations to manage data resources to meet the challenges of the "Big Data Problem" • Database technology enables the society and business organizations to develop organizational knowledge and to sustain organizational learning. Ch1-2
Data Are Resource of the Organization Data are valuable assets of the organization. There are many types of data: • Master data (e.g., customers) • Transaction data (e.g., sales) • Historical data (e.g., credit history) • Secondary data (e.g., industrial average) • Subjective data (e.g., marketing survey) Ch1-3	**Data, Information, Knowledge** • Data are raw facts. 　For example … • Information is a product of processed data in a given context. 　For example … • Knowledge is human interpretation of the real world. 　For example … Ch1-4
Database stores data, NOT information, or knowledge • Database stores data. • It generates information. • The user use the generated information to develop knowledge. • Data warehouse, so-called "knowledge base" …. are built on databases to deal with information and explicit knowledge Ch1-5	**Common Mistakes in Data Resource Management** (e.g., *use spreadsheets or poor designed database tools to store data*) **(1) No control of redundant data** **(2) Violation of data integrity** **(3) Relying on human memory to store and to search needed data** Ch1-6

Control Data Redundancy

- The central issue of database is data redundancy control
- **Data redundancy** occurs when the same fact is stored in more than one place

- (Note: Do not interpret data redundancy to be "the same number or the same text is stored in more than one place."

Ch1-7

Discussion on data redundancy and data integration

CUSTOMER - PURCHASE

CustomerNumber	CustomerName	CustomerAddress	CustomerPhone	Purchase	PurchaseTime	
123456	Smith	Westport Rd.	508999	$200	10/20/2014	09:45am
234562	Green	Eastport Ave.	509343	$300	10/23/2014	01:32pm
123456	Smith	Westport Rd.	508999	$150	11/08/2014	05:04pm

(a) Data redundancy occurs

Ch1-8

Discussion on data redundancy and data integration (cont'd)

CUSTOMER

CustomerNumber	CustomerName	Customer Address	CustomerPhone
123456	Smith	Westport Rd.	508999
234562	Green	Eastport Ave.	509343

PURCHASE

CustomerNumber	Purchase	PurchaseTime	
123456	$200	10/20/2014	09:45am
234562	$300	10/23/2014	01:32pm
123456	$150	11/08/2014	05:04pm

(b) There is no data redundancy if the data are stored in this form

Ch1-9

Database and Database Systems

- Objectives of database system:

- Controlled data redundancy
- Data consistency
- Data sharing
- Facilitate application development
- Wide-ranging data management functions

Ch1-10

Database System

Ch1-11

Database Management System (DMBS)

- DBMS is software that manages the database:
- Support database construction and data access
- Control data redundancy
- Provide data integration
- Maintain data independency
- Monitor and improve data retrieval performance
- Control data security
- Enforce business rules and maintain data integrity
- Manage concurrency control
- Perform backup and recovery
- Maintain data dictionary
- Facilitate restructuring database

Ch1-12

Commonly used DBMS for relational database

- (1) ORACLE is Oracle Corporation's product.
- (2) IBM DB2 (or DB2) is IBM's product.
- (3) MySQL is a popular choice of database for use in Web applications, because it is closely tied to the popularity of PHP, an open-source server-side programming language.
- (4) Microsoft SQL Server was Microsoft's entry to the enterprise-level database market, competing against ORACLE and IBM DB2 in about 1989.
- (5) Microsoft Access was released in 1992 as an end-user oriented DBMS in the Microsoft Office suite. It does not support many sophisticated database management functions.

Ch1-13

CHAPTER 2.
DATA STRUCTURE TECHNIQUES FOR DATABASE

Ch2-1

Data Secondary Storage – Disk

Ch2-2

File, Record, Attribute, and Key

Ch2-3

Pointer – a basic technique for data search

Ch2-4

Basic File Organizations

- File organizations on disk is critical for data access efficiency
- There are four basic file organizations:
  Sequential
  Random
  Linear indexed
  B-tree

Ch2-5

Sequential File

Ch2-6

Pros/Cons of Sequential Files

- Advantages of sequential files:
- (1) Saves space.
- (2) No record key is required.
- (3) Efficient when all of the records are sequentially processed (e.g. payroll processing).
-
- Disadvantages of sequential files:
- (1) It would take a long time to find a particular record.
- (2) It is difficult to update. For example, it is difficult to insert a record.

Ch2-7

Random Files

- Hashing function

Record key value → Hashing Function → Address of the record on disk

- Random files are less used in modern databases (See examples in the textbook).

Ch2-8

Pros/Cons of Random Files

- Random files are not common in modern databases
- Advantages of random files:
- (1) It can access an individual record very fast.
- (2) It is efficient in updating (e.g., adding and modifying records).

- Disadvantages of random files:
- (1) Sequential access is impossible.
- (2) A record key is necessary.
- (3) Wastes spaces.
- (4) Synonyms make the process slower.

Ch2-9

(Linear) Indexed File

Index Table	
Record Key	Address of Record
3081	1010
4123	0239
1056	4320
. . . .	. . . .

Disk

1010
3081 ABCD...
4320
1056 EDTY...
0239
4123 XMTH...

Ch2-10

Pros/Cons of Linear Indexed Files

- Advantages of indexed files:
- (1) It can be used in both sequential and random access. Processing speed is fairly good for both.
- (2) It is efficient in adding a record, sorting and updating the file, if the indexed file is not huge.

- Disadvantages of indexed files:
- (1) A record key is necessary.
- (2) If the data file is huge, then the linear index table becomes a sequential disk file, and processing will be slow.

Ch2-11

B-Tree

- B-tree is the major file organization used in modern databases
- You need to understand the B-tree makes databases so powerful in data search
- You need to understand how the computer constructs B-trees and maintains B-trees
- After this chapter, you may not return to hands-on questions of B-tree, but you need to keep B-tree in your mind

Ch2-12

B-Tree

This cylinder holds records
with key value of 1001 through 1056

Ch2-13

B-Tree:
Find record with key value of 6000

This cylinder holds records
with key value of 1001 through 1056

Ch2-14

Rules in B-Tree

- (1) A B-tree consists of index records that are organized into a tree. The tree has its root with one and just one index record on the top, and a number of levels.
- (2) Each index record accommodates the same number of pairs (4 in the example of Figure 2.7), and each pair can hold a key-value and a pointer.
- (3) Each index record is at least half full (in the example of Figure 2.7, at least 2 pairs in an index record are occupied with key-values and pointers, and the rest pairs can be empty).
- (4) In each occupied key-value-pointer pair, the pointer points to an index record at the next level or a disk cylinder if the pair is contained in a leaf index record, and the key-value is the maximum key value in the pointed index record or the maximum key value on the cylinder.

Ch2-15

B-tree construction – from bottom to up

- Step 1. List all given disk cylinders in the ascending order of their maximum key values of records.
- Step 2. Given a certain number of key-value/pointer pairs of each index record, determine the number of index records at the leaf level for the given cylinders, and create the index records.
- Step 3. Following the construction rules, fill each index record, and link the pointers to the cylinders.
- Step 4. Determine the number of index records for the next necessary higher level, and create the index record(s).
- Step 5. Following the construction rules, fill each index record, and link the pointers to the lower level index records.
- Step 6. Repeat Step 4 through Step 5 until the root of the tree has been reached.

Ch2-16

B-Tree Maintenance

Example: *Cylinder 6 is full and add Cylinder 9*

(a) No index record splitting

Ch2-17

B-Tree: Maintenance
Example: *Cylinder 5 is full and Cylinder 10 is added:
Splitting index records Splitting index records*

(b) Index record splitting and upper-level index record updating

Ch2-18

Summary of B-Tree

- In our examples, B-tree is used for indexing key values. Actually, B-tree can also be used for non-keys.
- A database management system can construct and maintain a huge amount of B-trees so that random data access would be efficient.
- On the other hand, significant computational resource is devoted to B-tree construction and maintenance.

Ch2-19

Chapter 3.
Data Models

Ch3-1

Data Models

- A data model is a representation of complex data structures of the target real world, or system (e.g., Student Information System), for database design.
- There are four data models in the DB field:
  - Hierarchical model for hierarchical databases;
  - Network model for network databases;
  - Entity-relationship (ER) model for relational databases; and
  - Object-oriented model for object-oriented databases.

Ch3-2

ER Model: Entity

- Entity – a class of objects
  - Physiomorphic entity is a physically existing object; e.g., customer, student, and inventory.
  - Event entity represents an event of routine operations; e.g., game and credit approval.
  - Document entity is an artificial abstraction; e.g., degree.

Ch3-3

Entity – E.g., STUDENT

- Attributes – describe the entity, e.g., StudentID, StudentName ....
- Data type – each attribute has its data type, e.g., text, number...
- Instance – a value of attribute, e.g., John Smith
- Primary key – unique identifier of the entity, e.g., StudentID

Ch3-4

Entity

STUDENT
* StudentID
StudentName
StudentAddress
StudentYear

Ch3-5

ER Model: Relationship

- Relationship – Association between entities
  - Binary
  - Unary
  - Ternary
- Cardinality - Maximum number of instances of entities involved in the relationship
- Modality - Minimum number of instances of entities involved in the relationship

Ch3-6

299

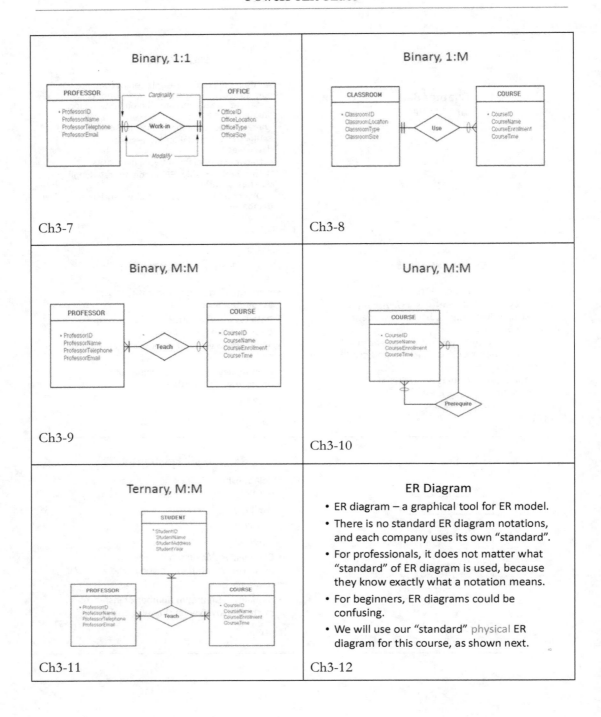

Ch3-7 — Binary, 1:1

Ch3-8 — Binary, 1:M

Ch3-9 — Binary, M:M

Ch3-10 — Unary, M:M

Ch3-11 — Ternary, M:M

ER Diagram
- ER diagram – a graphical tool for ER model.
- There is no standard ER diagram notations, and each company uses its own "standard".
- For professionals, it does not matter what "standard" of ER diagram is used, because they know exactly what a notation means.
- For beginners, ER diagrams could be confusing.
- We will use our "standard" physical ER diagram for this course, as shown next.

Ch3-12

ER Model

- (1) The relationships between the instances of entities along with the cardinalities and modalities are not given, but are modeled by the database designer using ER diagrams. They depend on the **business rules** of the business environment, or the **assumptions** made for the particular database.
- (2) The cardinalities and modalities will be used by the database management system to enforce the pertinent business rules.
- (3) In relational database, there is no way to present M:M relationships directly in the database. Any M:M relationship must be converted into 1:M relationships through the use of **associative entity**, as discussed in detail later in this chapter.

Ch3-13

Instrument for Implementing 1:1 and 1:M Relationships – Foreign Key

- For a 1:1 relationship, you can arbitrarily choose the primary key from either entity and place it as the foreign key to the other entity However, if one of the modalities is 0, it is better to place the foreign key into the entity with the 0 modality
- For a 1:M relationship, you place the primary key of the entity with the 1 cardinality into the entity with the M cardinality as the foreign key.
- Foreign key in a table and its corresponding primary key in another table have the same domain of values (e.g., both have 7 characters)

Ch3-14

Foreign Key for 1:1

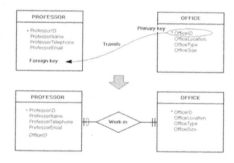

Ch3-15

Foreign key for 1:M

Ch3-16

Foreign key in unary 1:M

Ch3-17

Instrument for Implementing M:M Relationships – Associative Entity

- Foreign key only is incapable to implement an M:M relationship
- The associative entity converts the M:M relationship into two 1:M relationships which can then be represented in the relational database.

Ch3-18

Associative entity for implementing M:M relationship

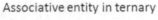

Rules of Associative Entity

- (1) Once an associative entity is introduced, the M:M relationship becomes two 1:M relationships, and the associative entity is on the M sides between the two original entities. The original M:M relationship disappears.

- (2) To distinct an associative entity from an ordinary entity, a diamond symbol is used.

Rules of Associative Entity (cont'd)

- (3) Follow the same rules of implementing 1:M relationships, place the primary key of the entity on the 1 side into the associative entity as the foreign key.

- (4) An associative entity usually has its unique attribute(s) that is not a part of either of the original entity but describes the characteristics of the associative entity, called **intersection data**.

- (5) Usually, the combination of the foreign keys in the associative entity is the primary key of the associative entity.
- However, one may add additional attribute(s) to the primary key, or use a new primary key for the associative entity.

Associative entity in unary

Associative entity in ternary

Summary of ER Diagram Notations

Summary of ER Diagram Notations (Cont'd)

(b) Physical ER Diagram Notations

Ch3-25

Start Point (A) for ER Diagram: Transcript

- Transcript of the system (see an example in the textbook)
- (1) Identify entity and its attributes through identifying **noun**.
- (2) Identify relationship through identifying **verb** or verb phrase.
- (3) Identify cardinalities and modalities through identifying **business rules**.
- (4) Make commonsensical **assumptions** if the transcript does not provide all information you need.
- (5) Construct a logical ERD for the case.
- (6) If there is an M:M relationship in your logical ERD, convert the M:M relationship into 1:M relationships by adding an associative entity along with its intersection data attributes.
- (7) Complete the notations for all primary keys and foreign keys.

Ch3-26

Example of Transcript and the ERD

The School wants to create a database to maintain data for the school. Student data should include identification, name, address, and the earliest enrollment year. Professor data should include identification, name phone number, and office. Each professor has her/his own office, and teaches many courses each semester. Several professors might form a team to teach a single course. Each student can take many courses each semester. Course data should include unique course number, title, and enrollment cap. Each course can have its prerequisites. Each course must have a classroom. The school wants to keep track of students' grades.

Ch3-27

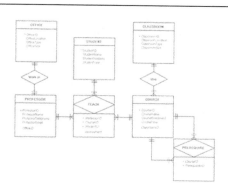

Ch3-28

Start Point (B) for ER Diagram: Sample Data Document

- Sample data documents (see an example in the textbook)
- (1) Identify the entities that have the attributes in the table.
- (2) Identify the relationships between the entities based on your understanding of the business environment.
- (3) Identify cardinalities and modalities based on commonsensical assumptions.
- (4) Construct a logical ERD for the case.
- (5) If there is an M:M relationship in your logical ERD, convert the M:M relationship into 1:M relationships by adding an associative entity along with its intersection data attributes.
- (6) Complete the notations for all primary keys and foreign keys.

Ch3-29

Figure 3.14. A Sample Datasheet for Construction of ER Diagram

Ch3-30

Redundant relationships in ERD

- A redundant relationship in ERD is caused by a **relationship loop**.
- However, a relationship loop not always introduces a redundant relationship.
- If a relationship loop introduces a redundant relationship, the loop must be broken up by deleting the redundant relationship.

Ch3-31

An ERD without Redundant Relationship

Ch3-32

An ERD with Redundant Relationship

Ch3-33

We will answer an important question in Chapter 5

Is there a criterion for judging whether an ER diagram is correct or wrong?

Ch3-34

Iterations of ER diagram construction

- Regardless whether the start point of an ER diagram is system descriptions or is sample datasheets, one-shot construction may not result in a good ER diagram.
- The construction of ER diagram and the normalization process should be carried out together.
- If a trial ER diagram is generated before the normalization process, this ER diagram might need to be revised after the normalization process to obtain the approved ER diagram for the database.
- If the start point is sample datasheets, one may perform the normalization process before constructing the trial ER diagram for the database. This fine point is illustrated in Technical Guide I through an example.

Ch3-35

Chapter 4.
Relational database

Ch4-1

Relational Data Model: Table

- In the relational data model, an entity is a relation, or a table.

Ch4-2

Properties of relation

- (1) The order of columns of a relation is not important

- (2) The order of row of a relation is not important

- (3) Each **cell** in the table can have only one single value. The value could be "**null**".

- (4) No two records in a relation have the same value of primary key.

Ch4-3

Candidate Key and Alternative Key

- A relation can have more than one attribute (or a combination of attributes) that can be used to identify the unique record in the table.

- For instance, if we assume StudentName (including first name, middle name, and last name) is unique in the database, then the STUDENT relation can have two **candidate keys**: StudentID and StudentName. If the DBA chooses StudentID to be the primary key for STUDENT, then StudentName is called the **alternative key**.

Ch4-4

Conversion of ER Model to Relational Data Model

(1)Constructing Tables
(2)Defining Constraints

Ch4-5

Constructing Tables

- It is a one seamless step procedure if our "standard" physical ER diagram is used

- (1) An entity in the ER model is a relation in the relational data model

- (2) The primary key of an entity in the ER model is the primary key of the corresponding relation in the relational data model

- (3) The foreign key in an entity in the ER model is an attribute of the corresponding relation in the relational data model.

Ch4-6

Convert ERD to Relations

Ch4-7

Defining Constraints

- (1) For a relationship with 1:M cardinality, no constraint is needed as it is the default case.

- (2) For a relationship with 1:1 cardinality, define the constraint using the following pseudo-code:

    Table {CONSTRAINT *foreign-key* UNIQUE}

    For instance, for the 1:1 relationship between PROFESSOR and OFFICE in Figure 3.7, the constraint is

    PROFESSOR {CONSTRAINT *OfficeID* UNIQUE}

Ch4-8

Defining Constraints (cont'd)

- (3) For a relation with 1 modality, no constraint is needed as it is the default case. Nevertheless, the following pseudo-code can be used to make the default explicit.

    Table {CONSTRAINT MANDATORY TO} The-Other-Table

    For instance, in the Figure 3.7 example, the following constraint imposes 1 modality to the OFFICE table.

    OFFICE {CONSTRAINT MANDATORY TO} PROFESSOR

- (4) For a relation with 0 modality, define the constraint using the following pseudo-code.

    Table {CONSTRAINT OPTIONAL TO} The-Other-Table

    For instance, in the Figure 3.7 example, the following constraint imposes 0 modality to the PROFESSOR table.

    PROFESSOR {CONSTRAINT OPTIONAL TO} OFFICE

Ch4-9

Data Retrieval from Relational Database

(1) Massive B-trees in a large database to support direct access of records (Chapter 2)

(2) Simple cases: Data retrieval from a single table each time - Trace primary keys and foreign keys to find needed data

Ch4-10

Example: Simple data retrieval path

Find the assessment made by professor Fred Brown for student Chris Smith in the Database Design & Implementation course.

Ch4-11

Data Retrieval from Relational Database (cont'd)

- (3) Highly integrated data retrieval – Join multiple tables using keys and foreign keys of the tables

Example: Given two tables:

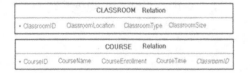

Ch4-12

Data Retrieval from Relational Database (cont'd)

List course ID, course title, course enrollment, course time for each course along with its classroom's data including classroom ID, classroom type, classroom size.

It is impossible to retrieve needed data by using a simple data retrieval path.

Ch4-13

Data Retrieval from Relational Database (cont'd)

Join operation

Merged Table:

COURSE-CLASSROOM

- The merged table contains redundant data
- However, the merged table provides data integration
- In Chapter 6, we will learn how the DBMS can provide integrated data while stores tables without data redundancy.

Ch4-14

Referential Integrity

- As the primary key in the 1-side table is the foreign key in the M-side table, there are potential violations of data integrity
- For example, when the user deletes a classroom records but the classroom has already been assigned to several courses, what should the database do?
- The DBMS controls the data integrity based on rules

Ch4-15

Delete Rule:

- (1) **Restrict** – If there is a record in another table that is relating to the record to be deleted, the deletion is prohibited.

CLASSROOM Relation
• ClassroomID ClassroomLocation ClassroomType ClassroomSize

COURSE Relation
• CourseID CourseName CourseEnrollment CourseTime (ClassroomID)

- A classroom record is allowed to be deleted only when it has not been assigned to any course.

Ch4-16

Delete Rule:

- (2) **Cascade** – All records in another table that are relating to the record to be deleted will be deleted as well.

- If one deletes a classroom record, all records of the courses which use the classroom will be deleted automatically.

Ch4-17

Delete Rule:

- (3) **Set-to-Null** - All records in another table that are relating to the record to be deleted will be updated by setting the FK attribute to NULL.

- If a classroom record is deleted, all courses that have been assigned to this classroom will be changed to "null" that means "no classroom".

Ch4-18

CHAPTER 5. NORMALIZATION AND LOGICAL DATABASE DESIGN

Ch5-1

Normalization

- **Normalization** is a process that evaluates the table structures and minimizes data redundancy.

Ch5-2

Functional Dependency

- **Functional dependency** defines the **determination relationships** between the attributes.
- The statement "*B is functionally dependent on A*" or "*A determines B*", where B is an attribute, A is an attribute or a group of attributes, means that "*if you know the value A, then you know the value of B.*"

A → B

Ch5-3

Examples of functional dependency

- StudentID → StudentName
- [StudentID+CourseID] → Grade

Ch5-4

Functional Dependency

- The functional dependencies for a database are assumed by the database designer based on her/his conceptual understanding of the relationships between attributes in the real world.
- The functional dependencies for the database are usually objective "common sense", but can also be assumptions which may or may not be totally objective.

Ch5-5

Normal Form

- A **normal form** represents a certain type of functional dependency property of tables.
- We will emphasize on **first normal form** (**1NF**), **second normal form** (**2NF**), and **third normal form** (**3NF**), although there are higher-level normal forms.
- Note that (1) if a table in 3NF, it must be also in 2NF; (2) if a table in 2NF, it must be in 1NF as well; (2) the database is in 3NF only if all tables are in 3NF.

Ch5-6

0NF

- A 0NF table has a missing value or multiple values in a cell, or has not primary key.

Student ID	Student Name	Course ID	Grade
1001	Chris Smith	ACT211	A
		MIS315	B
		MIS322	
10021	Anne Riley	ACT212	B
		MGT311	
		FIN312	A
10293	John Kerry	MGT212	B
		ACT211	A

Ch5-7

(b) Table with no primary key

Student ID	Student Name	Grade
10001	Chris Simth	A
10001	Chris Simth	B
10001	Chris Simth	B
10021	Anne Riley	B
10021	Anne Riley	A
10021	Anne Riley	A
10293	John Kerry	B
10293	John Kerry	A

Ch5-8

Conversion from 0NF to normal form

- **Step 1:** Eliminate missing values or repeating values in any cell.

- **Step 2:** Define all functional dependencies among the attributes based on the business environment or common sense. If there is an attribute without involving functional dependency (e.g., Grade in Figure 5.1(b)), you must create a functional dependency for it by adding a new attribute(s) (e.g., add CourseID for Grade in Figure 5.1(b)).

- **Step 3:** Identify the primary key for the table (e.g., [StudentID+CourseID] in Figure 5.2), so that if the value of the primary key is known then the value of any other attribute must be known.

Ch5-9

1NF

- A table is in **first normal form (1NF)** if it meets the following two conditions.
- (1) The table has no missing value or multiple values in a cell.
- (2) The primary key of the relation is identified based on assumptions of functional dependency among all attributes. These assumptions should be consistent with the **business rules** in the business environment.

Ch5-10

1NF

StudentID	StudentName	Major	Department	CourseID	CourseTitle	Grade
10003	John Smith	ACT	Accounting	ACT211	Fin Accouting	B
10003	John Smith	ACT	Accounting	ENG101	Intro.English I	A
10014	Anne Gold	CHM	Chemistry	CHM101	Intro.Chemistry	C
10014	Anne Gold	CHM	Chemistry	CHM231	Adv.Chemistry	B
12343	Bob Brown	GNS	Biology	BIO101	Intro.Biology	A
12343	Bob Brown	GNS	Biology	CHM101	Intro.Chemistry	B
12343	Bob Brown	GNS	Biology	BIO345	Genetics II	A
13345	Mike Green	ACT	Accounting	ENG101	Intro.English I	B
13345	Mike Green	ACT	Accounting	ENG201	Intro.English II	B
13345	Mike Green	ACT	Accounting	ENG345	Literature	C

StudentID ——▶ StudentName
StudentID ——▶ Major
StudentID ——▶ Department
CourseID ——▶ CourseTitle
Major ——▶ Department
StudentID+CourseID ——▶ Grade

Ch5-11

Data redundancy in 1NF table

- Data redundancy in 1NF

  (e.g., the fact that 1003 is John Smith repeats)

- Data redundancy causes modification anomalies

Ch5-12

Data modification anomaly

(1) **Update anomaly**

If a repeated fact is changed, all redundant values must be changed in each place they are stored.

(2) **Insertion anomaly**

A table with data redundancy could preclude useful facts.

(3) **Deletion anomaly**

A deletion of record from the table can cause unintentional deletion of facts.

Ch5-13

Data redundancy in 1NF table (cont'd)

- The root of this problem is known as **partial key dependency**
- Student data depend on StudentID only (not [StudentID+CourseID])
- Course data depend on CourseID only (not [StudentID+CourseID]).
- A partial key dependency occurs when the value in a non-key attribute of a table is dependent on the value of a part, but not the whole, of the table's combination primary key.

Ch5-14

Normalize 1NF table

Ch5-15

Steps of normalizing 1NF table

- **Step 1:** Make a list of potential individual keys derived from the primary key of the table in 1NF. For example, for the table in 1NF in Figure 5.2, thee potential individual keys can be derived from [StudentID+CourseID]: they are: StudentID, CourseID, and [StudentID+CourseID] itself.

- **Step 2:** For each attribute in the table in 1NF, assign it to the pertinent functionally dependent potential individual key. Using the example of Figure 5.2 and Figure 5.3, you can assign StudentName to StudentID, CourseTitle to CourseID, Grade to [StudentID+CourseID], and so on. The final result of the two steps is shown in Figure 5.4.

- **Step 3:** Revise and preserve the given functional dependencies. A functional dependency might be lost as a result of the normalization process. One must revise and preserve the functional dependencies.

Ch5-16

Table in 2NF

- The normal form of 1NF table without partial key dependency is called 2NF.
- A table in 2NF can still contain data redundancy. For instance, the STUDENT table has repeating facts about major and department.
- This problem is caused by **non-key dependency** (or **transitive dependency**);
- A non-key dependency occurs when the value in a non-key attribute of a table is dependent on the value of another non-key attribute.

Ch5-17

Normalize table in 2NF

- The normal form of a table that is in 2NF and contains no non-key dependency is called third normal form or 3NF.

Ch5-18

Normalize 2NF into 3NF

- **Step 1:** Identify any non-key dependency in the table in 2NF. In the example of Figure 5.4, Major → Department is a non-key dependency.
- **Step 2:** Create a new table (e.g., OWNERSHIP in the Figure 5.5 example) for the attributes involved in the non-key dependency (Major and Department in this example), and assign the primary key for this new table (Major in this example).
- **Step 3:** Keep the determinant attribute involved in the non-key dependency (Major in the Figure 5.5 example) in the original table (STUDENT) as the foreign key from the new table (OWNERSHIP), and delete other attributes involved in the non-key dependency (Department in this example) from the original table (STUDENT).
- **Step 4:** Revise and preserve the given functional dependencies. A functional dependency might be lost as a result of the normalization process. One must revise and preserve the functional dependencies.

Ch5-19

Determine normal form of non-0NF table

- 1. If the given table has partial key dependency, then it is in 1NF.
- 2. If the given table does not have partial key dependency and has non-key dependency, then it is in 2NF.
- 3. If the given table does not have partial key dependency and does not have non-key dependency, then it is in 3NF.

Ch5-20

The normalization procedure

Ch5-21

Higher-level NF

- Tables in 3NF could still have data modification anomalies due to other types of functional dependencies.
- **BCNF (Boyce-Codd Normal Form)** addresses the "reverse" dependency problem in a 3NF table
- **4NF** addresses multivalued dependency problem.
- 5NF and domain-key normal form (DKNF) exist

Ch5-22

Requirements on Normalization

- The minimum requirements on normalization would be 3NF in general
- However, many professionals insists that a database must meet 4NF
- MIS majors need to know the concepts of BCNF and 4NF
- Your course project of database design should meet 4NF

Ch5-23

"Reverse" Dependency in Tables in 3NF

- "Reverse" dependency: a non-candidate-key attribute is the determinant of an attribute of the primary key.
- A reverse dependency occurs when the value of a part of the combination key is reversely determined by the value of another non-candidate-key attribute.
- This causes redundancy.

StudentID	Major	Advisor	MajorProject
10014	CHM	Brown	3.5
10014	GNS	Green	3.1
13346	ACT	Smith	3.2
12343	GNS	Green	3.7
13469	ACT	Jones	3.4

StudentID+Major ──► Advisor   Advisor ──► Major ["Reverse" dependency]
StudentID+Major ──► MajorProject

Ch5-24

Normalize Table in 3NF into BCNF

STUDENT

StudentID	Advisor	MajorProject
10014	Brown	3.5
10014	Green	3.1
13345	Smith	3.2
12343	Green	3.7
13469	Jones	3.4

StudentID+Advisor ⟶ MajorProject

ADVISOR

Advisor	Major
Brown	CHM
Green	GNS
Smith	ACT
Jones	ACT

Advisor ⟶ Major

Ch5-25

Normalize 3NF into BCNF

- **Step 1:** Identify any reverse dependency in the table in 3NF. In the example of Figure 5.7, Advisor → Major is a reverse dependency.
- **Step 2:** Create a new table (e.g., ADVISOR in the Figure 5.8 example) for the attributes involved in the reverse dependency (Advisor and Major in this example), and assign the primary key for this new table (Advisor in this example).
- **Step 3:** Make the determinant attribute involved in the reverse dependency (Advisor in the Figure 5.8 example) to be a part of the combination primary key of the original table (STUDENT), and delete other attributes involved in the reverse dependency (Major in this example) from the original table (STUDENT).

Ch5-26

Multivalued Dependency Problems of Tables in BCNF

- Multivalued dependency problem.

- StudentID →→ Major
  StudentID →→ Minor

  The same facts are repeated
  (e.g., 10014 has MKT major
  10003 has SPA minor)

STUDENT

StudentID	Major	Minor
10003	MKT	SPA
10003	FIN	SPA
10014	MKT	FRA
10014	MKT	GER
23546	CHE	BUS
35462	ENG	BUS

StudentID ⟶ Major
StudentID ⟶ Minor

- A multivalued dependency occurs when the table is in BCNF and the value of an attribute determines a set of more than one possible value of the other two attributes in the table.

Ch5-27

Normalize Table in BCNF into 4NF

MAJORS

StudentID	Major
10003	MKT
10003	FIN
10014	MKT
23540	CHE
35462	ENG

StudentID + Major ⟶

MINORS

StudentID	Minor
10003	SPA
10014	FRA
10014	GER
23540	BUS
35462	BUS

StudentID + Minor ⟶

Ch5-28

Normalize BCNF into 4NF

- **Step 1:** Identify any MVD in the table which is in BCNF. In the example of Figure 5.9, StudentID →→ Major and StudentID →→ Minor are MVD.
- **Step 2:** Create a new table (e.g., MAJORS in the Figure 5.10 example) for the attributes involved in the MVD (StudentID and Major in this example), and assign the combination primary key for this new table ([StudentID+Major] in this example).
- **Step 3:** Delete the multivalued attribute involved in the MVD (i.e., the right hand side of the MVD, Major in this example) from the original table (STUDENT in this example), and rename the table (e.g., to MINORS in this example).
- **Step 4:** Repeat Step 1 through Step 3 for the table resulted in Step 3 (e.g., MINORS in this example) until no MVD exists in all resulting tables.

Ch5-29

Logical Database Design

- **Logical database design** is the process that defines the databases structures to meet the data requirements of the business.
- **Step 1.** Generate an initial ER model
- **Step 2.** Convert the initial ER model into a preliminary set of tables.
- **Step 3.** Perform normalization on the preliminary set of tables into normalized tables (see the procedure in the previous section).
- **Step 4.** Revise the ER model based on the normalized tables.
- **Step 5.** Convert the normalized tables into the internal model for a selected DBMS.
- **Step 6.** Attach pertinent constraints to applicable tables.
- **Step 7.** Confirm that the internal model for the selected DBMS is consistent with the ER model.

Ch5-30

Three Important Points

- (1) The logical database design for a database is an iterative process. If the design process starts with data samples, Step 1 might be skipped, as explained in Technical Guide I.

- (2) The ERD of a database is a blueprint for the database. It is used for human communication. More importantly, because it is difficult for human to verify whether the computer internal model is consistent with those normalized tables without a blueprint, the ERD must be used. Technical Guide II shows more about this.

- (3) Logical database design ensures the data needs for the business, but does not take the performance of database into account. The ultimate consequence of data in higher-level normal forms is the inefficiency of data retrieval. To solve this problem in a large database, physical database design must be applied, as discussed in Chapter 7.

Ch5-31

Logical Database Design

Ch5-32

CHAPTER 6. DATABASE PROCESSING
AND SQL

Ch6-1

SQL

- **SQL (Structured Query Language)** is a universal language for querying and updating databases.
- SQL integrates features of data definition languages (DDL) and data manipulation languages (DML).
- When using other computer languages (such as COBOL, C, Java, ADO.NET) to develop business process software that is connected to databases (Oracle, DB2, etc.), one must write SQL code

Ch6-2

SQL Examples

- The toy database for the examples

Ch6-3

```
CREATE TABLE tblStudent
  (StudentID CHAR(8),
   StudentName CHAR(20),
   StudentAddress CHAR(20),
   StudentEnrolYear INT,
   PRIMARY KEY (StudentID));
```

Listing 6.1. CREATE TABLE

Ch6-4

```
DROP TABLE tblStudent;
```

Listing 6.2. DROP TABLE

Ch6-5

```
INSERT INTO tblStudent
  VALUES ('01234567', 'John',
          '285 Westport', 2018);
```

Listing 6.3. INSERT a Record

Ch6-6

```
UPDATE tblStudent
   SET StudentAddress = '300 Eastport'
   WHERE StudentID='01234567';
```

Listing 6.4. UPDATE a Record

Ch6-7

```
DELETE FROM tblStudent
   WHERE StudentID='01234567';
```

Listing 6.5. DELETE a Record

Ch6-8

Sample Data Used for Examples

StudentID	StudentName	StudentAddress	StudentEnrolYear
01234567	John	285 Westport	2018
02345678	Anne	287 Eastport	2020
03456789	Robert	324 Northport	2019

tblStudent

CourseID	CourseName	CourseEnroll
ACT211	Financial Accounting	35
ACT212	Cost Accounting	28
MIS315	Information Systems	40
MIS322	Systems Analysis & Design	38
MIS432	Database Design	30
MKT311	Principles of Marketing	25
MGT490	Special Topics	20

tblCourse

StudentID	CourseID	Grade
01234567	ACT211	A+
01234567	ACT212	A
01234567	MIS315	B
02345678	ACT211	B+
02345678	MIS323	C
03456789	ACT212	B
03456789	MIS432	A
03456789	MKT311	A

tblGrading

Ch6-9

Find the student's name and address of student ID 01234567 from the student table.

```
SELECT StudentName, StudentAddress
FROM tblStudent
WHERE StudentID = '01234567';
```

StudentName	StudentAddress
John	285 Westport

Listing 6.6. SELECT to Select Specified Data from a Table

Ch6-10

Find the student's entire record of student ID 01234567 from the student table."

The "*" sign represents all attributes of the table.
```
SELECT *
FROM tblStudent
WHERE StudentID = '01234567';
```

StudentID	StudentName	StudentAddress	StudentEnrolYear
01234567	John	285 Westport	2018

Listing 6.7. SELECT to Select an Entire Record from a Table

Ch6-11

Find distinctive student enrollment years from the student table.

```
SELECT DISTINCT StudentEnrolYear
   FROM tblStudent;
```

StudentEnrolYear
2018
2019
2020

Listing 6.8. DISTINCT to Eliminate Duplications

Ch6-12

List the names of those students who enroll to the program after 2017.

```
SELECT StudentName
FROM tblStudent
WHERE StudentEnrolYear > 2017;
```

StudentName
John
Anne
Robert

Listing 6.9. Comparison - Greater Than

Ch6-13

List the names of those students whose ID numbers are greater than 00234567 and who enroll to the program after 2017 or before 2005.

```
SELECT StudentName
FROM tblStudent
WHERE StudentID > '00234567'
AND (StudentEnrolYear > 2017 OR
StudentEnrolYear < 2005);
```

StudentName
John
Anne
Robert

Listing 6.10. AND and OR Operators

Ch6-14

Find the student records for those students whose street names contain 'Westport'.

Here, the percent sign "%" is a wildcard to represent any collection of characters. Note that, Microsoft Access uses "*" for this type of wildcard.

```
SELECT *
FROM tblStudent
WHERE StudentAddress LIKE '%Westport%';
```

StudentID	StudentName	StudentAddress	StudentEnrolYear
01234567	John	285 Westport	2018

Listing 6.11. LIKE Operator and Wildcard "%"

Ch6-15

Find the student record for each student whose name has the letter 'o' as the second letter of the name.

Here, the wildcard sign "_" represents any one character. Note that, Microsoft Access uses "?" for this type of wildcard.

```
SELECT *
FROM tblStudent
WHERE StudentName LIKE '_o%';
```

StudentID	StudentName	StudentAddress	StudentEnrolYear
01234567	John	285 Westport	2018
03456789	Robert	324 Northport	2019

Listing 6.12. LIKE Operator and Wildcard "_"

Ch6-16

Find the student whose ID is '01234567', '00234567', or '00034567'.

```
SELECT StudentName
FROM tblStudent
WHERE StudentID IN ('01234567',
'00234567', '00034567');
```

StudentName
John

Listing 6.13. IN Operator

Ch6-17

SQL-User Interaction

- SQL is mainly embedded in host computer programming languages (C++, Java, .NET, COBOL...)
- SQL can be used on PC and includes user input request, depending on versions.
- For example:

```
SELECT StudentName
FROM tblStudent
WHERE StudentID=[Please input student ID:];
```

Ch6-18

List all student records in the reverse alphabetic order
by student name.

```
SELECT *
FROM tblStudent
ORDER BY StudentName DESC;
```

StudentID	StudentName	StudentAddress	StudentEnrolYear
03456789	Robert	324 Northport	2019
01234567	John	285 Westport	2018
02345678	Anne	287 Eastport	2020

Listing 6.14. ORDER BY Clause

Ch6-19

Find the total student records in the student table.

```
SELECT COUNT(*)
FROM tblStudent;
```

Expr1000
3

Listing 6.15(a). COUNT Function

Ch6-20

Find the total student records in the student table.

```
SELECT COUNT(*) AS CountOfStudents
FROM tblStudent;
```

CountOfStudents
3

**Listing 6.15(b). Use AS Keyword to Define Result
Name**

Ch6-21

What are the smallest enrollment number, largest
enrollment number, total enrollment number, and
average enrollment number in the course table?

```
SELECT MIN(CourseEnrollment),
       MAX(CourseEnrollment),
       SUM(CourseEnrollment),
       AVG(CourseEnrollment)
FROM tblCourse;
```

Expr1000	Expr1001	Expr1002	Expr1003
20	40	216	30.8571428571429

Listing 6.16. MIN, MAX, SUM, and AVG Functions

Ch6-22

Find the total number of courses taken by **each** student,
and only include students who have taken at least 2
courses."

```
SELECT StudentID, COUNT(*)
FROM tblGrading
GROUP BY StudentID
HAVING COUNT(*) > 1;
```

StudentID	Expr1001
01234567	3
02345678	2
03456789	3

Listing 6.17. GROUP BY Clause and HAVING Clause

Ch6-23

Find the total number of courses taken by **each** student, and
only include students whose ID are greater than '01234600'
and have taken at least 2 courses.

```
SELECT StudentID, COUNT(*)
FROM tblGrading
WHERE StudentID>'01234600'
GROUP BY StudentID
HAVING COUNT(*)>1;
```

StudentID	Expr1001
02345678	2
03456789	3

**Listing 6.18. Apply WHERE Clause before GROUP BY
Clause**

Ch6-24

Arithmetic Operations

- The major purpose of SQL is data retrieval from the database together with simple data manipulations.
- Complicated manipulations on the retrieved data and information presentations shall be implemented by the application programs that host SQL scripts.
- Nevertheless, SQL provides **arithmetic operations**. Addition (+), subtraction (-), multiplication (*), and division (/) can be used in the SELECT clause.

Ch6-25

Arithmetic Operations (cont'd)

List the course ID, course enrollment, and seats available for each course, assuming that the normal cap for each course is 30.

```
SELECT CourseID, CourseEnrollment,
30-CourseEnrollment AS SeatsAvailable
FROM tblCourse;
```

CourseID	CourseEnrollment	SeatsAvailable
ACT211	35	-5
ACT212	28	2
MGT600	20	10
MIS315	40	-10
MIS322	38	8
MIS432	30	0
MKT311	25	5

Listing 6.19. Arithmetic Operations

Ch6-26

Join – Merge Tables

- (1) A condition associates two tables, and the general format is:

  [TableOnOneSide].[PrimaryKey] =
  [TableOnManySide].[ForeignKey]

- (2) If *n* tables are used in the query, then *n*-1 conditions are needed and are tied by the AND operator.

- (3) To differentiate the same names in different tables, the table name followed by a period sign is used for an attribute name (e.g., tblStudent.StudentID) to **qualify** the attribute name. In other words, the table name must be quoted to specify what table the attribute belongs to.

Ch6-27

List the names of those students who receive "A" or "A+" in any course.

```
SELECT DISTINCT tblStudent.StudentName
FROM tblGrading, tblStudent
WHERE
tblStudent.StudentID=tblGrading.StudentID
AND (tblGrading.Grade='A+' OR
     tblGrading.Grade='A');
```

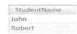

StudentName
John
Robert

Listing 6.20. Join Two Tables

Ch6-28

```
SELECT *
FROM tblStudent, tblCourse, tblGrading
WHERE tblStudent.StudentID = tblGrading.StudentID
AND tblCourse.CourseID = tblGrading.CourseID;
```

Listing 6.21. Join Multiple Tables to Integrate Related Data

Ch6-29

Who (student ID and name) receives "A+" or "A" grade in which course (course ID and course name)? List the results in order of student ID.

```
SELECT tblGrading.StudentID, tblStudent.StudentName,
tblGrading.CourseID, tblCourse.CourseName,
tblGrading.Grade
FROM tblGrading, tblStudent, tblCourse
WHERE tblStudent.StudentID=tblGrading.StudentID
AND tblCourse.CourseID=tblGrading.CourseID
AND (tblGrading.Grade='A+' OR tblGrading.Grade='A')
ORDER BY tblStudent.StudentID;
```

Listing 6.22. Query with Multiple Table

Ch6-30

318

```
SELECT DISTINCT tblStudent.StudentName
FROM tblStudent
INNER JOIN tblGrading
ON
tblStudent.StudentID=tblGrading.StudentID
WHERE (tblGrading.Grade='A+' OR
       tblGrading.Grade='A');
```

Listing 6.23. Explicit Format of Inner Join

This format is not recommended for beginners.

Ch6-31

Outer Join (-outer join is not used often)

List the course ID and course name for all grades. Include all courses in the results. For courses that do not have grade records, omit the grade.

```
SELECT tblCourse.CourseID, tblCourse.CourseName,
       tblGrading.Grade
FROM tblCourse LEFT JOIN tblGrading
   ON tblCourse.CourseID=tblGrading.CourseID;
```
Listing 6.24. Query with Left Outer Join Clause

Ch6-32

Subquery

(1) Reduce computational workload of join operation
* Avoid join operation

```
SELECT tblStudent.StudentName
FROM   tblStudent
WHERE  tblStudent.StudentID IN
           (SELECT tblGrading.StudentID
            FROM tblGrading
            WHERE (tblGrading.Grade='A+'
            OR tblGrading.Grade='A'));
```

StudentName
John
Robert

Listing 6.25. An Example of Subquery that Avoids Join Operation

Ch6-33

Subquery
* Make the joining tables smaller

List all student grade records, including only the student numbers, the student names, the course numbers, and the grades.

```
SELECT tblStudent.StudentID, tblStudent.StudentName,
       tblCourse.CourseID, tblGrading.Grade
FROM
(SELECT tblStudent.StudentID, tblStudent.StudentName
 FROM tblStudent) tblStudentSmall,
(SELECT tblCourse.CourseID
 FROM tblCourse) tblCourseSmall,
 tblGrading
WHERE tblStudentSmall.StudentID=tblGrading.StudentID
AND tblCourseSmall.CourseID=tblGrading.CourseID;
```

Listing 6.26. An Example of Subquery in the FROM Clause

Ch6-34

Subquery

(2) An alternative to the GROUP BY clause.

Show each student's name along with the number of courses she/he has taken.

```
SELECT tblStudent.StudentName,
    (SELECT COUNT(*)
     FROM tblGrading
     WHERE
     tblStudent.StudentID=tblGrading.StudentID)
    AS NumberOfCourses
FROM tblStudent;
```

StudentName	NumberOfCourses
John	3
Anne	2
Robert	3

Listing 6.27(a). Subquery for Groups

Ch6-35

GROUP BY seems to be easier

The SQL in Listing 6.27(b) does the similar work using GROUP BY clause

```
SELECT tblStudent.StudentName,
       COUNT(*) AS NumberOfCourses
FROM tblStudent, tblGrading
WHERE
tblStudent.StudentID=tblGrading.StudentID
GROUP BY tblStudent.StudentName;
```

Listing 6.27(b). GROUP BY for Group

Ch6-36

Subquery

(3) A subquery represents a variable

Find the percentage of the enrollment of MIS432 out of the total enrollment of all courses.

```
SELECT SUM(CourseEnrollment)/
  (SELECT SUM(CourseEnrollment) FROM tblCourse)*100
  AS MIS432EnrollmentPercent
FROM   tblCourse
WHERE  CourseID = 'MIS432';
```

MIS432EnrollmentPercent
13.8888888888889

Listing 6.28. An Example of Subquery as a Variable

Ch6-37

Subquery

(4) Determine uncertain criteria

Which students with ID numbers greater than '02000000' have the earliest enrollment year of such students?

```
SELECT StudentName
FROM   tblStudent
WHERE  StudentID > '02000000'
AND StudentEnrolYear=
      (SELECT MIN(StudentEnrolYear)
      FROM tblStudent
      WHERE  StudentID > '02000000');
```

StudentName
Robert

Listing 6.29. An Example of Subquery for Uncertain Condition

Ch6-38

List student names, course names, and grades of those students whose ID numbers are greater than '02000000' and have the earliest enrollment year of such students.

```
SELECT tblStudent.StudentName,
  tblCourse.CourseName,        tblGrading.Grade
FROM tblStudent, tblCourse, tblGrading
WHERE tblStudent.StudentID=tblGrading.StudentID
AND tblCourse.CourseID=tblGrading.CourseID
AND tblStudent.StudentID > '02000000'
AND tblStudent.StudentEnrolYear=
  (SELECT MIN(tblStudent.StudentEnrolYear)
  FROM tblStudent
  WHERE  tblStudent.StudentID > '02000000');
```

StudentName	CourseName	Grade
Robert	Database Design	A
Robert	Cost Accounting	B
Robert	Principles of Marketing	A

Listing 6.30. An Example of Join and Subquery

Ch6-39

Two important points of subquery for uncertain condition

- First, when the right side of the WHERE clause is uncertain (e.g., MIN, MAX, SUM, AVG, COUNT), you must use a subquery to replace the uncertain condition.
- Second, in Listing 6.29, you can see that the condition StudentID>'02000000' in the host WHERE clause repeats in the condition in the subquery. If the second WEHRE clause is omitted, the query is quite different from the original meaning, and stands for *"which students with ID numbers greater than '02000000' have the earliest enrollment year of all students?"*

Ch6-40

UNION Operator

List the course ID and course enrollment for each course that has enrollment greater than 35, or the student name and student ID for each student who enrolled after 2019.

```
SELECT CourseID AS Name, CourseEnrollment AS Data
FROM tblCourse
WHERE CourseEnrollment>35
UNION
SELECT StudentName AS Name, StudentID AS Data
FROM tblStudent
WHERE StudentEnrolYear>2019;
```

Name	Data
Anne	02345678
MIS315	40
MIS322	38

Listing 6.31. UNION Operator

(This example is merely to demonstrate how the UNION operator works. The query result is a kind of "orange" and "apple".)

Ch6-41

Tactics for Writing Queries

- (1) Read the query carefully. Determine what data are to be retrieved and what attributes are to be included in the SELECT command.
- (2) If a variable is needed, use a subquery as the variable.
- (3) Determine what tables are will be used in the FROM clause.
- (4) If two or more tables are involved, use a join operation(s) (match the primary key in one table with the foreign key in another table) in the WHERE clause.

Ch6-42

Tactics for Writing Queries (cont'd)

- (5) Construct the WHERE clause by including all conditions that are linked by AND or OR. Never use any aggregate function in the WHERE clause directly.
- (6) If a condition has an uncertain criterion (MAX, MIN, AVG, SUM, COUNT) on the right side of the condition, use a subquery.
- (7) Consider GROUP BY (for each group) with HAVING condition, ORDER BY clauses, and other operators (e.g., DISTINCT) if needed.
- (8) For hands-on practices, you may construct test tables with a limited number of test samples to test the SQL script to see if it generates the expected result.

Ch6-43

SQL Embedded in Host Computer Programming Languages

- Computer application programs in large languages (e.g., COBOL, C++, Java, and .NET) often deal with relational databases directly and host SQL script.
- To make a connection to the databases and process the embedded SQL, specific database connection software must be integrated into the system.
- (We have a demo of ASP.NET that access a database. You may take a course to learn more about server-side programming for Web application development.)

Ch6-44

Search Access Database in the Internet Environment - An Example of ADO.NET

Ch6-45

CHAPTER 7. PHYSICAL DATABASE DESIGN

Ch7-1

Physical Design

- **Physical database design** is to alter the logical database design and improve the database performance

- **Response time** – the time delay from the database access request to the result appears;
- **Throughput volume** – the data access output in a given time period;
- **Security** – the data protection.

Ch7-2

Physical Database Design Techniques

- Unlike logical database design, physical database design is more or less artistic and depends upon the specific situations of applications of the database.
- The support functions for physical design vary depending on the DBMS. Large DBMS such as Oracle and DB2 have rich functionalities for physical database design, but end user oriented DBMS for tiny databases, such as Microsoft Access, have few physical design features.
- We discuss 10 physical database design techniques

Ch7-3

Adding Index

- For example, if the user finds students from the STUDENT table often by StudentName, then StudentName should have an index although it is not the primary key.

- The downside of adding indexes is the increase of computation overhead for maintenance of B-trees.

Ch7-4

Adding Subschema

Students' Subschema   Professors' Subschema   Bursar's Subschema

Tables of Database

Ch7-5

Clustering Tables

- If two or more tables are used together so often, these tables should be **clustered**; that is, are placed close each to other (e.g., on the same disk cylinder).

- The downside of clustering is that it might increase the "distances" between one of the clustered table and other tables because not all tables can be clustered.

Ch7-6

Merging Tables

- If two or more tables are repeatedly joined through the join operations, then **merging** these tables into a large table might be necessary to reduce the valuable computing time spent on the repeating join operations.
- The **combined table** becomes a **denormalized** table and usually contains data redundancy.
- To keep the data sufficiently accurate, re-merging could take place from time to time.

Ch7-7

Horizontal Partitioning Table

- In **horizontal partitioning**, the rows of a table are divided into parts, and the parts are stored separately for many reasons, such as different access frequencies of the parts and different security requirement of the parts.
- For instance, if the STUDENT table is huge, it can be divided into two parts: one sub-table contains records of active students and the other sub-table contains records of inactive students.
- The downside of partitioning is that the computation overhead would be increase when the entire table is used.

Ch7-8

Horizontal partitioning

Ch7-9

Vertical Partitioning Table

- In **vertical partitioning**, the columns of a table are divided into parts, and the parts are stored separately because different users require different attributes.
- For instance, if the STUDENT table is huge, it can be divided into two parts: one sub-table contains attributes StudentID, StudentName, and StudentYear; and the other sub-table contains attributes StudentID, StudentName, and StudentAddress.
- The concepts of vertical partitioning and adding indexes are different.

Ch7-10

Vertical Partitioning

Ch7-11

Creating New Primary Key

- Combination primary keys make data retrieval process slower, especially when the combination key involves too many attributes, because it makes too many indexed attributes in the B-trees.
- For example, in Figure 3.13, [StudentID+CourseID+ProfessorID] is a combination key for the associative entity TEACH. One may create a new primary key, say, OccurrenceID, to replace it.
- Note that the table still keep the attributes of the original combination key.

Ch7-12

Substituting Foreign Key

- If an alternative key of the table on the 1-side is more often used for data retrieval than the primary key, this alternative key could be used as the foreign key of the table on the M-side.
- For instance, in the database represented by Figure 3.9, considering ProfessorName is an alternative key of the PROFESSOR relation, and is used more frequently than ProfessorID, *ProfessorName* can substitute *ProfessorID* as the foreign key in the TEACH relation.

Ch7-13

Duplicating Table or Parts of Partitioned Table

- When multiple users try to access the same table, the response time of the database will slow. To reduce the bottleneck effect, the technique of **duplicating tables** (or parts of partitioned tables) is used at the risk of overt data redundancy.
- The duplication should be temporary for the access peak hours, and should be fully managed by the DBMS.

Ch7-14

Storing Information (Processd Data)

- If a piece of information (or processed data, e.g., total) is requested frequently and/or by many users in a short period, the system would waste much computation resource.
- **Storing** information is to reduce the unnecessarily repeating computation.
- Apparently, the stored piece of information should be of short life to keep the information updated.

Ch7-15

Implementation of Physical Database Design

- The implementation of physical database design highly depends on the DBMS.

- (1) **Storage-related construction**.
- (2) **SQL-related construction**. SQL allows the user of the database to create VIEW. This makes it possible to create a VIEW of multiple tables for security, or to create partitions of a single table.
- (3) **Query optimizer**. Many DBMSs support SQL ANALYZE command to analyze database performance statistics. A DBMS has its own algorithms for determine the most efficient way to execute SQL.

Ch7-16

CHAPTER 8. DATABASE
ADMINISTRATION

Ch8-1

DBA Responsibilities

- Data Planning and Database Design
- Data Coordination
- Data Security, Access Policies, and Data Ownership
- Data Quality
- Database Performance
- User Training
- Data Standards, Data Dictionary, and Documentation
- Database Backup and Recovery
- Data Archiving
- Database Maintenance
- Managing Business Rules

Ch8-2

Data Quality:
Data quality is evaluated by

- accuracy
- objectivity
- believability
- reputation
- access
- security
- relevancy
- value-added
- timeliness
- completeness
- amount of data
- interpretability
- ease of understanding
- concise representation
- consistent representation.

Ch8-3

Data Dictionary

- A data dictionary stores **metadata**, namely data about the data in the database.
- There is no universal standard for data dictionary. Individual DBMS has the data dictionary in its own way.
- A **passive data dictionary** is used for **documentation** purposes.
- An **active data dictionary** is a sophisticated one that interacts with the "mother database" in a real-time fashion.

Ch8-4

Simple Example of
Data Dictionary

Ch8-5

Learn Data Dictionary from Your Microsoft Access Project

- Following Technical Guide II for using Microsoft Access, you can find a way to retrieve the DMBS generated data dictionary for the database in Microsoft Access. If you build a database for your course project, you can learn a variety of metadata that are useful for database management.

[Demo Data Dictionary in Microsoft Access]

Ch8-6

Backup and Recovery Approaches

- Mirrored databases – Too expensive
- Re-do transactions – for a large scale disaster
- Un-do transactions – for a small scale error

Ch8-7

Re-Do Transactions

Ch8-8

Un-Do Transactions

Ch8-9

Data Archiving

- Special needs for data retention
- Business laws and government laws requirements for data retention
- Data archive is a place where a set of certain data stored
- Data archive does not belong to the database, but should be traceable from the database

Ch8-10

Database Maintenance

- Hardware and software upgrading
- Other changes in the environment.
- Long-term maintenance policies
- Short-term maintenance plans
- The responsibility of dealing with cost issues and the relationships with vendors

Ch8-11

Managing Business Rules

- A **business rule** is a statement that aims to influence or guide business in the organization.
- Business rules include business regulation, organization structure, job responsibility, business procedure, security, database, and others.
- One of the DBA roles is to manage the business rules related to the database design.
- (1) Functional dependencies between the attributes of entities.
- (2) Cardinalities and modalities attached to the relationships between the entities.
- (3) Referential integrity rules for record insertion and deletion

Ch8-12

CHAPTER 9. DATABASE IN COMPUTER NETWORKS

Ch9-1

Centralized Database in the Local Area Network Environment

Ch9-2

Centralized Database in the Internet Environment

Ch9-3

ODBC – An important component

Ch9-4

Distributed Database

Ch9-5

Distributed Database (cont'd)

- Location transparency - The DDBMS takes care of data physical locations and data migration, and makes the users feel the database is centralized in somewhere.
- Data deployment

(1) **Partitioning** – A table may be split up through **horizontal partitioning**, **vertical partitioning**, or the combination of horizontal and vertical partitioning, and each **fragment** is subject to placement.

(2) **Placement** – A table or a fragment of table should be placed at the site where the table or the fragment is used most frequently, and the site takes the major responsibility for its data integrity control as well as backup and recovery.

(3) **Duplication** – A table or a fragment of table may have a replicated copy at the site where the table is used frequently.

Ch9-6

Example of data deployment

- Given the situation described in the textbook of the database:

- There are headquarter (Boston) and 4 region offices

Ch9-7

Situations

- *GreenAppliance retail company has the database as described in Figure 9.5(a).*
- *Its headquarters is set in Boston.*
- *There are four region offices: Providence, Toronto, New York, and Seattle.*
- *Each region office manages dozens branches in the region. Each region sells unique products.*

Ch9-8

Situations (cont'd)

- *The CEOs of the company monitor the sales across the company on the daily basis, and also make decisions on the selection of suppliers regularly.*
- *The senior managers of each region office take the responsibility of sales and the performance of its branches, but do not deal with the suppliers directly.*
- *What is your strategy of deployment of the tables for the distributed database?*

Ch9-9

Data Deployment Matrix

Locations / Tables	Headquarters Boston	Region Offices Toronto, Miami, Seattle, Providence
MANUFACTORY	The table is placed in Boston.	
BRANCH	The table is placed in Boston.	
REGION	The table is placed in Boston.	
SALES	A duplicated table is placed in Boston which merges the four segments of the horizontally partitioned parts of the four regions.	A horizontally partitioned part is placed in each region. The H.P. is based on the values of BranchName that are related to the region (the value of RegionName through BRANCH.
PRODUCT	The table is placed in Boston.	A duplicated horizontally partitioned part is placed in each region. The H.P. is based on the values of ProductNumber that are related to the region (the value of RegionName) through SALES and BRANCH.

Ch9-10

Data deployment Graph

Ch9-11

Justification

- (1) The REGION and BRANCH tables are mainly used by the headquarters and are rarely used by any region office. Thus, these two tables are placed in Boston.
- (2) As the headquarters makes decisions on suppliers, the MANUFACTORY table is placed in Boston. Region offices might access the MANUFACTORY table occasionally, but the usage is low since they do not assume the responsibility of selection of suppliers.

Ch9-12

Justification (cont'd)

- (3) As each region office takes the responsibility of sales and its performance, the SALES table should be horizontally partitioned for each region office. The individual sub-table is placed to the corresponding region office. The headquarters also needs to access the SALES table on the daily basis but not in the real-time mode. Thus, a duplication SALES table, which merges the four sub-tables of the four region offices, is placed in Boston.

- (4) As the headquarters takes the responsibility of selection of suppliers, the PRODUCT table is placed in Boston. However, each region office must access the PRODUCT table as well for monitoring sales activities. As each region sells unique products, the PRODUCT table is duplicated for each region office for only a horizontally partitioned part which is relevant to the products for that region.

Ch9-13

Distributed Database

- Data integrity control

- Distributed join operations - Join operations in distributed databases would become more time consuming because the joined tables may not be located in the same place. Many heuristic algorithms are employed to "optimize" **distributed join operations.**

Ch9-14

Interfaces of Databases

Ch9-15

XML for databases

Ch9-16

XML

- The XML data model is hierarchical, not relational. The conversion of data from a relational database into the XML format might not be straightforward.
- The use of XML involves several companion tools, such as XSLT or CSS, XML Schema or DTD, and is not as simple as it should be.

Ch9-17

Example of XML

```
<?xml version="1.0" standalone="yes"?>
<StudentTable>
<Student
        StudentID="01234567"
        StudentName="John"
        StudentAddress="285 Westport"
        StudentEnrolYear="2018" >
</Student>
<Student
        StudentID="02345678"
        StudentName="Anne"
        StudentAddress="287 Eastport"
        StudentEnrolYear="2020" >
</Student>
<Student
        StudentID="03456789"
        StudentName="Robert"
        StudentAddress="324 Northport"
        StudentEnrolYear="2019" >
</Student>
</StudentTable>
```

Listing 9.1. XML Document for the STUDENT Table in Figure 6.2

Ch9-18

CHAPTER 10. DATA WAREHOUSE AND DATA MINING

Ch10-1

Data Warehouse

- In a large organization, it is unlikely to have just one database.
- People need a variety of types of data which may not be normalized or may not be current.
- A **Data warehouse** holds all kinds of data for supporting decision making activities.
- A data warehouse can be divided into **data marts**, and each data mart serves a particular functional division (e.g., finance, accounting, human resource management, etc.).
- **High-dimensional** data

Ch10-2

Multidimensional Data and Data Cube

Sales data cube

Ch10-3

Creating Data Cube from Relational Database: Star Schema

Star Schema for Generating High-dimensional Data Cube

Ch10-4

Star Schema

- The **fact table** is the center of the star, and is SALES table in this example that keeps sales data for the data cube.
- The query *"Find all monthly sales which are generated by every branch for every existing product within the past four months"* will generate a sales data cube.

Ch10-5

Snowflake Design

Snowflake design is 1:M relationship chains towards the center of the star

Ch10-6

Snowflake Design

- **Snowflake design** is an extension of star schema design of multidimensional data for data warehousing.
- Since the relationships between tables are always 1:M towards the fact table, the snowflake design makes meaningful very high dimensional data cubes possible.

Ch10-7

OLAP

- **OLAP** (Online Analytical Processing) is one of the most popular business intelligence techniques in organizations.
- The word "**online**" means data availability.

Ch10-8

Elemental Techniques of OLAP

(1) Query

(2) OLAP operation: **Slicing** is to reduce the dimensionality of data by fixing the level(s) of one or more dimensions to create **slices**. **Dicing** is to divide the data cube into sub-cubes (so called **dice**) for comparison, (e.g., actual vs. plan, this year vs. last year). Combinations of slicing and dicing with other methods (such as queries) are also called **drill-down**, which means investigating information in increasing details.

Ch10-9

Slicing

Ch10-10

Dicing

Ch10-11

Elemental Techniques of OLAP (cont'd)

(3) Statistical analysis

(4) Data visualization

- A complex OLAP task can be accomplished by using a combination of these elemental techniques.

Ch10-12

OLAP in Microsoft Office Environment

Ch10-13

Example (Technical Guide C):
Data cube in pivot table form

Ch10-14

Example (Technical Guide C):
(1) Query

Ch10-15

Example (Technical Guide C):
(2) OLAP cube operation –
Slicing, Dicing, Drill-down

Ch10-16

Example (Technical Guide C):
(3) Statistical analysis

Ch10-17

Example (Technical Guide C):
(4) Data visualization

Ch10-18

Example (Technical Guide C):
Examples of interesting and useful
information discovered through OLAP

- *"Anna of East Branch was the Laptop record-sales manager in both Mar and Apr, although other branches (West and Central) had the same sales levels in one of the two months."*
- *"East Branch has a significant increase of sales of DVD in Apr compared with Mar by ((73-57)/57=28%)."*
- *"The difference of sales between West Branch and South Branch is insignificant, although the average sales of West Branch is slightly higher than sales of South Branch (by (30.5-29)/29=5%)."*
- *"Over the time period, the fluctuation sales patterns of DVD and PDA are similar, while the sales of other three products are increasing after March."*

Ch10-19

Business Intelligence and Data Mining

- **Business intelligence** is a broad category of applications and technologies of gathering, accessing, and analyzing a large amount of data for the organization to make effective business decisions.
- Data mining is the process of trawling through data in the hope of identifying patterns.

Ch10-20

A Data Mining Story

- There is a well-known supermarket data mining story that *consumers who purchase diaper are more likely to purchase beer at the same time.*
- This story sounds interesting because such a purchase pattern is unsuspected.
- Apparently, these consumers may not be the typical ones. This story is an example to demonstrate to people how data mining could help the business to catch opportunities although such an unsuspected fact might be regional or short-lived.

Ch10-21

Closing Episode

Ch10-22

CPSIA information can be obtained
at www.ICGtesting.com
Printed in the USA
FFHW01n0932210818
47767267-51472FF